The Miracle of Lourdes

FROM THE REVIEWS

"Mrs. Cranston deserves the gratitude of the Church, the medical profession and the world at large for the careful way in which she has clarified all this. It was a happy day for all of us when she decided to go to Lourdes to make a thorough study of what has happened there in the century which has passed since the Beautiful Lady appeared and the miraculous cures began; to see for herself what is happening there today; and then to write about all this for the benefit of those who cannot take such a journey and make such investigations, or who have done so timidly, hastily or skeptically. It would be hard to imagine anyone more ideally suited for such a task: as a Protestant she cannot be accused of propaganda; as a keen observer and careful student little escapes her; as an experienced reporter she knows how to interpret and record her observations. She is candid, she is fair, she is logical, and she is so objective that at times she would seem almost detached were it not for her earnestness; and she presents facts and figures in a way which not only commands respect but arouses interest."

—SATURDAY REVIEW

"The reader will join with the pilgrims in feeling that the true spirit of Lourdes is best expressed in constant prayer and penitence, the spiritual hope and revelation the living meaning to all mankind of its faith, hope and charity. A valuable rendition in factual form of what takes place in a famous little corner of the world."

—SACRAMENTO BEE

"Her descriptions of the town, the processions, the natives and visitors, the sensations felt by the sick and the dying when they enter the icy baths of miraculous water are remarkably vivid."

—LOUISVILLE COURIER-JOURNAL

RUTH CRANSTON

The Miracle of Lourdes 🖋

Updated and Expanded Edition by the Medical Bureau of Lourdes

WINNER OF THE CHRISTOPHER AWARD AND THE MARIAN MEDAL

IMAGE BOOKS
Doubleday
New York
1988

Library of Congress Cataloging-in-Publication Data

Cranston, Ruth.
    The miracle of Lourdes/by Ruth Cranston; updated and expanded
by Bureau médical.
        p.   cm.
    ISBN 0-385-24187-9: $8.95
    1. Christian shrines—France—Lourdes.   2. Mary, Blessed Virgin,
Saint—Apparitions and miracles—France—Lourdes.   3. Spiritual
healing—France—Lourdes—Case studies.   4. Miracles—Case studies.
5. Lourdes (France)—Church history.   I. Bureau médical (Lourdes,
France) II. Title.
BT653.C67 1988
232.91'7'094478—dc19

                                                            87–16105
                                                            CIP

*To the Valiant and Devoted Men Who Have
Established, Developed, and Maintained the
Medical Study of the Cures at Lourdes, Thus
Performing an Inestimable Service to Science,
to Religion, and to All Mankind*

*The year 1958 will mark the end of the first
hundred years of a rewarding devotion of joy to
the Blessed Mother of God at the Shrine of Lourdes.
It was in 1858 that she appeared there to the young
and innocent daughter of a French miller.*

Lourdes
May 20, 1986

Just as Monseigneur Pierre Marie Théas, the former Bishop of Tarbes and Lourdes, did in 1955,

I, in my turn, today and in the same capacity, am very pleased to pay warm homage to the author of The Miracle of Lourdes *for her testimony in favor of a more intrinsic knowledge of Lourdes and its Message.*

It is certainly appropriate that a new edition of this book, carefully brought up to date and completed, be published in 1988.

I gratefully thank all of those who took this initiative and brought it to fruition, for the benefit of its readers, both in the United States and elsewhere.

They will thus be better able to respond to Our Blessed Lady's invitation.

†*Henri Donze*
BISHOP OF TARBES AND LOURDES

CONTENTS

Preface to the Image Edition

Dear Reader,

When Ruth Cranston's book was published for the first time, in 1955, surely no one could have predicted that I would finish out my professional life here in Lourdes as the (ninth) Permanent Doctor of the Medical Bureau, succeeding some very outstanding physicians. Even more unlikely is that I should write a preface for a new, updated edition of Mrs. Cranston's book. Writing in English is not one of my stronger talents, so I must beg your indulgence. The republication of *The Miracle of Lourdes*, however, is the most important focus here.

There are a number of good reasons for publishing a revision of this book. There have been very few books about Lourdes written in English, and they are now quite hard to find. This book had great success and a profound influence throughout the United States when it was first published.

As Permanent Doctor of the Medical Bureau, I am called upon to do many different things. Though it may seem strange, my principal function is as a sort of "public relations" person. Each year, I meet and greet large numbers of people coming from all over the world, some of them from the United States. Among the latter are about twenty people who come to Lourdes each year as "helpers" or "volunteers." These people live in all parts of the United States, from the Atlantic to the Pacific, and some of them have been coming here regularly for as long as twenty years. There are some doctors (perhaps not very many, given the number of physicians in the United States) who have faithfully stood by some hundred or so sick pilgrims. And there are groups including doctors and pilgrims, like the Marist Brothers' Lourdes Bureau, of Boston, which come to Lourdes regularly. Also, there are many people who have heard one or more of Mrs. Winifred Feely's lectures in the United States who have come to Lourdes or have become benefactors of the Shrine.

All of them have led me to believe that there is a potentially large number of Catholics—and perhaps others as well—who, prevented by distance and difficulties from coming to Lourdes, would very much appreciate an opportunity to have a current, not-too-technical account of what I know best, i.e., the medical facts of Lourdes, along with true documentation about the cures and miracles here.

I found the help I needed for this project from some English-speaking friends and colleagues who are well informed about what I really wanted to make known.

—Mrs. Winifred Feely, who is a lovely friend to me and to the Medical Bureau. She had the privilege of knowing and talking with Ruth Cranston when the author was in Lourdes in the early 1950s. Mrs. Cranston died in 1956, just after publication of the book; Mrs. Feely, a little younger, kept coming to Lourdes every summer (the pilgrimage season), has been a real witness, and has been the "lecturing lady" in the United States each winter. A more detailed history of Mrs. Feely's involvement with Lourdes, and particularly the Medical Bureau, appears in Appendix A, and she has contributed a "Testimonial," which appears after this Preface.

—Dr. Barbara Coventry is a British general medical practitioner who came to Lourdes in 1960. She is now a Councillor to the Hospitalité Notre Dame de Lourdes. Here in Lourdes, she is most closely associated with the Piscines (Baths). She has also contributed to this new edition. "Lourdes, Then and Now" appears as Appendix B of this volume.

—Dr. Vivienne d'Andria is also a British general medical practitioner. She is the doctor in charge of the Leeds Pilgrimage, from England. It is she who pulled together much of the information on each of the cures described in the new sections, as well as many of the more historical facts on the changes and improvements at Lourdes.

This new edition of *The Miracle of Lourdes* consists of a total reproduction of the original book with some new, as yet unpublished supplements. These are to be found in Chapters 11, 27 and 28, and in all of the Appendixes (A–F). The purpose of these additions is to make known what has happened at Lourdes since the original book was published and to introduce some of the people who have been instrumental in those events. There are a lot of new facts, cures, miracles, and changes. Generally, the changes have been made by the authorities of the Shrine, though there have been some made by, or for, the pilgrims themselves.

The new material is centered on what really unites us . . .

—a genuine and living Catholicism, and in fact, concern for others. In spite of our differences of culture, sex, nationality, and language, we have in common the care and service of others—those who are deprived of health, the lonely, the infirm, the crippled, the handicapped, all of whom have only a marginally secure autonomy.

—a medical formation which, besides the necessary qualifications, favors the care of the whole patient (not just the disease) and listens to his/her wishes, hopes, complaints and fears, whether they are physical, existential, or spiritual.

—a really discerning view of events and mentalities; of changes, in general or in particular; a judgment that can be appreciated because it is candid, observant, and just.

Our task is not expressly to commend the merits of Lourdes, or naïvely to praise all the "Lourdes miracles," but to add our competence and our witness regarding what has come about in the past thirty years here.

The most famous and still the most frequently asked question, of course, is, "Are there still miracles in Lourdes?" And only one answer is possible: "Yes." There is not one of us who has not experienced, at least once, an extraordinary and benevolent occurrence that we attributed to God—so we are all *"miraculés,"* in a sense. And there are still many wonderful cures.

The next question is often "Why, in more than a century, have there been only sixty-four miraculous cures recognized by the Church?" To answer this question, one must point out the arduous process by which the Church discerns and then pronounces a miracle. There are four major stages involved in the investigation of a cure at Lourdes. These will be described in much more detail in the book itself. For now, it should suffice to say that each of these stages requires painstaking research and documentation, and therefore, time. And if a particular cure does not "pass" one of these stages, then no matter how wonderful and miraculous it may seem to the recipient, it will not be officially declared "miraculous" by the Church. Even if it does pass, there is much investigation to be done by already busy people—and none of these decisions is lightly made. It is clear that the road to official Church recognition of a miracle is long and filled with obstacles.

Since the earliest cures, in 1858, it is of interest to note that

—the first seven miracles were proclaimed in January 1862 by Msgr. Laurence, the Bishop of Tarbes at the time of Bernadette,

—the next thirty-three were proclaimed by twenty-three different bishops, between 1907 and 1914,

—the last twenty-four, between 1946 and 1979, were proclaimed by twenty other bishops,

—cures have been occurring all along, and at least two thousand of them have been acknowledged by doctors as "inexplicable."

Here, as elsewhere, it must be said that the human limitations of the spokesmen for the official Church simply do not allow them to make a complete and faultless discernment of all the interventions of God. Cardinal Lambertini, the famous canonist and legislator of the eighteenth century, gave us a warning about miraculous cures. This man of genius, particularly well informed and well advised, who became Pope Benedict XIV, could hardly be suspected of any irreverence toward the Church, yet he wrote, "A fact may actually be miraculous, even in God's eyes . . . and yet not seem so for the Church."

I hope this book will help you to part with some obsolete ideas, if you have held them, about the concept of miracles.

—It is certainly not faith which causes the miracle; but indeed it is faith which recognizes it!

—Nor is a miracle a "challenge" to science.

—As Fr. Xavier Léon-Dufour, S.J., a contemporary theologian, said, "A miracle is only a more surprising manifestation than usual of the relationship which unites God and His creature in impoverished condition . . . in which the believer discerns God acting in a special way . . . and the superabundance of the love of God."

For whatever purposes it pleases God to use all of this!

Dr. Theodore Mangiapan
President, Medical Bureau of Lourdes

Testimonial: Mrs. Winifred Feely

Mrs. W. A. Feely has, since 1950, been utterly devoted to Lourdes. It was in that year that she experienced a physical cure, a grace, though she never sought to have this recognized. Since then, she has consecrated all her energy and resources—her thoughts, breadth of vision, and sense of humor—to others. With the passage of time, she has become a unique witness, the "living memory" of the Medical Bureau, epitomizing the grace of Lourdes in the way she so kindly welcomed all the English-speaking pilgrims. This she did faithfully until retiring in 1985.

Testimonial

Many years have passed since Mrs. Ruth Cranston, author of *The Miracle of Lourdes,* came to see me at Lourdes.

For me, now, the future looks short and limited, but the past, with its huge vistas of memories, seems boundless. Some of these memories have dimmed with the years, but not all. Ruth Cranston, I have never forgotten.

She came to Lourdes with an introductory letter, dated April 8, 1953, from Francis Cardinal McIntyre, D.D., Archbishop of Los Angeles, to His Excellency, the Most Reverend Pierre Marie Théas, D.D., Bishop of Tarbes and Lourdes, asking "that help be given to a resident of our Diocese, who is contemplating some writings on the subject of Lourdes. . . ." Bishop Théas, since he spoke no English, sent her to me. At that time, I was a volunteer helper at the Medical Bureau.

Dr. Leuret, of Bordeaux, was the President of the Medical Bureau. He met me in 1950 when I was cured in the Piscines (Baths) of Lourdes. He heard that I intended to offer my services as a volunteer helper, as a thanksgiving, and he suggested that I help in the Medical

Bureau. He needed someone who was bilingual, who could interpret and translate for the doctors, and more generally for all visitors who could not fluently speak French—or English.

Thus I met Mrs. Cranston, who had already published articles in *Harper's Magazine,* as well as *The Delineator* and *Century.* She had been active in Red Cross activities in 1928, was a member of the World Foundation of Churches and was also active in the World Conference on Religions. Both these organizations had headquarters at Geneva. In 1945, *World Faith,* her story of the religions of the United Nations, was published.

Ruth Cranston was a good-looking woman, fair-haired, reserved, and smiling. She was interested to hear that I was born in China, for she, too, had spent some of her young years in China. Her father, she told me, was a Methodist bishop who visited missions in that unforgettable country.

She told me that she had gone to see Dr. Smiley Blanton, a well-known doctor and psychiatrist in New York, to ask his advice about a book she planned to write on "faith healing." It was he who suggested she visit Lourdes; he had worked there with other doctors and was most enthusiastic about it all. She was herself much impressed as soon as she arrived. She was eager to write about the famous Shrine of Lourdes; she told me that no book had yet been written in English about the various facets of the work and atmosphere at Lourdes, the reactions of the sick pilgrims, the charity and kindness of the volunteer helpers, men and women, from all over the world. She was an excellent listener, had endless patience, a kind and comforting manner, and immense tact. The sick pilgrims with whom she talked were at ease with her, for she never made them feel she was invading their privacy. With the permission of some of the cured pilgrims, she went to visit them in their homes. Some of these visits are beautifully recorded in her book. Nothing was too much trouble for her! Dr. François Leuret was deeply affected by both her genuine interest in the medical side of the work and her thoroughness in research.

For my part, I was happy too that she did not seem to think of Lourdes as a place where only physical cures took place. She very quickly realized that cures and miracles were indeed few compared to the millions who come to Lourdes, the sick so humanly praying and hoping and wanting to be cured. She recognized from her conversations with the sick pilgrims that there was a beautiful light in suffering, which gave those who were not cured courage, serenity, peace, and hope. In keeping with the message of Our Lady: "Let the people come . . . let them pray for sinners . . . and make penance," she soon came to agree with my opinion that no one goes away from Lourdes empty-handed. Mrs. Cranston was visibly moved when, in answer to her question as to what I thought was a miracle of Lourdes, I replied that the words of Fr. Ronald Knox summed it up for me: "Prayer is perhaps not trying to make our voices heard above the Chorus of Angels, but hoping that in all the noise their inadequacy [will] go unnoticed."

There is at Lourdes a profound listening silence.

On November 26, 1954, she wrote to me (a very long letter):

> I'd greatly like your opinion in relation to Catholic readers. The American editors and especially the *Reader's Digest* are keen on "personal history" stories, which is why I went to Lourdes. I was so deeply attracted I couldn't stay away. This is what I saw and have to report from there. It isn't told quite as crudely as that, but that is the general idea. They think it goes over much better than a purely factual . . . "Down in the South of France, there is a wonderful town called Lourdes. Here is to be found, etc., etc. . . ."
>
> Do you think the personal side will "put off" the Catholics? I have never been enthusiastic about it, but the editors say everybody nowadays wants to "consciously travel along with the writer." It is making me a lot of trouble! However I've no doubt they know better than I do. Please give me your opinion. . . .
>
> . . . When I see you I want to have a long talk about so many Lourdes things, things that really get into the heart and really matter. . . .
>
> . . . I went to an interesting three day Conference of doctors, clergymen and psychotherapists (about 50 in all) while I was in New York, and was astonished to see what strides both the medical profession and the clergy have made on the subject of spiritual healing. They were very respectful about Lourdes—though not very well informed about it. . . .

On July 9, 1955, she wrote to me about her desire to have an Imprimatur from the Bishop of Lourdes for her book, and said:

> Through my tribute to the Bishop of Lourdes (Chapter 10) and what has been called by Catholics "the finest chapter in the book" (Chapter 20) . . . my sincere admiration for Catholic work and the Catholic Church expressed throughout the book has already brought down upon my head the criticism of Protestants who ask if I am "going over to Catholicism"!
>
> But my praise is sincere and comes from what I saw and from my honest conviction—so it stands unaltered by the criticism. . . . I don't know whether the Bishop will like the final Chapter [now Chapter 26] or not. It is really an "answer" to the skeptics and unbelievers of this generation—Catholics of course don't need it, but many of my readers will.

On February 24, 1956, she wrote to me from California, telling me of a difficulty with French publishers concerning her book, saying, "I do not believe that Our Lady and Bernadette will allow this book to remain unpublished in France."

The last time I saw Ruth Cranston was when I lunched with her in California some days after that—I remember it so well! As we walked down the steps leaving the restaurant, she said to me, "When you are [back] at Lourdes, please speak to the Lady about the pain in my back . . . and ask her to help me." I said I would and that I would light a candle—for me, a prolongation of prayers—at the Grotto. And never did I forget her request.

On April 2, 1956, at the age of sixty-seven, Ruth Cranston returned to God.

The Miracle of Lourdes was published in December 1955 in the *Reader's Digest.* It also appeared in *McCall's Magazine.* It had a tremendous success. For my part, I felt that her book had put Lourdes on the map. Many had never heard of Lourdes, had no idea that the place existed.

In his review of *The Miracle of Lourdes,* which appeared in the Chicago *New World,* Rev. Francis J. Filas, S.J., said, "This is one instance where one can confidently assert that the Digests, excellent as they were, did not do full justice to the book itself. Mrs. Cranston, a Protestant, has written of Mary's Shrine with a reverence that every faithful Catholic would desire to imitate. May Our Lady reward her for her Service."

A fortnight after her death, one of Ruth Cranston's sisters wrote to me.

> Dear Mrs. Feely, I regard my sister's book as Ruth's personal "miracle" . . . for, as you may know, she had sight in only one eye (restored after an operation for cataract), and the task of going through thousands of Records in French at Lourdes would have daunted many a researcher with normal vision.
>
> I wish you might see, if you have not already done so, the laudatory review of the book appearing in the *Saturday Review* for March 3rd, written by Frances Parkinson Keyes. I am glad that Ruth read it. . . . She also knew of the Christopher Medal Award, and had had a most inspiring reception in Dallas and New Orleans, and so went out on the crest of the wave.
>
> How could we have wished it otherwise?
>
> Yours with every good wish,
>
> Ethel Cranston Mitchel

Heaven gave me, thirty years ago, the great privilege of helping a dear Protestant to write, in English, a beautiful book on Lourdes. Now, in 1986, I have been asked to collaborate in bringing that book up-to-date. Who would ever have thought of that? I certainly never did!

And on April 2, I shall have a special thought and prayer for Ruth Cranston, for it will be the thirtieth anniversary of her homegoing to God. What memories will throng into my mind—of our talks, our discussions, her reactions to the atmosphere of Lourdes, and all the things she so beautifully expressed in that book. It enabled the English-speaking world to have a glimpse of "another" world, one which I feel is a place suspended between Heaven and Earth: the Shrine of Our Lady of Lourdes.

Finally, and beyond the fact of the separation of our bodies, may I direct some words to her—a "message" (it will be the last explicit one from me) which will call to mind our innermost union and sharing concerning the work and mission we accomplished together—that of making known the Truth of Lourdes.

March 1986

Dear Ruth Cranston,

The air is woven and interwoven like a thread of song throughout every recollection, and you are in so many of those memories!

I am now on the last lap of my long and eventful life, so it may not be so long before we meet in Eternity. How lovely it will be to relive our memories of Lourdes, that hallowed place we loved so much.

And perhaps our eyes will shine brightly, like those countless candle-flames at the Grotto, which whisper to Our Lady of the hopes, the requests, and the love of millions of pilgrims from all over the world.

Until then, I do not forget you, dear Ruth Cranston, and please remember me.

Your affectionate Chère Amie,

Winifred Feely

Foreword
[to the First Edition]

In the southwest corner of France, near the Spanish border, is one of the most beautiful little towns in the world—and one of the most famous: the town of Lourdes.

Famous because hundreds of people have been reported cured there—cured instantly, permanently, completely: cured of practically every known disease. And this without treatment of any kind. They have been cured at the Shrine of Lourdes—many people believe—miraculously.

Two million persons visit the Shrine each year. They are from every faith and nation, for this is a universal shrine of all the world. They come with one common longing: to be healed of their miseries; there, at that simple altar in the rock, to be made whole.

The cures are not, as is commonly supposed, of hysterical or neurotic patients. They are cures of diabetes, tuberculosis, blindness, tumors, bone disease, cancer.

The day is past when professional men could scoff at such things. Five thousand doctors have banded together in an international medical association for the scientific study of the cures at Lourdes. They are from many countries: Australia, Argentina, India, Egypt, Turkey, Spain, Sweden, England, the United States, and many others. Investigations of the cures are as precise and methodical as the analyses at any first-class hospital. A Medical Commission of twenty distinguished physicians and surgeons of various countries passes upon these records before a cure is finally and officially declared. When it *is* declared, you may be sure it is authentic and rests on unimpeachable evidence.

Why should the everyday active person take time to read about such a place? Because it has an answer not only for the physically sick and suffering but for the ills and problems of us all. It has an answer for the world sickness, and for our individual sickness also.

Come and take a look at it. Whatever your special burden or secret malady, you may find a solution here. You may find that you, too, if you will, can be cured at Lourdes.

ACKNOWLEDGMENTS

I am especially grateful to

- –Miss Jean Taneyhill, Ruth Cranston's niece and legatee,

- –Miss Patricia Kossmann, our editor, and

- –Mr. Hugh A. Markey, our kind, patient, generous friend and intermediary.

Without their help and encouragement, our project, modest as it may appear—though precious and promising in our minds—might never have been written and published.

Dr. T. Mangiapan

Author's Acknowledgments

Thanks are due primarily to Monseigneur Théas, Bishop of Lourdes, for his gracious approval of this undertaking, and for permitting access to the records and all facilities at Lourdes. Also to the Rector of the Sanctuaries, Monseigneur Ricaud, and to the President of the Hospitallers, the Count de Beauchamp, for help with much valuable material.

I am especially indebted to Dr. Oberlin and Dr. Grenet of the International Medical Commission of Lourdes for their kind counsel and assistance in connection with medical records and appraisals. To Dr. Francois Leuret, President of the Medical Bureau during my stay in Lourdes, and to Mademoiselle Leuret, then Secretary of the Bureau and curator of the dossiers, my debt is incalculable. Also to Dr. Pelissier, Dr. Olivieri, and Dr. Niewdam—most kind advisers.

Among Catholic friends and leaders in America, besides those already mentioned, I am particularly grateful to the Reverend David McAstocker, S.J., and to Mrs. Fulton Oursler for initial help and suggestions; to the Reverend Michael O'Sullivan and Dr. A. E. Gourdeau for valuable advice and checking of facts and figures; and to the Maryknoll Sisters for precious books and for their constant prayers and inspiration.

Deep appreciation goes also to Ruth and to Maxwell Aley, who occupied from the first a central place in the project; to Marguerite Bowman for months of devoted and tireless secretarial service; and to Winifred Feely for special research and assistance along many different lines.

When it comes to acknowledging quoted material, one is in real difficulty. Lourdes material has been quoted and requoted so many times, it is hard to know where some of it actually originated. I have done my best to acknowledge original sources, and to give proper credit to the authors and publishers who have kindly allowed me to quote from their publications.

Foremost among these, thanks go to Dr. Auguste Vallet and Dr. Henri Guinier for the use of substantial portions of their very important writings: Dr. Vallet who as President of the Medical Bureau from 1927–1947 gave such wonderful service, and whose writings are among the most valuable on the cures and on Bureau procedure.

I am much indebted also to M. Louis Abadie of the *Journal de la Grotte* for permission to use material from former issues of the paper— especially stories of the cures and of the Big Pilgrimages. And to the Maison Viron and Maison Lacaze for similar generous help with pictures, old and new.

Special thanks are due Dr. Smiley Blanton for permission to use portions of his paper before the American Psycho-Analytic and Psychiatric Associations on the cure of Charles McDonald; and to Mr. McDonald himself and his publishers for their very kind cooperation in furnishing material from his personal account of his cure. Also to the Catholic Truth Society for permission to reprint substantial portions of Mr. John Traynor's writings from their booklet *I Met a Miracle.*

To the Cures themselves and their relatives, I am indebted for much generous help with personal material and photographs—especially to Jeanne Fretal, Fernand Legrand, Francis Pascal, Madame Leydet, and Madame Joucan.

In conclusion, I am well aware of some of the dissatisfactions that will be felt in regard to this book. Catholics no doubt will miss certain Catholic overtones and cherished references. But there are many Catholic books in which they will find them; and I believe they will agree that the important thing with a book like this is to get the Lourdes story over to the general public as simply and concisely as possible.

Protestants, on the other hand, may object that the writer—though a Protestant—repeatedly uses Catholic terms, such as the Blessed Sacrament, the Last Rites, the Blessed Virgin, and so forth. The reason for this is obvious. Lourdes is a Catholic shrine, and its religious ceremonies and observances are Catholic. It is therefore not only courteous but inevitable to use Catholic terms in describing them.

Many people will urge that I should have written more about Bernadette. I have not done so for two reasons: first, limitation as to time, and the great amount of research that would be necessary to write of her at all adequately; second, many writers have written volumes about her, and very beautifully—far better than anything I might add. The reader is referred to these books in which he will find detailed and fascinating stories of this beloved and remarkable person. The present book has to do especially with accounts of Lourdes cures and the Pilgrimages.

Again referring to time limitations, I would ask my readers—especially doctors—to have in mind the enormous amount of material that had to be gone over, translated, and abridged in connection with these accounts. Any apparent gaps or omissions should be put down not to a lack in Lourdes records but to my own physical limitations of time and energy. The complete records are there for anyone who cares to take the time and trouble to read them.

In the midst of preparing this manuscript, word has come of the death of Dr. Leuret, from 1947 to 1954 President of the Medical Bureau. His passing is a terrible loss to all friends of Lourdes, myself among them.

Here was an ideal combination of exacting man of science and unassuming follower of religion. Dr. Leuret never "talked religion." But he himself was such a humble and honest Christian, he gave one great respect for his faith. Every day before morning office hours I saw him trudging across the Square to Mass. Every day, broiling sun or slashing rain, I saw him walk the long mile down and back along the Esplanade, in the Procession—and always at the very end; after all the priests and bishops, nuns and organizations, all the pilgrims, came Dr. Leuret—last in line.

Something tremendously touching about that modest figure, so unobtrusive, so vitally important—for his sharp probing eye watched constantly for some significant move or sign of possible cure among the sick—even while his devout knee bent in earnest and sincere worship.

Without his unending kindness and help, this book would never have been written. It is dedicated to him especially—together with the other "valiant and devoted men" who have served Lourdes and the Bureau so faithfully.

PART ONE

Early Cures
and Organization

1

We Go on Pilgrimage

I went to Lourdes out of an irrepressible curiosity.

For years I had been interested in the power of religious faith in the relief of human ills, and had made a special study of it. I had visited a good many healing centers in America and other countries, inquiring into different methods and philosophies.

But until recently I knew very little about Lourdes, although I had spent a good part of my earlier life in France. At that time I was not interested in such things.

Then came that bright morning when my eye fell on an item in a newspaper lent me by a French friend:

IDIOT CHILD CURED AT LOURDES. BOY OF SEVEN REGAINS FULL INTELLIGENCE AFTER THREE YEARS LIVING LIKE AN ANIMAL.

Accounts of other cures followed: cancer of the stomach, peritonitis, ununited bone fracture, lung tumor. I read them, every word. They stirred my imagination. I wanted to know more about them. I wanted to know more about Lourdes.

I asked the Sisters at a nearby convent. They lent me books. I sent to France for other books. The more I read, the more interested I became. There was something in this place and in these stories—between the lines as well as within—that drew me; as it draws hundreds and thousands of people from all over the earth.

"Nonsense!" says the "rational" everyday mind. "A lot of pious exaggerations. Don't be carried away. It's probably nothing but our old friend autosuggestion—nervous emotionalism at a beautiful spot and an historic shrine."

But that wasn't enough. As I got deeper into it, I found the facts so impressive, and the whole picture so challenging, I began to want to see and study Lourdes for myself.

Now of course there are many books on Lourdes. However, most of them are either stories about Bernadette and her visions—volumes keyed especially to religious devotions, or they are early histories written in the romantic style of the nineteenth century: books that would strike the modern reader as old-fashioned and outdated. Or they are written in French. Recent fine accounts such as those that stirred my interest—Dr. Leuret's *Guérisons Miraculeuses Modernes,* Dr. Vallet's *La Vérité sur Lourdes;* Dr. Molinery's *Le Fait de Lourdes,* and several other excellent volumes—are all in French. There seemed to be no up-to-date factual story in English of this astonishing place and the prodigious things going on there. I wanted to write that story.

I talked it over with my friends. I told them the tremendous impression accounts of this place had made on me. I mentioned my years of residence in France and my knowledge of French and the French people, which should prove useful.

"But you are not a Catholic!" was the immediate objection— Lourdes being of course a celebrated Catholic shrine.

I asked whether that might not be an advantage rather than a limitation. Catholic leaders whom I consulted seemed to think it might not be a bad idea to have a book on Lourdes written by a Protestant.

"A modern book on Lourdes by a Protestant—excellent!" said a genial Catholic professor. "Go ahead. We'll help in any way we can."

The idea kept tugging at me; I kept turning it over in my mind. The main point that roused my curiosity was the change in attitude of many physicians. I knew that in times past, even as late as the early part of this century, Lourdes was considered a place for crackpots and hysterical women who were "cured" of a lot of imaginary nervous troubles through a sort of religious mass-suggestion. Most reputable medical men refused to get involved with it. What had happened to change this viewpoint (as I found it had, radically, changed)—to make not merely a few hundred but thousands of first-rate doctors today take a different stand, and study Lourdes cures with interest and respect?

No one can read Alexis Carrel's case history of Marie Bailly in *Voyage to Lourdes*—one doctor's unforgettable experience—without being brought up sharp before the tremendous implications for all doctors of this extraordinary place.

There were the astounding physical cures; there was also the dramatic and moving human-interest side of the story: the joining together of many nations and classes in simple human helpfulness—hundreds of thousands of volunteer workers coming here year after year to devote their time and services to the sick. There was the colorful pictorial side; continual pilgrimages from all over the world, the great Eucharistic processions, the vast torchlight processions by night; the quaint costumes, the fraternizing among different peoples—Buddhist and Moslem peoples, as well as Bretons and Dutch, Indians and Argentines; the unceasing prayers in every language under the sun; the many vivid human incidents.

It was all too much—for a person with any imagination. I decided I must have a first-hand look at the place.

I met with plenty of opposition from friends and associates. "Lourdes, eh? Why on earth should anybody want to go to Lourdes? Mediaeval superstition . . . ecclesiastical trumpery . . . old wives' tales!"

"Most depressing spot I ever visited," said one. "All that pomp and mummery, all those rows and rows of sick people lying about. . . . Why in the world do you want to go there?"

"Eyewash," said another. "Obvious charlatanism. . . . Big piece of smart Catholic propaganda. Don't waste your time on it."

The more they talked, the firmer I became—the more determined to go and see for myself. Was this truly, as the French authors presented it, a place of simple sincerity and wonderful deeds? Or was it a gigantic hoax, a marvelously planned propaganda piece, cleverly conceived by astute ecclesiastics to lead erring followers back into the fold? Was it a mass delusion, an hallucination as great, though as sincere, as that of which Bernadette herself was accused? Or was it an amazing and extraordinary fact—as it has been called now for a hundred years, the Fact of Lourdes: a challenge to medical men and to all men and women of this skeptical twentieth century?

I intended to go there and find out. I had no ax to grind. I belonged to no organization—religious, medical, or metaphysical. I was just an ordinary citizen with an inquiring mind and a friendly (if wary) spirit, out on my own special quest and pilgrimage.

In the spring of 1935 I started out. Catholic friends instead of creating opposition, had given sympathetic encouragement. Cardinal

McIntyre, Archbishop of my own region of Los Angeles; Father Bunn, President of Georgetown University; Father Gardner and Father Lafarge of the magazine *America;* and in England, Father Martindale and the Lourdes Association of Great Britain helped me most generously with letters, long talks, good counsel. When I reached Lourdes, the kindness and active, practical help of Monseigneur Théas, the Bishop of Lourdes, and of Dr. Leuret, President of the Medical Bureau, opened every door—made this book possible. Nurses, Cures, and the sick themselves cooperated wholeheartedly.

Protestant physicians and friends of Lourdes also made valuable contributions. So this book, created with so much friendly assistance and goodwill from so many sources, has been written—in the hope that the story of Lourdes may become a little better known, and the Fact of Lourdes better appreciated by people generally.

The question may be asked: Why this special, strong attraction to Lourdes above all other healing centers? Why go six thousand miles, when many remarkable cures are claimed around the corner, so to speak, right here at home? How does Lourdes differ from other healing places? What are its peculiar characteristics in relation to unusual cures?

The outstanding characteristic of the healing center at Lourdes, and the one that made it of particular interest to me, is the medical *controle* or checking of alleged cures through an elaborate and rigorous scientific machinery involving large numbers of doctors, some of them religious, some not. Second, the powerful influence of the organized group work—the Hospitallers and nurses—in relation to the large numbers of sick; the comradeship and extraordinary sense of unity of these masses of sick for each other.

Then there is the special atmosphere in which the cures take place: the beauty of the surroundings, the pageantry and ritual of a great Church bringing dignitaries and endless caravans of common folk from all over the world. But above all, the perpetual prayer, going on day and night, on the part of vast numbers of people—so that the very air is charged and vibrant with it.

These are some of the things that characterize Lourdes; that give it, in my opinion, a special appeal. The reader can, if he chooses, take it as the study of one healing center among many, and can compare it with others he may have investigated. But I hope that he will study it impartially and fairly, making it for the time being a personal pilgrimage of his own.

2

How the Shrine Began

There it lies, a shining jewel of a town, slipped into the velvet pocket of the Pyrenees—spires, towers, green trees and gleaming gardens, dazzling in the brilliant southern sunlight. Smiling country—lush fields, flashing streams; crisp keen air resounding all day with the songs of pilgrims, the tramp of hurrying feet.

In this town of sturdy Bearn mountain folk, about the middle of the nineteenth century, something extraordinary happened. The story goes that one day (February 11, 1858) the Virgin appeared to the child of a poor peasant family in the region—a girl of fourteen named Bernadette Soubirous—while she was out gathering firewood. Bernadette saw "The Lady" in a sort of radiant mist, high up on a rock in a grotto above the river. She was a young and very beautiful lady, in a white robe with a blue sash. The girl saw her so vividly that she could not understand why everyone else did not see her too.

After the first day The Lady came to Bernadette in a series of visions, or Apparitions, as they have traditionally been called. She spoke to the child in the Lourdes dialect, saying: "Please come here every day for a fortnight. Go and tell the priests to build a chapel on this spot. I want people to come here in procession . . . Pray—tell them to pray! Prayer and penitence! (The Lady stressed this over and again.) . . . Go and drink in the spring and wash in it," she commanded. "I am the Immaculate Conception. I desire a chapel here."

The Spring was invisible and unknown till The Lady pointed it out to Bernadette and led her to dig in the earth and make it gush forth. At first it was a mere trickle, no thicker than a finger. Soon it became a powerful stream, made famous by the cures which took place there.

From the first, the country people believed in Bernadette. She communicated her intense faith to them and they followed her implicitly, praying with her at the grotto at each of the "apparitions" of The Lady. They gathered in small bands at first, then in crowds from all over the surrounding country. They set up a rude little shrine and brought candles and flowers and small gifts. Local clergy at first were cool and aloof. Civic authorities scorned the visions, threatened Bernadette and her family, closed the grotto, confiscated the shrine.

But then the miracles began. A blind man who washed his eyes in the spring water regained his sight. A mother, neighbor of the Soubirouses, dipped her dying child in the waters, and the child not only lived but became well and robust for the first time. People began to bring their sick from all over the land. It was reported that the son of the Emperor Napoleon III had been cured by the application of Lourdes water. The grotto, which had been closed by police order, was declared by the Emperor open to the public. After the first cures the crowd trebled. Hotels sprang up, churches were built—all the fanfare of a tourist and pilgrimage center quickly developed.

Finally the Bishop of the diocese set up a commission of investigation to look into the matter. The commission—hard-headed and skeptical men—after four years' study came through with a complete vindication of Bernadette and a declaration that certain cures that had occurred at the shrine definitely must be considered miraculous—i.e., contrary to all known biological laws and medical science.

In January, 1862, the Bishop of Tarbes and Lourdes issued a decree: "We declare that Mary the Immaculate, Mother of God, did in reality appear to Bernadette Soubirous on February 11, 1858, and on certain subsequent occasions, to the number of eighteen in all, in the Grotto of Massabieille near the town of Lourdes . . . and that the faithful are justified in believing it certain."

Bernadette was canonized (1933) in a magnificent ceremony at St. Peter's, the Pope and all the College of Cardinals participating. She had died years before (1879), in her convent at Nevers—a person remarkable for her independence of spirit, absolute honesty and courage, who had stood by her visions and her convictions despite threats of prison and insane asylums, persecutions and humiliations of all sorts. The transformation of her life and character, under the influence of her visions and alleged contact with the heavenly Lady, her change from an ignorant, undeveloped little peasant girl into a woman of extraordinary strength and reserve, is one of the amazing facets of this altogether amazing story.

The Church capitulated; the medical profession did not. Doctors pronounced Bernadette "hallucinated"—some said demented. Any physician who dared speak a believing word for the cures at Lourdes was himself considered hallucinated and undeserving of a scientific reputation. Professor Pitrès, Dean of the Faculty of Medicine at the University of Bordeaux, told his students: "If ever people talk to you about the so-called miraculous cases of Lourdes, know that it is mere exploitation of human stupidity."

The Spring was called "fixed," the patients "sentimental neurasthenics." "Hysteria" . . . "self-hypnosis" . . . "autosuggestion" . . . "false diagnosis" . . . these were some of the explanations given for the remarkable things going on there. Lourdes became a focal point for the bitter battle between freethinkers and believers raging in Europe during the latter half of the nineteenth century. Doctors scorned the idea of any real cure coming out of the place. They considered it a resort for dupes and charlatans and called its defenders quacks and fakers.

In 1905, a young doctor was turned out of the University of Lyons Medical Faculty because he stated that a case of tuberculous disease in which he was interested had been miraculously cured at Lourdes.

"With such views, sir," said the Dean coldly, "you can hardly expect to be received as a member of our Faculty!"

"In that case," said the young physician, "I must look elsewhere."

He came to New York, to the Rockefeller Institute, and in 1912, as result of his researches there, received the Nobel Prize. His name is Alexis Carrel.

In 1912, another medical student at Lyons, Madame Jeanne Bon, was rejected on her thesis for her doctorate—"not for lack of merit, but because it dealt with the cures at Lourdes, with the miraculous." Eighteen years later, 1930, Henri Monnier received his doctorate (and very honorable mention) from the University of Paris with a thesis on the same subject. What had happened during those eighteen years?

To go back a little: After the vindication of Bernadette and the Church's recognition of the miracles, the Spring of the Grotto by order of the Bishop was channeled to fill the reservoir with twelve taps and five piscines, or pools, to receive the sick for bathing. This of course greatly increased the number of pilgrims and declared cures.

In 1872, the first National Pilgrimage was organized; and in 1884, the first "Hospitality" Association for the transportation and care of the sick. In 1885 came the establishment of the Medical Bureau—for professional study and verification of alleged cures. This gave the place a much more serious atmosphere, from the medical point of view. Curiosity brought to the Bureau doctors of all beliefs, and the number of visitors for a while doubled each year.

In 1893, the celebrated French neurologist Charcot gave his interpretation of the cures at Lourdes under the title: "The Faith Which Heals." In 1894, Zola published his novel *Lourdes* in which he deliberately falsified accounts of certain famous cures, but which again focused public attention on the place.

In 1906, Paris editor Bonnefon launched a bitter press campaign to close Lourdes in the name of hygiene. He met with an unexpected and thunderous reply. Dr. Vincent of Lyons got together the signatures of three thousand doctors testifying to the invaluable services rendered by Lourdes to the sick "whom we doctors have been powerless to save," and insisting that nothing be done to interfere with them.

A number of books appeared, by medical men of high reputation, discussing the phenomena of Lourdes and giving well-documented accounts of some of the outstanding cures: *Medical History of Lourdes,* by Dr. Boissarie; *The Facts of Lourdes,* by Dr. Marchand; *Medical Proof of the Miraculous,* by Dr. Le Bec; and various others.

All these things gradually—one might say painfully, and with slow and stubborn impact—wore away the early absolute resistance and broke down bit by bit the implacable professional prejudice against Lourdes.

But the most powerful force in this gradual transformation of public and professional opinion was that of the Cures themselves. They constituted a living argument difficult to explain away.

3

Early Cures

One of those to be shaken out of his early skepticism was Bernadette's own physician, Dr. Dozous.

This Dozous was an unusual fellow to be found in a little French mountain town in the middle of the nineteenth century. When the strange goings-on were first reported about his young patient, the Soubirous girl, he was as incredulous as other good citizens. But Dozous was a real scientist. Instead of turning his back, with a flat denial, he took the trouble to investigate and see for himself.

He went to the Grotto with his chronometer—the only scientific instrument available to him then—to observe Bernadette in her "visions." The unearthly beauty of her face during her trances made a deep impression on him. After the first experience he went every day and watched her intently, clocked her psychological states, and made careful notes of his observations.

His devotion was rewarded. For, while watching, he witnessed one of the first important Lourdes cures. And this happened to another of his patients—a little neighbor of Bernadette's, Louis-Justin Bouhohorts.

Louis-Justin was eighteen months old. Bernadette's mother was often called in by his frantic mother to help, during the child's terrifying seizures. The little boy had a disease which resulted in complete paralysis of his legs. Dr. Dozous in his notes on the case wrote: "Diagnosis hesitates between meningitis and poliomyelitis." The child could not walk, stand, or sit up. He had violent convulsions and high fever, with increasingly serious attacks. Finally the doctor said, "It is only a matter of hours."

The child moaned and gasped in his crib, and his father said to the mother, who was trying to help him, "Let him alone. Can't you see he is very nearly dead?"

He went to get a neighbor to assist with the burial arrangements. She soon arrived, with linens to make the shroud. But the mother would not give up.

She snatched the child from the cradle, rolled him in her apron, and ran to the Grotto. She found the piscine that the workmen had dug a few days before; and in that icy pool she plunged her baby up to the neck, for fifteen whole minutes. Neighbors looked on, aghast. Dr. Dozous, who was there with his chronometer watching Bernadette, counted the minutes for Mother Bouhohorts, too. When she took the baby out, the little body was all stiff and blue.

His mother carried him home and put him in his crib again. When his father saw him, he said harshly: "Well, are you happy now? Have you finished killing him?"

The mother knelt and prayed beside the cradle. At the end of a few minutes she pulled her husband's sleeve. "Look—he is breathing!" And the child *was* breathing—quietly and normally. He went to sleep and had a very good night. The next morning, his mother said, he ate a good breakfast. She put him back in his crib while she did her housework.

Some minutes later she heard a slight noise. She looked around. It was Louis-Justin. He had climbed out of his crib and was *walking*—toddling toward her like any normal child.

Later in the day Dr. Dozous and Dr. Lecrampe examined him, the former producing his notes on the case. "I examined this child three days ago," he said. "No change at that time. I wrote here: 'Still paralysis of the thighs.' I gave him twelve hours to live. And here he is—*walking!*"

"Yes, yes, go to Lourdes," said Professor Pèis. "You will see there some fine cases of autosuggestion, with all the flowers and candles and incense, the collective prayers and so on."

But for Louis-Justin Bouhohorts there were neither flowers, nor chants, nor prayers, nor incense—just a few curious people standing about, more or less skeptical, and an observing physician definitely distrustful. And then—eighteen months old! Is it possible that at eighteen months one can make an act of faith and be subject to autosuggestion?

The case of the Bouhohorts child made a profound impression on Dr. Dozous. He was one of the first medical witnesses of the acts at Lourdes, and has been called the first operator in the medical verification work there.

An interesting sequel to the story: Louis-Justin Bouhohorts, aged seventy-seven, was one of the honored guests at the great ceremony of the canonization of St. Bernadette at Rome in 1933. He owed her a long and healthy life.

Also in the early days came the sensational cure of Joachime Dehant. Joachime, twenty-nine years old, had suffered for twelve years from a frightful ulcer on her right leg. She came from Gesves, Belgium. Dr. Marique and Dr. Froidebise, who attended her there, furnished precise details in their certificates describing her condition when she left for Lourdes.

They stated that the right leg showed an ulcer 12 inches long by 6 inches broad, extending to the bone. During the years, the muscles of the leg had been partly destroyed, the bone deadened. Foul-smelling pus discharged constantly from the wound. The foot, lacking all support, was inverted, the knee joint rigid—the whole limb could be represented by the figure 4. On the train the odor from the wound revolted everybody.

But Joachime was so sure she would be cured at Lourdes that she took a pair of boots with her to wear on her way home. On reaching Lourdes, she was carried to the Grotto and her leg was immersed in the waters of the pool for some thirty minutes. Nothing happened. Without losing heart she returned some hours later, bathed the leg for another thirty minutes. Agonizing pain followed—but then a feeling of great ease and the disappearance of all suffering. The wound was completely cured, the skin reformed, and a perfect scar developed.

Mademoiselle Dorval, who had accompanied Joachime to the baths, the Abbé Devos who had cared for her in the train, and many pilgrims who had shrunk from her previously, all verified her sudden and radical change. The right leg had resumed its normal straightness and shape, and functioned naturally. When Joachime alighted at Gesves on the return journey, she was wearing her boots and could walk as well as anybody. She has made forty-five pilgrimages of thanksgiving to Lourdes since her cure, and always in the best of health. The Church lists Joachime Dehant as one of its fifty-one recognized Miraculous Cures.

When French pension offices start paying out money—and big money—you can be sure they believe an injury is genuine. That's what they did in the case of Gabriel Gargam, a railway post-office clerk.

On a cold evening in December, the Orleans Southwest Express was racing through the night on the run between Bordeaux and Angoulême. In the postal car, up near the engine, the clerks worked swiftly and silently, sorting the mail. Gargam worked quietly and expertly with the rest. In a few hours he'd be home, stomping into his own house hungry and tired, sitting down to the excellent soup his mother always kept for him in the big iron pot on the back of the stove. Off with his boots, on with his slippers—a good pipe, a nip of cognac, a glance at the papers, and then to bed. So he dreamed contentedly, sorting his letters, humming a little tune.

Suddenly, a deafening shriek. The train buckled. Cracking timber —lamps smashing—people screaming—a bridge crashing into the ravine. Gargam felt a searing pain in his back. Then—blackness.

He woke up in a hospital, bandaged from head to foot, paralyzed from the waist down. He had been crushed almost to death—his spine injured beyond any hope of recovery. The least movement produced vomiting. They had to feed him through a tube, which caused terrible suffering. The tube could be inserted only once a day. Not eating, he became very weak and emaciated. Gangrenous sores formed on both feet. His physician, Dr. Decressac, declared in his certificate that the spinal disease would inevitably result in death.

The doctors of the Orleans Railroad and the Postal Administration placed exhaustive reports before the court that judged the case. The patient was awarded the then substantial amount of 6,000 francs annuity—the court pronouncing him "a human wreck who would henceforth need at least two persons to care for him day and night."

After twenty months in the hospital he was growing weaker every day. He could no longer swallow. The sores on his feet grew worse, and the doctors warned his family that death was near.

Gargam was completely unreligious and had not set foot in a church for fifteen years. But his mother was a deeply religious woman. Because of her entreaties he agreed to enroll for the pilgrimage to

Lourdes. The journey was accomplished with great suffering, on a stretcher.

On his first afternoon at Lourdes he lay on the route of the Procession of the Blessed Sacrament—very weak, and soon entirely unconscious; his features relaxed, cold and blue. But at the moment when his nurse thought him dying, suddenly he opened his eyes, raised himself on his elbow, fell back again—but made another effort. Now he was up. He took several steps after the Blessed Sacrament, but he had no clothes or shoes. He was stopped and put back on his stretcher.

Never mind. Nothing they could do to him mattered now. He was cured! His paralysis was gone. He had recovered complete freedom of movement.

His entrance into the Medical Bureau was dramatic. Sixty doctors, many newspaper correspondents, believers and unbelievers, surrounded him. "Gargam arrived on his plank," says the record, "wrapped in a long bathrobe. He stood before us, a specter. Big, staring eyes alone were living in his emaciated colorless face." Emotion ran so high, and the crowds were so great they had to defer his examination till the next day.

Now Gargam came no longer on his plank, but in a new suit, and walking. The sores on his feet, yesterday open and suppurating, were closing perceptibly. He walked without much difficulty. The doctors examined and questioned him for two hours.

X-rays showed the compression of the lumbar vertebrae where spinal-cord injury had caused the paralysis of the lower part of the body. Now he was able to put aside his feeding tube and to eat normally. In a few days he gained 20 pounds in weight, four inches in the circumference of his leg. From the first, his endurance was astonishing. The crowd and the reporters besieged him. He answered them all calmly and never wearied.

Gargam's return home was a stirring event. The news of his cure had spread through all the stations of the Orleans road. It was verified by the physician of the Post-Office Department who told him he should immediately resume his post.

The case created a sensation. The sixty physicians who examined him at Lourdes all agreed: the cure was scientifically inexplicable. One might have expected the railroad to make some effort to recover the annuity. Instead, Gargam had great difficulty in persuading the incredulous railroad officers to take back their money.

He came to Lourdes each year for many years and served as

stretcher-bearer, sturdily carrying other patients on his once gangrenous feet.*

A cure of blindness is especially moving.

Madame Biré of Lucon, hard-working country woman and mother
of six children, woke up one morning not to the light but to total
darkness. For a long time she had been having violent headaches, hemorrhages from the stomach, queer confused dizzy feelings. She knew
she was seriously ill. But she never dreamed of this. *Blind!*

The doctor tried to comfort her in her terror. Maybe it was only
temporary. These things happened sometimes—"nervous blindness," it
was called . . . "The delicate mechanism of the eye, susceptible to
inner strains, tensions,"—and so on.

After the examination the doctor's voice was grave, compassionate.
"I hate to tell you, madame, but there has been a complete wasting of
the optic nerves—on both sides. I'm afraid there's no cure for that, and
no recovery." In his notes Dr. Hibert put down: "Luminous reflexes
entirely destroyed. Blindness from double papillary atrophy."

The papillae are the optic discs at the end of the optic nerves;
normally a beautiful, bright orange-red, a network of strong, fine fibers;
in Madame Biré's case they were grayish white and wasted away to a
mere thread.

Her doctor told her, in effect, that the mechanism of vision itself
had been destroyed.

How would you feel? How would anybody feel? Working people
—the children—so little money—and *blind!*

Madame Biré grew rapidly worse. The emotional disturbance
brought on more serious hemorrhages. She couldn't eat—continuous
vomiting and lack of food produced dangerous weakness. And this
went on for six months. Her family and Dr. Hibert were deeply concerned.

Finally she decided to join the Vendée Pilgrimage to Lourdes. Her
doctor and her eldest daughter accompanied her. In the train during the
night she had prolonged fainting spells, and arrived at Lourdes in a
nearly dying condition.

In the morning she was taken to the baths, but the crowd was so

* He was there in 1951—but died in 1952, at the ripe old age of eighty-three.

great she had to return to the Grotto, where she remained for some time, lying back in her little carriage and praying with the other sick.

Mass ended at 10:15 and the Sacred Host was taken back into the Church of the Rosary. As the priest passed beside her, Madame Biré suddenly stood up and said in a weak voice: "Ah, I see the Blessed Virgin!" She fell back into her carriage, fainting. A little blood oozed from her lips. Her daughter thought she was dying.

But Madame Biré soon came to her senses. She saw the statue of the Virgin there in the niche—"less white and brilliant than the first time," she said. But—she could see!

Crowds flocked around her. She was taken to the Medical Bureau with her certificate from Dr. Hibert, stating the fact of her complete blindness for months past. Several doctors at the Bureau examined her, among them Dr. Lainey, an oculist from Rouen. He entered his report in the Bureau record:

> Examination of the eyes with the ophthalmoscope showed on both sides a white pearly papilla, devoid of all color. The veins and the arteries, thrown to one side, were thin and threadlike. The diagnosis was forced upon me: here was white atrophy of the optic nerve, of cerebral cause. This, one of the gravest affections, is recognized by all authorities as incurable. But Madame Biré had recovered her sight that morning. She could read the finest print, and her distant vision was just as good.

She had recovered her sight but the lesions remained, to disappear shortly afterward.

Ten doctors made a second examination next day, with the findings: the organ still atrophied and lifeless, the sight clear and perfect. Questions followed thick and fast, with many scientific words the patient did not understand.

"How *can* you see, madame, when you have no papillae?" one doctor asked impatiently.

"I beg your pardon—the Blessed Virgin has given me some!" Madame Biré replied with spirit. "Listen, gentlemen, I am not familiar with your long, learned words. I have just one thing to say"—and she said it in nearly Biblical terms: "For nearly six months I could not see; I could not see even yesterday morning; and now I *can* see. That is enough for me."

It had to be enough for her questioners also. They acknowledged that the cure appeared complete. The future would tell whether it was permanent.

A month after her return home the Medical Bureau asked Madame Biré to go to Poitiers where three specialists, among them Dr. Rubbrecht, a Belgian oculist, examined her. The Bureau wished to know whether she was still seeing with "dead" eyes. Dr. Rubbrecht found the phenomena had ceased. "All traces of papillary atrophy," he wrote, "have disappeared. There are no longer any lesions, and the cure is complete."

From the hour of her cure Madame Biré could eat normally; she recovered her strength at once. During the following year she gained fifty pounds, could do all her housework and was perfectly well.

The next year she came back to Lourdes. Dr. Lainey again examined her. He found the back of the eye normal, and the sight perfect. The register stated: "Madame Biré is now in splendid health." The President of the Bureau, Dr. Vallet, saw her twenty years later. Her sight was still excellent. And a Canonical Commission, after lengthy investigation, had pronounced her one of the Miraculous Cures of the Church.

Dr. Mariaux of Belgium, discussing this case at the Medical Bureau, said: "The instantaneous return of sight and the restoration of the sclerosed optic nerve is a fact absolutely inexplicable from a clinical point of view." All the doctors who studied the case unanimously set down the same opinion.

In two fine drawings, afterward photographed, Dr. Lainey showed Madame Biré's eyes as they were the first year he examined her, and again the second year. An American physician, Dr. J. Arthur Reed, of Pasadena, California, who recently operated on my own eyes, declared on reading the Medical Bureau record and seeing the drawings:

"Such a case is medically impossible. By all means publish it. Any eye doctor would be dumfounded before such a cure. Cases of optic atrophy, such as the one in the photograph, just don't recover."

Other extraordinary cures baffled the doctors during those early years of the Shrine. Little Yvonne Aumaitre, daughter of a Nantes physician, was cured at the age of two of double clubfoot. Her father recorded the case for the Medical Bureau files. Constance Piquet was cured of cancer of the breast—an advanced case pronounced inoperable by Doctors

Laverne and Morlet, of Paris. Madame Pecantet was healed of cancer of the lower lip. For two years she could feed herself only liquids, through a small pipe. After several days' washing with Lourdes water, the hideous sore disappeared and the lip became completely normal.

Marie Le Marchand, her face half eaten away by a tuberculous skin disease, came out of the piscine with only a long red scar to remind her of her former malady. Dr. d'Hombres gives a vivid account of the Before and After appearance of this case.

With such impressive evidence it was not surprising that public interest steadily increased, and that even doctors who were most antagonistic had to shift their position somewhat. A place where such things happened could no longer be dismissed as merely a resort for charlatans and crackpots.

The early 1900's saw the spectacular cures of Madame Biré, Gargam, Adele Gofette (another sensational accident case), Marie Borel, Henriette Hauton, Marie Bailly of whom Carrel wrote, and many others. The cures were studied with increasing interest by physicians in France and other countries.

In 1930, a British doctor wrote: "The attitude of the medical profession as a whole toward Lourdes has changed very considerably of late years. The change is from skepticism and incredulity to an acknowledgment, not necessarily of the supernatural, but that cures in connection with Lourdes do occur which cannot be explained by any known biological laws."

In December, 1931, at the very same university where Professor Pitrès had pronounced his scathing indictment of Lourdes, a meeting was held by the Society of Medicine and Surgery of Bordeaux for the serious and very respectful study of Lourdes cures.

Dr. Pierre Mauriac, brother of the famous academician and dean of the Faculty of Medicine of Bordeaux, presented the history of a severe rheumatic case, with resulting deformities, which had progressed steadily for three years which was cured suddenly after a pilgrimage to Lourdes. At the same meeting Professor Portman reported the cure of a cancer of the upper jaw; Professor Duverguey, that of a large varicose ulcer; Dr. Moulinier, the sudden amelioration of a young girl suffering from tuberculosis—the cure still in effect after nine years; while Dr. Gourdon told of a nurse who fell from an elevator on the third floor, sustaining concussion, fracture of the pelvis and both legs—the fractured bones failed to unite and a fatal end appeared certain. The patient went to Lourdes, against strong objections from her doctor. On the fourth day there, all pain ceased, and two days later she could stand. She resumed her work and was still working—active and in the best of health—several years after her accident.

All this may sound like a medical fairy tale, but the telling of fairy tales within such a hardheaded and first-rate organization as the Society of Medicine and Surgery of Bordeaux—narrated also in the *Fortnightly Gazette of Medical Science of Bordeaux*—seems very unlikely.

The truth was that forty years of steady, conscientious plugging away by the doctors of the Medical Bureau had had their effect. In 1927 came the founding of the International Medical Association of Lourdes, an organization for the scientific study of Lourdes cures, with a membership that rapidly spread to include physicians of many lands. A large correspondence developed, with letters of inquiry pouring in from all parts of the world. The President of the Medical Bureau was invited to hold conferences in Ireland, Holland, Belgium, Luxembourg, Switzerland, Italy, Algeria, Morocco, and Egypt, and but for the war would have continued to South America and the Antilles.

Requests came from Japan for an account of Lourdes cures to be submitted to a celebrated physician of that country, who desired to study the subject before coming to Lourdes himself. There were pilgrimages to Lourdes from Ceylon, from Dakar, from the United States, from Trinidad, from Denmark, from Lithuania, and many other countries.

In 1950, Dr. Vallet, the retiring President of the Medical Bureau, was made an officer of the Legion of Honor.

All this does not mean that there was no longer any opposition or hostility. There was plenty—and still is to this day. It takes courage (as several American doctors have assured me) to introduce the subject of Lourdes at a medical meeting or doctors' dinner party. One is still met with looks of pity, astonishment, or downright impatience in some quarters.

"But," as Dr. Marchand wrote, "the time of systematic contempt has passed. Many doctors have visited Lourdes, arriving there as absolute skeptics and irreconcilable adversaries of the miraculous. They have left convinced by the evidence, not ashamed to avow that they have witnessed facts accomplished before their eyes which they were totally unable to explain."

$$\approx 4 \approx$$

Lourdes Today (1955)

Modern Lourdes is a thriving town of some 13,000 residents, busy and prosperous with its huge tourist and pilgrimage trade.

If you are lucky, you arrive there as I did—in the radiant early morning: the sun just rolling up into a dazzling sky, birds singing, silver streams rushing along between rows of swaying willows; the mountains soft and hazy, still shrouded in their morning mist; and in the distance a slender spire, just visible against the rounded hills.

For an hour the train had been speeding through rich, waving cornfields dotted with red-roofed farmhouses and clumps of dark-green cypress trees. Nearing Lourdes, we saw that a pilgrimage train was arriving just ahead of us—a train evidently with a large number of sick patients. As it pulled into the station, from every window faces looked out, filled with hope and expectation, greeting their promised land: the dear land where their miseries were to be left behind—or at least forgotten for a few blissful days; for which they had endured the bitter sufferings and hardships of the long journey, most of them on the hard wooden benches during a night of "sitting up" in third-class.

But they seemed amazingly cheerful. Someone started a hymn—the "Song of Bernadette." It caught fire. Car after car took it up, till the whole long train rang with it.

"Avé, Avé—Ave, Mariá
Avé, Avé—Ave, Mari-ia!"

The train swung forward, and on this wave of joyous praise and hope we moved into the Lourdes station.

Groups of leather-harnessed stretcher-bearers hurry along the platform to the compartments reserved for the very sick. Blue-caped nurses appear at the car doors. The pilgrims who are well line up with their Director to show their tickets and to see their invalids safely established in the hospital ambulances.

I show my own ticket and pass through the station along with the rest. I rattle up to my hotel in the hotel bus, and find the usual French hotel room with its brass bed and red carpet and walnut wardrobe. I deposit my belongings, then go down and out into the street to see the town.

From that moment on, nothing is usual—or like any place I ever saw before. For this is a city of pilgrims, and they are everywhere; people who have come from the four corners of the earth with but one purpose: prayer, and healing—for themselves or for their loved ones. The city exists for them. One is surrounded by them, and steeped in their atmosphere every moment of existence in Lourdes. A great block of them closes in on me the minute I step outside my hotel.

Out into the thronged streets and hot summer sunshine, blinking up at the high white plaster houses, the old stone walls, the crowds and the banners and the weaving cars and *charabancs*. Masses of people everywhere: peasants, many of them, in their Sunday clothes, looking a bit dazed and uncomfortable; flocks of little girls and boys in provincial costume—lots of young people; Sisters and priests of many different Orders.

It is a town of steep hills and sudden, dramatic vistas—a town rich in history. On the hill to the right is the square old fortress, built by the Romans two thousand years ago, and claimed by many different rulers. The Moors took it around the year 800. Charlemagne then laid siege to it, made a truce with the Moors; the Saracen chief was converted to Christianity and became the city's first governor.

The town of today is divided into two parts: the commercial and residential district containing the shops, hotels, civic buildings, houses of the year-round residents and business people; and the second section known as "the Domaine," or Fief of Notre Dame. The busy "Main Street," ancient Rue de la Grotte, is a typical mountaintown thoroughfare, narrow, bustling, shouting; people and their vehicles jostling each other in good-natured confusion; shops with their varied wares crowding one another off the narrow sidewalks: Lourdes souvenirs, water bottles, perfumes, *patisseries,* notions. Pilgrims tramp up and down here all day long, with their knapsacks and lunchboxes.

At the top of the hill is the Square with the War Monument, the banks, the post office; the dry-goods stores, the bookshop, two or three cafés; and everywhere you look, hotels—scores of them.

At the bottom of the hill, Main Street runs into the Avenue Bernadette—equally crowded, equally noisy, and which leads directly to the Domaine. All day and every day, a continuous throng surges in this direction—people of many tongues, in many different costumes: a Scotch stretcher-bearer in a kilt, a Swiss pastor shepherding his picturesque flock with their wide lace headdresses; English curates, Italian *monsignori,* American and Irish bishops in colorful purple; city dwellers, peasants, soldiers and senators, mechanics and miners; the gentleman who gets out of his luxurious touring car, the wool salesman who comes in his truck.

The old and the new jostle at every turn: donkeys carrying huge bundles of laundry to the convent on the hill; young men tearing through on motor bikes; groups of humble village priests trudging along barefoot; an actress in a smart convertible, en route to Pau or Cauterets; big blue *charabancs* filled with tourists from Biarritz.

At the corner, hundreds of cars and buses rush by. All at once a girl with a big herd of sheep appears in the middle of the road. All halt, resignedly, and wait for her to go through. At Lourdes, a couple of cows can hold up traffic any time of the day. After all, it is still Bernadette's country town. This whole thing was started by a girl with a flock of sheep.

And here, now, directly in front, is the realm which her visions sanctified. Cross the perilous, tooting highway, enter at the big iron gate, and there you are at the Domaine: a long sweep of land stretching for a quarter of a mile from the beginning of the town near the station, straight up to the Sanctuaries; bounded by the river Gave on the one side; on the other, the seething modern auto route of the Boulevard de la Grotte.

The Domaine was bought and set aside by the Church in the early days of the Shrine—to keep it apart and forever inviolate for the worship of God and The Lady. Within the high iron grille that surrounds it are the Sanctuaries, a hospital or "refuge" for the sick, the Medical Bureau, the printing press, quarters for hospital attendants and stretcher-bearers and, most important of all, the Grotto itself. Higher up on the hill to the left are the ecclesiastical offices presided over by the Rector of the Sanctuaries, the Episcopal residence of the Bishop of Lourdes, and various other buildings connected with the complex administration of the shrine and the pilgrimages.

All day long, cars and buses tear up and down the boulevard—tradesmen and hawkers blare their traffic with the world outside. All day long the pilgrims come streaming into the Domaine, turning their backs upon that noisy world, giving themselves gladly, wholeheartedly to three days—or at least one day—of prayer and meditation.

Directly on entering this consecrated area, one feels more peaceful. The Esplanade opens its wide green lawns with their welcoming statues—Archangel Raphael, protector of travelers, Gabriel opening his book to the Ave Maria, Michael crushing Satan under his powerful foot—gazing down benevolently upon humble humankind and surrounding one with sunlit serenity. The marble figure of young Bernadette nearby offers a homely human touch. And in the very center of the Esplanade and the Domaine is the statue of Notre Dame de Lourdes—regal, benign, encircled day and night with pilgrims from every corner of the world sending their petitions and whispered supplications heavenward.

Standing there at the center, the newcomer faces the big Square which leads to the three Sanctuaries: the Church of the Rosary, the Crypt, and the Basilica—built one above the other, culminating in the Basilica at the top, with its pointed spire and its clock that strikes the Avé every hour. A great horseshoe Rampe sweeps out from the churches, making a promenade for pilgrims and a wonderful spot from which to see the processions and the town of Lourdes. On both sides of the Rampe underneath are various useful little bureaus and offices for the assistance of pilgrims.

Magnificent trees surround the whole place, and all about are rolling hills and the dreamy beauty of the gray-green countryside. Under the arcades of the Rampe, to the right, are the famous piscines, or baths, where the pilgrims come to be plunged into the waters of the Spring The Lady showed to Bernadette.

Pass the fountains where thousands of pilgrims come to drink and to carry away Lourdes water; walk a little farther under the trees beside the busy rushing river, and there you are at the Grotto: "that fiery hollow in the rock beneath the Basilica, a flaming cave burning in its side." An insignificant hole in the wall, it once was—a jagged rent in the mountain, unheeded, dark, forbidding, feared even by the populace; today the shrine most visited in all the world.

And here is the niche, the cleft in the rock where Bernadette first saw The Lady and heard her give the directions which resulted in all this vast structure and present activity. In that dark cavern where now a statue of the Virgin stands, one can well imagine The Lady shining forth from her niche, the child below on her knees, worshiping. Today thousands of people worship perpetually. The sides of the Grotto are worn smooth by all the hands and lips that have touched its sacred stones. Hundreds of flickering candles, tall pyramids of creamy white flowers, offer their perpetual praise. Along one side are heaps of crutches, plaster jackets, and steel braces, labeled "Thank You!" by the jubilant ones who discarded them.

The entire impressive edifice of the Basilica rests physically, as it does spiritually, on the Grotto. The one lofty and imposing (the mighty Church); the other simple and humble, close to nature, like Bernadette. All day long, people are praying here, absorbed, withdrawn. Procession after procession comes and goes—pilgrims from Brussels, from Bordeaux, from Strasbourg, Luxembourg, Madrid, Dublin. . . . Those who are praying do not look up—lost in recollection.

In the pulpit yonder, a priest from one of the pilgrimages is preaching, leading the people in this great lifting of the heart: peasant women on their knees, saying their rosaries; monks, Boy Scouts, taxi drivers, housewives; Breton pastors, Basque farmers, Dutch sailors, American college students; endless streams of people singing, kneeling, praying.

"I want people to come here in procession. . ."

And all because a young girl had a vision, and was faithful to it to the end.

The great moments of the day at Lourdes are the morning Masses, the Baths, the Procession of the Blessed Sacrament in the afternoon, the Torchlight Procession at night.

At dawn the hospitals begin to hum. Nurses and orderlies swiftly and skillfully wait upon their sick. Patients are washed, dressed, carried to Mass, carried back again. The morning trek to the Baths begins. The very sick are taken on stretchers, others are wheeled sitting up; the little carriages, each with its burden of agony, hopes and fears, rolled along by devoted stretcher-bearers or nurses. These are often praying aloud as they push their patients; the patients too are praying. One meets them swinging along the Esplanade in the morning sunshine.

Here are the sights that wring the heart: pathetic forms, worn but eager faces—some with closed eyes, motionless, numb. A young man with hollow cheeks and gray lips, his leg strapped to a wooden splint; mothers holding their children, some in heavy casts, some with huge lolling heads—pop-eyed, and Mongoloid; a girl with beautiful classic features peering out from a plaster cage imprisoning her from head to foot; a woman in a black veil, trying to conceal a face covered with flaming red sores; a priest, white and shrunken, in the last stages of tuberculosis; a little boy with black bandages covering his eyes; an old man hobbling along on two hideously twisted stumps. Literally, the lame, the halt, and the blind.

In front of the piscines, relatives and friends with their rosaries, praying audibly. Songs and prayers are heard also at the Chapel of Bernadette around the corner. As I pass those tragic little carriages, I pray too—that good may come to those poor souls. Surely a kind and good God could not but be touched by so much suffering.

All morning patients are being wheeled to and from the Baths and the Grotto. By eleven they are back in their hospitals for the midday meal and to rest until the events and ceremonies of the afternoon. Some visit with their families. Some are examined at the Medical Bureau. From two to four, the journey to the Baths begins again.

Soon after three, the stretcher-bearers start to clear the Square and rope off areas for the sick, for the Procession. Crowds gather with their camp-stools, milling along the Esplanade and up the Rampe, making sure of a good place.

At four, the bells begin to peal—the Procession begins to form. The priests in their varied robes assemble at the Grotto. "Everything starts from the Grotto," I am told over and again.

The Bishop appears with the monstrance, under the sacred canopy. Always it is a visiting Bishop or Archbishop who officiates—usually one accompanying a Pilgrimage. It is a great honor to carry the canopy. The first day I was at Lourdes it was carried by a Japanese, a Belgian, a famous Cure of former years, and a Negro with one of the most beautiful faces I have ever seen.

The loud-speakers open up. A great hymn rolls out, the huge crowd joining in unison, magnificently. The Procession begins its long impressive way down one side and up the other of the sunny Esplanade. First the Children of Mary, young girls in blue capes, white veils—girls of different pilgrimages, many nationalities. Then come the banners: Birmingham, Liége, Turin, Lisbon. Then forty or fifty priests in black cassocks—priests of all ages and features—some very fine faces among them. Other priests, in white surplices—the Chaplains of the Sanctuaries. Then come the Bishops in purple—ten or fifteen of them, and finally the officiating Archbishop in his white and gold robes under the golden canopy. Bringing up the rear, large numbers of men and women of the different Pilgrimages, Sisters, Nurses, members of various religious organizations; last of all, the doctors. The head doctor—the President of the Medical Bureau—walks always at the very end of the line.

Hymns, prayers—fervent, unceasing. In the Square the sick lined up in two rows—reaching from the Statue of Notre Dame all the way up to the entrance to the Rosary Church. Every few feet, in front of them, kneeling priests with arms outstretched praying earnestly, leading the responses. Nurses and orderlies on their knees, praying too—the same prayers, first in Latin, then Italian, then English, then Dutch, finally French:

"Lord, we adore Thee; Lord, we worship Thee; Lord, we love Thee. Lord, if Thou wilt Thou canst make us whole. Lord, Thy will be done! Lord, we believe; increase our faith!"

Ardor mounts as the Blessed Sacrament approaches. Prayers gather intensity, here at this spot where Christ is besought with the same cries as on the borders of Galilee:

"Lord, if Thou wilt, Thou canst heal me. Lord, he whom Thou lovest is sick . . . Lord, that I may see! Lord, that I may hear! Lord, that I may walk!"

The Bishop leaves the shelter of the canopy, carrying the monstrance. The Sacred Host is raised above each sick one. The great crowd falls to its knees. All arms are outstretched in one vast cry to Heaven. As far as one can see in any direction, people are on their knees, praying, in the form of a cross.

The sick raise their terrible faces, for the Blessing. Some pray that their own cure be forgotten, while imploring that their neighbor shall be healed. Souls long sealed within crushing agonies and suppressions open to the influx of divine and abundant Life. This is the moment when a sick one sometimes rises, and, pale but triumphant, follows the Procession with calm victorious tread up the steps and into the Church.

Sometimes—but not today. The Bishop blesses the last sufferer, and mounts the steps of the Rosary Church to bestow the final benediction. Priests and chaplains follow him in. The crowd begins to disperse.

The sun is going down. Nurses and orderlies take up the little carriages. The sick take up their burden of suffering again. People move off toward the Spring, to fill their bottles with Lourdes water; to the Way of the Cross on the hill, to do the Stations; to the statue of Notre Dame or of Bernadette. They talk in quiet groups.

There was no miracle today—except the only miracle The Lady asked for: Prayer and Penitence—mankind on its knees, in earnest common supplication.

5

Conditions for the Sick

Two million travelers and thirty thousand sick people pass through Lourdes every year; many of the sick in the last stages of some mortal disease. But in the hundred years since the Shrine's establishment, the city has never had an epidemic, there has never been a case of contagion, and the mortality rate has been not more than eight to ten persons per year. Certainly an amazing record.

True, the Lourdes sick do not travel with other passengers. Special pilgrimage trains protect both the patients and the general public, and are a guaranty for the public health. At the time when an anti-Lourdes movement was afoot in an effort to close the Shrine "for the sake of hygiene," Dr. Piraud of Poitiers wrote:

> The movement of trains of sick across France affords no disadvantage to public health. As a member of the municipality of Poitiers and Vice-president of the Board of Health of this city, where hundreds of thousands of pilgrims have stopped and sojourned since the foundation of the National Pilgrimages, I declare that our city has remained absolutely free from all contagion and infection.

Lourdes hospitals are models of cleanliness—wards, kitchens, everything immaculate. Each pilgrimage brings its own nurses, but the two hospitals have also their permanent staff of Sisters. The Hospital of

Our Lady of Lourdes, on the Esplanade, is staffed by the Sisters of Nevers, Bernadette's own Order; the Hospital of the Seven Sorrows—just a few steps from my hotel—by the Sisters of St. Frai.

During the season, 1,200 to 1,300 invalids follow each other continuously in the wards—patients with all sorts of diseases—each pilgrimage staying only three to five days. The wards are remarkably neat and tidy, considering the poverty of many of the patients and the pathetic informality of their luggage—often just a cardboard box or string bag.

The dining halls are big, airy apartments, spotlessly kept; the kitchens the last word in modern equipment, with huge ovens and enormous round metal pots for cooking. Three enormous refrigerators keep the provisions fresh and appetizing. The chef has only one assistant. During the season, with the Sisters and nurses serving, a thousand are fed at each meal.

Regarding conditions at the baths, there has been at times heated discussion. Dr. Boissarie (in 1905) maintained that conditions at Lourdes were better than those at the typical hot springs—"where the pool is a large body of water in which the patients bathe all together, fifty or more at a time; where there is general contact, the water is not renewed, and the air soon becomes vitiated."

At Lourdes, he said, "the patients are bathed one at a time. Their immersions take only a minute. The sick person is protected by a curtain, the air circulating freely around him, and instead of a common pool he is dipped in a bath. Those seriously ill, those with heart disease and so forth, are not plunged in the baths, but are partially washed or 'lotioned.' Sores which might be contagious are bathed at the end of the session. With the large and experienced staff that directs the baths we are sure that every precaution is taken."

During 1953, 244,055 patients were immersed. There has never been an accident. Some 2,500 persons are given the baths each day.

The fact remains, as some writers have emphasized, that the water at the Lourdes baths is not changed after each patient. Some say it is not changed all day. It has been described as "dark and malodorous," "purplish," "inky," "a dreadful broth," etc. Where two thousand patients are bathed in four hours, one follows swiftly upon another. Persons suffering from syphilis, cancer, tuberculosis, and all manner of diseases are immersed in the same bath water.

The strange thing is that no infection ever results. When I was bathed, the water looked clear and clean. But the composition of Lourdes water has long been a matter of impassioned argument, from more than one angle.

The pools and the Spring are of course a vital element in the life of Lourdes. Many of the greatest cures have occurred there. Before Bernadette discovered the Spring it was unknown. It appeared on February 25, 1858, during the sixth apparition of The Lady. The Lady said, "Go drink at the fountain, and wash there." Bernadette dutifully followed instructions and scooped out the sand in that spot—though everyone mocked and laughed at her. A small amount of water appeared—first a trickle, then a stream, finally a rushing torrent. People stopped laughing.

On the following Sunday, workmen came voluntarily and dug an excavation about 3 feet long and 1 1/2 feet deep. The water that was conducted there by means of a small channel served as piscine in the early days, and here the first cures took place. (The Bouhohorts' baby, blind Bouriette, Blaisette Soupène, etc.) Later a small turbine engine was installed to provide a reservoir for the excess water and to meet the demands of the big pilgrimages.

The Spring is at the back of the Grotto to the left of the altar, behind a double grating fastened with a padlock. The water is conducted by pipes to the fountain in front of the Grotto, to the taps where the pilgrims come to drink and to fill their bottles; and to the piscines or baths. Each year, many thousands of bottles are sent to all parts of the world, by the chaplains' service.

The Spring furnishes 19 gallons a minute, 1,400 gallons an hour, and some 30,000 gallons every twenty-four hours. Many sick have been cured while being immersed or "lotioned" with Lourdes water; many others without drinking the water or taking the baths at all: at the Procession, at the Grotto, and so on. However, there is no doubt that the water has a powerful psychological influence.

Symbolically water is a sign of regeneration. In the Old Testament, Naaman the Syrian was cured in the Jordan; in the New Testament, John the Baptist plunged repentant sinners into it, and even Jesus went through this ceremony of purification. In ecclesiastical symbology, water stands for Christ, the angels, Gospel teaching, the science of the Saints—above all, as the symbol of the Holy Spirit. It does have a powerful suggestive value apropos of spiritual cleansing and restoration.

Chemically, however, the water of the Spring at Lourdes contains no curative or medicinal properties whatever.

In the early days some of the canny Lourdes citizens had rosy visions of exploiting the Spring and turning the town into a flourishing resort—like Aix-les-Bains or Vichy. They were bitterly disappointed when analysis revealed that the water contained nothing remarkable.

Professor Filhol of the Faculty of Sciences at Toulouse was engaged to make an analysis. He sent in the following report:

Carbonic acid	8 cc.
Oxygen	5 cc.
Nitrogen	17 cc.
Ammonia	Traces
Carbonate of lime	0 Grams 096
Carbonate of magnesium	0 Grams 012
Carbonate of iron	Traces
Carbonate of sodium	Traces
Chloride of sodium	0 Grams 008
Chloride of potassium	Traces
Silicate of soda and	0 Grams 018
Traces of silicate of potassium	
Sulfate of potassium, of soda	Traces
Iodine	Traces
Total	0 Grams 134

"The result of this analysis" (Professor Filhol noted) "is that the water from the Grotto of Lourdes has a composition that may be considered as a drinking water similar to most of those found in the mountains where the soil is rich in calcium. The water contains no active substance giving it marked therapeutic properties. It can be drunk without inconvenience." (Signed, Filhol, Toulouse, August 7, 1858.)

In a letter to the Mayor of Toulouse, Professor Filhol added: "The extraordinary effects which are claimed to have been obtained following the use of this water cannot, in the present state of science, be explained by the nature of the salts of which the analysis shows the existence." In 1934, a new analysis was made by Dr. Moog of the Faculty of Toulouse. The results were the same.

In 1938, Professor Lepape of the College of France undertook an exhaustive research to discover the possible existence of radium or radioactivity in the water. He writes to Dr. Vallet, with his report: "I send you herewith the report concerning the measurements of radioactivity which I have made on the water that you sent me. The search for radium did not disclose the presence of any radioactive element. From the point of view of radioactivity the water is entirely insignificant, containing only 0.7 millimicrocuries of radon at the point of emergence. Yours very truly, A. Lepape, Paris, November 16, 1938."

A bacteriological study of the water from the baths of the sick did, however, bring a remarkable discovery. As we have said, while only a small percentage of the sick who go to the baths are cured, the uncured suffer no harm or any further infection after their immersion.

The doctors at the Medical Bureau wished to check the why of this, objectively, by facts. During the years 1934 to 1935, Dr. Vallet, with several other physicians, arranged to conduct specific investigations. Two samples of water were taken from the last bath where men's wounds are bathed, and these were sent with all proper precautions, one to the laboratory of Dr. Bertrand of Anvers, the other to the Provincial Laboratory of Bacteriological Analyses of the Province of Gand, in Belgium—neither office having any knowledge of the place of origin.

The resulting reports were identical. They stated:

"The water contains microbes of the most varied order—colon bacillus, staphylococcus, pyocyaneus, etc. But none of these microbes, after culture, showed itself pathogenic to the guinea pig." Experiments made the same year at Tarbes, nearer home, produced a similar report: colon bacillus, streptococcus, staphylococcus, diplococcus, cocobacillus. That is to say, water polluted in the extreme.

Six months after being inoculated with this water, all guinea pigs were living and normal and in healthy condition. In short, Lourdes water, even when polluted, remained perfectly harmless. Billions of bacilli were found, but they were inert.

At the same time, guinea pigs inoculated with water from another source containing much the same bacilli, died.

Dr. Vallet arranged for similar experiments to be made with guinea pigs inoculated with water from the river Seine. A sample of water was taken from the river near the Concorde Bridge at eleven o'clock in the morning, and was examined by Dr. Deinse of the Pasteur Institute. It was found to contain the same microbes as those reported in Lourdes water: streptococcus, colon bacillus, staphylococcus, etc. Three guinea pigs were injected with this water. They developed fever of 104 degrees, with rapid breakdown of tissue. Two out of three died.

Easy to understand, in the light of all this, how Lourdes water came to be considered "miraculous." And here is a dramatic footnote:

Many a Lourdes devotee—the stretcher-bearers and nurses especially—at the end of the day, will scoop out a glass of water from the baths and drink it down as an act of faith. Maybe this will be too strong a "dose" for the average reader—but at Lourdes it is an everyday fact.

The old Count de Beauchamp, President of the Hospitallers and now eighty-seven, said: "I have drunk a whole hospital-full of microbes, but I have never yet been sick!"

Naturally everyone wants to see the baths and to have a bath himself, if possible. Walking along the Esplanade to the right of the Sanctuaries, you come to the pointed-roofed bathhouses.* They are divided into compartments—two for men, three for women and children. Each compartment has a sort of vestibule where the stretcher-bearers or nurses help the patients to undress. Three of the walls are plain; at the far end on the fourth side is the shallow stone bath, with three steps leading down into the water. Those who can walk use these steps; others are lowered into the bath on their stretchers or in the arms of their attendants. Immersion in the icy water lasts barely a minute.

All morning and most of the afternoon, a steady stream of people come to be bathed. Bath attendants are in these tiny wet compartments for hours at a time, helping first one and then another. Outside, the space in front is filled with the stretchers and carriages of the sick, stretcher-bearers praying with them and encouraging them as they wait their turn. Behind them the tightly packed mass of friends and relatives, praying passionately, each for his own, and for all the invalids: "the assault on Heaven," as it is called at Lourdes.

Usually some pilgrimage priest leads the prayers, and with what fervor they pray, these poor country curés, flinging themselves on their knees with arms outstretched, invoking the Virgin with loud cries and imploring her to heal the patients who are being bathed.

"Mary, we love thee! Blessed Virgin, hear our prayers! Holy Virgin, save our sick! Jesus, save us or we perish!"

---

* At present new baths are being built, and a number of improvements created for the easement of the crowds around the Grotto.

One after the other the ambulances roll in, bringing their pitiful cargo of human wreckage: the dropsied, the consumptive, the maimed, the paralyzed. Creatures who seem scarcely human any longer, so hideous and grotesque are their deformities.

A good place to view the scene is from the terrace up above—the top of the rocky cliff which falls sheer to the roofs of the bathhouse buildings underneath. I used to stand there for hours, watching the endless file of stretchers being carried in. Even from up there one can see those tense white faces of the sick, eager or twisted with pain, as they lie waiting, the crowd milling around them.

Loud above the shuffling feet come cries of the priests—who stand now in a long row facing the people, with arms extended, always in the form of a cross. Now and again a burst of singing from the Grotto, where Masses are being said continuously—a great crescendo as the Gloria rings out.

And all around, the soft green countryside—the little white farmhouses, wide meadows, golden fields just ready for the harvest; the mountains, the sheep, the gray convent on the hill—everything Bernadette knew and loved.

The exquisite beauty of nature throws into sharper relief the agonies of those pain-racked bodies down below. One after another is passed along—lowered to rest briefly before that fateful door.

This is the moment. For this they have lived and planned, sacrificed and waited, for long weary months. And now—? This is where those others were cured. Will *I* be a chosen one? Will I too drop the intolerable burden of pain and agony within these damp walls, and come forth whole?

A lifetime of yearning and expectation is behind those closed eyelids, those lips silently moving in prayer. One by one the stretchers are lifted and swung gently over the threshold.

A person who is well hesitates to take up space that might be given to the needy sick. But such visitors are also permitted to have a bath when there is time for them; and one is not considered a real Lourdes pilgrim until he has had a dip in the piscine. So, in the afternoon when the crowds of sick had almost finished, I took my place with the waiting women on the benches near the bathhouse door.

"Partial or complete, madame?" asked a kindly, gray-haired stretcher-bearer.

"Oh—complete." If I was going to do it, I had better do it properly.

Two or three women ahead of me moved along toward the door. One by one they were beckoned in. "And you, madame!"

I slipped through the portal into the tiny dressing room. Here, in a space not more than five by seven, eight women—in various stages— were undressing. At one end, behind the heavy curtain, at three-minute intervals two sturdy attendants were helping the bathers down the steps into the pool. The cries were not reassuring.

We were told to take off all our clothes and to go into the water *en chemise*—in nothing but our vests. Just before we stepped in, one attendant swiftly slipped the vest over our heads, while the other threw a wet towel around us—the same towel that had covered the last person.

The women encouraged one another. "It's not so bad. Oh, it's only a moment. You won't really mind it—I've done it three times!"

The square, stone pool—a picture of Notre Dame de Lourdes opposite—some prayers and invocations on the wall. The attendants praying without ceasing.

Down into the icy water. Gasps—cries—screams. "Now, now, madame, it's nothing. Just an instant. But really nothing, madame!"

"Hail Mary, full of grace . . . Pray for us, poor sinners . . . now and at the hour of our death. Lord, if thou wilt Thou canst heal me. Lord, that I may see . . . Lord, that I may walk . . . Mary, Mother of God, pray for us. Saint Bernadette, pray for us. Lord, hear our prayer!"

My turn. The two pleasant-faced women grasp me firmly by the arms. One step down—two—*e-e-eh!* The water's freezing! In with the shoulders. Remember—this is where Joachime and the little Yvonne and Constance Piquet and Marie Lemarchand and all those others got their cure. This slippery wet little hole. Lord, help me to pray too. Help me to understand.

Up again. Quickly into one's clothes, damp, shivering. You aren't supposed to dry yourself after the bath. I know I must let Lourdes water dry on me. Six more timid, pink-fleshed women struggling into or out of their clothes. A stretcher-case being plunged in—a hunchback . . . Next, a woman with a dreadful, cancerous face. *"Lord, if Thou wilt. Hail Mary!"*

Out into the warm afternoon sunshine . . . the crowds, the kneeling pilgrims. More people going in—stretchers, little carriages—brancardiers skillfully moving their charges along. Through the crowds, past the kneeling priests, past the woman selling candles, out into blazing Square. . . . Glowing, a bit bewildered, moved in spite of oneself, wondering, hoping, praying for all those others—the really sick, waiting out there—the paralytics, the crippled, the idiots, the monsters, the blind. . . .

"Lord, if Thou wilt—oh God, for Your sake, please do heal them all!"
I have had a Lourdes bath.

6

Hospitality and Nursing Services

But how is all this organized? Who heads it? Who pays for it? What is the directing power behind it all? These questions naturally arise in the practical everyday mind. I asked them of the Rector of the Sanctuaries, soon after my own arrival.

We were sitting in his little office in the Administration Building—the unending procession of pilgrims winding past, up the hill, on their morning climb to the Way of the Cross. The Rector, a spare man with quiet dark eyes and a quizzical smile, regarded me benevolently across the plain deal table.

"Lourdes and its inner workings, eh? Very well—we'll begin at the beginning: The Bishop. He is supreme authority for all matters within the Domaine. Under him are the Rector and the corps of chaplains."

"And how many are they?"

"Fourteen, in permanent residence. In summer we call in twenty or thirty more, to hear confessions and give general assistance. These priests work very hard. Sometimes they are hearing confessions all night as well as all day. You see, hundreds of people want to confess at Lourdes who have not confessed for many years."

"I suppose each pilgrimage has its own priests, too?"

"Certainly. The number of pilgrims determines the number of priests who accompany it. Usually a pilgrimage runs from five hundred to a thousand persons; sometimes as high as sixty thousand, with the Rosary and the French National, for instance."

"And how does a person go about it when he wants to organize a pilgrimage? Suppose my friend Professor X, for example, wants to organize one, what does he do?"

The Rector shook his head. "Your friend Professor X can't organize a pilgrimage—nor your friend Madame Y, either, no matter how pious or devoted they may be. All pilgrimages must be organized under diocesan authority, and under the local priesthood.

"If a priest wants to organize a pilgrimage, first he gets authority from his bishop. Then he writes the Secretary-General at Lourdes to say how many pilgrims he wants to bring and at about what time. The Secretary-General arranges the schedule for all pilgrimages, and when you see the tremendous list—with three or four pilgrimages arriving every day—you realize what a terrific job it is.

"Look at that sheet of statistics here on the wall," he added. "In the year 1953, five hundred and fifteen pilgrimage trains came to Lourdes within the seasonal six months—not to mention planes and cars and other vehicles. They brought altogether two million pilgrims. That," said the Rector, laying the tips of his long fingers together, "is, in your language, 'a whale of a lot of people!' "

"Who," I asked, "makes the arrangements for all these people—the travel bookings, hotel accommodations and everything?"

"Again, the local pilgrimage priest and director. He is responsible for all arrangements. The Secretary-General simply gives that all-important thing: a date."

"What if a priest or group should arrive without the proper authority, or without fulfilling all the necessary requirements? I suppose that does happen sometimes?"

"They would not be admitted. You can understand how we would very soon be in chaos if these great numbers of people arrived helter-skelter, without complying with the regulations, or without the necessary staff to look after their sick members."

Each pilgrimage, he said, brings its own doctors, nurses, nurses' assistants and stretcher-bearers. The hospitals furnish free beds and shelter—as their name (Asile, or Refuge) implies. They provide food at a modest price, but no medical or nursing care. That is entirely up to the pilgrimage.

"What about the matter of expenses in general?"

"Each pilgrim's expenses are borne by himself or his family—sometimes by a local Society of Notre Dame de Lourdes in the city or region that he comes from. The cost of a trip to Lourdes, for a sick person in France, ranges from thirty to fifty dollars, and for a well pilgrim about the same. Even the pilgrimage nurses and stretcher-bearers pay their own way, and consider it an honor and privilege to serve. All these are volunteer workers—most of them have to put in a fairly long apprenticeship before they are recognized as full-fledged yearly helpers.

"But as you know," concluded the Rector emphatically, "the backbone and central pillar of the volunteer work at Lourdes is the organization of the Hospitallers. That is an organization of which we are all very proud—a remarkable group of people."

Everybody here knows the husky, brown-faced men—popularly called brancardiers, or stretcher-bearers—who constitute a sort of combination nursing and policing service; and who serve the sick indefatigably from morning to night, asking nothing for themselves but the privilege of serving. The Rector told me something of their background.

Early in the Shrine history it became evident that some permanent organization was needed to give assistance of various kinds to pilgrims, and to maintain order. In 1884, the Association of the Hospitallers of Our Lady of Lourdes was established to meet these needs.

The Order had a picturesque beginning.

One day a poor woman, alone and helpless, arrived at the Lourdes station. An old pilgrim, Count Roussy de Sales, saw her getting down from the train with much difficulty. He went to help her into the little carriage that she had brought. She was looking for someone to wheel her to the Grotto. Roussy de Sales offered his services, and took her across town. The way was long and difficult in that hilly place; several times he stopped to rest.

On the Place Marcadal he saw, sitting in the Café Français, two young men whom he recognized and who, returning from a wedding in tail coats and top hats, looked at Roussy de Sales in amazement. "You really ought to lend me a hand!" he told them, smiling. They got up at once, and all three pushed the carriage to the Grotto.

Their task done, they began to discuss the need for organized assistance for the sick pilgrims, and thus the foundation of the Hospitallers was laid. In the early days it was in the hands of the French aristocracy, and these servants of the poor came from some of the noblest families in the land: the Count de Combettes de Luc, Count de l'Epinois, the Marquis de Luranes Castelet, the Viscount de Four de Pibrac, the Count de Villalba, and Baron de Saint Maclou. These formed the first Council, the heart of the great movement that followed.

The story goes that these early brothers prayed together for a long time at the Grotto; then, going to the Spring, they took a goblet, filled it with Spring water, and drank to the success of their project. That success went far beyond their hopes.

A year later, in 1885, the work was well advanced, and the Bishop of Tarbes received the first authorized members. The Order is based upon the old Knights Hospitallers of St. John for the sick at Jerusalem. The Hospitallers join the service with an act of consecration, and pledge themselves to give a certain amount of time and work every year. They are governed by a top ecclesiastic appointed by the Bishop of Lourdes, and administratively by a president, a secretary, and a certain number of councilors. They pay all their own expenses and give their services without any monetary compensation. There are now more than 2,000 in the permanent Association. They are assisted by the volunteer stretcher-bearers attached to every pilgrimage. (In 1954 these numbered 10,393.)

Three main virtues are enjoined: Charity, Piety, Discipline. Every Hospitaller is given a small handbook containing the rules he is to follow. He "must be ready to bear cold and heat, sun and rain, hunger and thirst, and long waits. He must not exceed a walking pace when in charge of invalid chairs. He must not smoke when in charge of sick persons. He must know how to carry the sick so that they suffer the least possible jolting." Last but most important: *"He must pray without ceasing."*

A brancardier is on duty from dawn until midnight, and sometimes later. His tasks are heavy, his meals uncertain, his rest slight and often broken by emergency calls. He may get his dinner at nine or ten o'clock —or not at all. He may be sent to the end of town or back to the station after a long and wearying day.

The President of the Order, Count de Beauchamp, records proudly: "In the course of thirty years' service, I have never once been refused by a brother brancardier, or even heard a murmur from him, when I asked him to perform still one more hard job at the end of the day." Some inner force seems to carry these men along and enable them to live at an almost superhuman pace while they are at Lourdes.

The work of the Hospitallers is organized in military fashion because of the large numbers of invalids to be helped and the size of the crowds to be controlled; and during their period of duty they take their meals together in a sort of officers' mess. They come from all walks of life—generals, judges, bankers, civil servants, sharing tasks and quarters with grocers, clerks, mechanics. They seem to work with extraordinary comradeship and harmony. At their office under the Rampe, a group is constantly in waiting to go wherever they may be needed.

Each morning, the president has posted on the door of the office the Order of The Day regulating the services—at the station, the hospitals, the Grotto, the outside and inside of the baths, the Esplanade and the Procession; so that everybody knows precisely what his duty is.

The brancardiers are the first people the sick see on arrival, and the last to see them off when they leave. Those on duty at the station help the invalids out of the cars with utmost care and gentleness, especially the stretcher cases who are lifted through the windows with great skill. Then they are placed in automobiles and carried to the hospitals. Sometimes the brancardiers are at the station for sixteen hours at a stretch. In the crowded season, as many as twenty-two pilgrimage trains a day are served.

In the hospitals the Chief of Service begins his work in the very early morning. First he goes through the wards and arranges to have Holy Communion brought to those who desire it. Then he sees to it that the sick are placed on stretchers or in carriages and are taken to the Grotto at the appointed time, the Rosary being recited by the whole caravan.

The Chief of Service at the Grotto, in the meantime, must have the space in front of the Grotto cleared and ready, and a set of stewards in waiting for those who are to receive Communion there. Thus, on arrival of the sick, everything is arranged for the hearing of Mass—after which the patients are grouped on the Esplanade and given their breakfast. This over, the move back and forth between the Grotto and the baths goes on till the return to the hospitals toward eleven o'clock. In the afternoon a similar service is in operation until time for the Procession.

This is the most strenuous hour of the day for the Hospitaller. He has to look to the safety of the sick in the midst of a crowd which sometimes numbers 40,000 to 50,000 pilgrims. When a cure takes place, the crowd may be carried away with excitement. The Chief of Service on the Esplanade has a large staff of assistants, posted so as to form barriers when necessary, and to prevent onrushes of the people. Well ahead of time, they have cleared the Square and the spaces on the Esplanade reserved for the sick, and these are then lined up in perfect order on each side, awaiting the great event of the day.

The Blessed Sacrament passes before each invalid whom the Chief of Service presents, and each receives a blessing. What jubilation when a patient is cured! And what a blessing when one can utter a word of help, give some bit of encouragement, or just tell a joke or a story to make the others forget their troubles for a few minutes and win a smile or a laugh from one of that suffering multitude.

All this service is wonderful enough just in a material way—of keeping order and making things a little easier for the sick. But over and above that, the spirit of self-dedication and constant prayer in which these brothers work, their powerful faith, their intense personal interest in every patient—in his physical welfare but especially in his spiritual estate, and in his getting all possible help and inspiration from these few days that have cost him so much pain and sacrifice to achieve: all this is deeply impressive and moving. Observing the gentleness, the tenderness with which these big men serve, day after day—many of them former invalids and Cures themselves—you begin to understand some of the factors that go into the making of that magic spirit of Lourdes.

Touching—and sometimes amusing—incidents color the life of a brancardier. Often the sick are very grateful for all this service and want to show it. Sometimes they offer a tip. One woman with more money than good sense offered a brancardier ten francs to get her in first at the baths. This one was rather curtly rebuffed.

Another time, a poor woman painfully took from her purse a ten-franc piece and said to the brancardier who was wheeling her: "Here, take it—for you!"

"But no, madame—keep it. I do not need anything."

"Oh," said the sick woman tearfully, "I understand. You won't take what I offer because it's too little. But I am too poor to give more."

"But no, madame—never!" And the brancardier took from her hands the little coin, respectfully, reverently, and put it into his wallet. The widow's mite—the alms of the poor! He could not refuse.

A favorite story of the brancardiers concerns two Oriental associates. Two Hindus presented themselves one day at the office of the Hospitallers and asked to speak to the secretary in charge. They had fine features and gentle manners, but their clothes were in tatters—their worn sandals tied up with string, their shirts clean but faded and full of holes. Evidently the poorest of the poor.

They explained in halting French that they had come from the middle of India to make a pilgrimage to Lourdes and that they wished to serve for those few days as brancardiers. The brancardier whose duty it was to inscribe volunteer helpers hesitated to enroll them, but was touched by their modest and imploring attitude and sent them to a certain Chief of Service, asking him to keep a special eye on these recruits who seemed a bit out of the ordinary.

The new brothers went to work and performed their duties with a zest and devotion, the Chief reported, "simply admirable"; and this went on for about a week. At the end of their time they came again to the office to return their equipment, and found there the same brancardier who had received them the week before.

He stared at them, amazed. There were at Lourdes just then only two Hindu brancardiers—these must certainly be his two friends. But what a transformation! He saw before him two distinguished-looking gentlemen faultlessly dressed in handsome suits, wearing gold watchfobs and magnificent scarf-pins, and with valuable rings on their fingers.

"But how is this?" stammered the brancardier. "I had thought you were—"

"We are two bankers from India," the men replied, smiling. "We wanted to make a real pilgrimage to Lourdes, especially to give ourselves to serving the sick. We wanted to put ourselves in the same state as the poorest of them, in order to live their life and really understand them. So we decided to dress as miserable people, the better to carry out our plan."

The brancardiers marveled at the insight and sensitivity displayed by these visitors from afar, who had so thoroughly grasped the Lourdes spirit, and given themselves so perfectly and wholeheartedly to it.

The work of the Hospitallers extends beyond Lourdes itself into many dioceses and faraway regions where local Associations have been formed. These are now to be found in eighty-five dioceses of France, also in Belgium, England, Switzerland, Holland, Italy, Spain, and Portugal. These local societies collect the sick, raise funds for them, prepare them, both spiritually and materially, for the pilgrimage, see that they get to Lourdes and safely home again. During the year the local organizations hold Lourdes conferences and reunions, monthly religious services and retreats in common. Many help at home who cannot go to Lourdes, but their help is just as important. Thus a vast network of Hospitality and knightly service is spread over France and various foreign countries.

About the same number of nurses as brancardiers—that is, around 2,000—belong to the permanent organization. The women's membership has been a vital part of the Hospitality from the very beginning.

This too was originally under the direction of women from the great families of France and Italy especially. Today its nurses and nurses' aides (known as "hand-maids") who come with the pilgrimages each year, are recruited from all classes: the wealthy and the nobility, but also salesgirls and stenographers, dressmakers and filing clerks—all serving together in devoted comradeship just like the men. Many women Cures of former years, come back each season as nurses, or to help as scullery maids and with other menial jobs in the hospitals. Often 1,800 people a day are served in the women's section at the baths, several hundred helpless and stretcher cases among them.

"I think," says the Comte de Beauchamp, "there is no service more meritorious and more humbly accomplished than that of these servants of the sick, both men and women, who for three consecutive hours of the morning and evening, behind curtains in an unpleasant atmosphere, aid the helpless, undo and afterwards remake the dressings of the most painful sores, and keep praying constantly."

The quiet order and efficiency of all this work is the more admirable when you remember that the assistant stretcher-bearers and nurses change every three or four days with each new pilgrimage; and that the men and women Hospitallers come not only from different parts of France, but from many different nations.

✨ 7 ✨

The Medical Organization*

Down to the right, on the Esplanade, stands the unpretentious gray building that houses the famous Bureau of Medical Verifications. That first day, I walked across the Square and toward its open door with mounting excitement. Inside those plain gray walls were the documents I had come six thousand miles to see. Here, for me, next to the Grotto itself, was the vital center.

Here in the court outside, patients with their families or physicians are waiting to be examined—stretchers, wheel chairs, little carriages lined up against the wall. Here visiting doctors come to register and get their official badges permitting them to visit the hospitals, talk to the sick, study the records—in short, to have the run of the place.

And here, during the next few minutes, I met the keen-eyed, cordial group of men who make up the staff of the Medical Bureau: half a dozen capable scientists, some seasoned veterans who return year after year, devotedly giving their time and skill; some strapping young interns just out of medical school, eager to learn all they can. The wife of one of them runs a little shop in Lourdes so that her husband can come in the summer and give his services at the Bureau.

* (Ed. Note: This chapter describes Lourdes as it was in 1955, along with some of its history. For some details on Lourdes today, see Chapter 11. For a history of physical changes since 1955, and short biographies of the presidents of the Medical Bureau since then, see Appendix A, p. 315ff.)

These were to be my friends and generous helpers during the weeks to come—and a gold mine of valuable information.

They gave me a very kind welcome.

"Come in, come in, madame!" said the President, Dr. Leuret. "Monseigneur has told us about you. Everything here is at your disposal. Madame has come all the way from America to do a book on Lourdes," he explained to the others, beaming. "The sort of book we like—careful, precise, well-documented."

He took me over to the office and opened a cabinet containing the precious dossiers. "Here you will find what you have crossed the ocean for," he said proudly. "And I believe you will find that you have not come in vain!"

This President of the Bureau is a remarkable person: Legion of Honor, Croix de Guerre, Councilor of France, Professor of Medicine; he is also head of a large clinic in Bourdeaux—the worst section, which he has turned into a thriving parish house as well as hospital. A square, stocky man with sharp eyes and a heart as big as a cathedral, himself father of twelve children, he would pick up his little patients with infinite tenderness, talk to them, coax them as if they were his own, get them to tell him their pitiful little symptoms. Mothers gave their burdens into his charge with a sigh of absolute trust and confidence.

Sitting on a bench in the sunlight, after his morning office hours, he told me the story of his beloved Bureau.

"First and foremost: the medical work at Lourdes is run entirely by doctors and supported by doctors. Never forget that. Some are Catholics, some are Protestants; some are agnostics or unbelievers; others, followers of non-Christian faiths. There is only one criterion for membership in this work: the members believe that the study of Lourdes cures is something important which deserves their help."

He stopped to lend a hand to a stretcher-bearer who was rolling a little girl in a heavy steel brace out onto the boardwalk, then went on.

"Our beginnings were humble, though from the first the Bureau was served by men of the first rank. A certain Dr. St. Maclou who came to Lourdes with his wife on pilgrimage—that was in 1885—strongly felt the need for a permanent medical man on the spot, to examine the alleged cures. He offered himself for the post, and remained here till his death, a man of austere scientific standards and highest character.

"After him came Dr. Boissarie—the 'lion of Lourdes' he was called —one of the most brilliant young Paris interns of his time. He gave up several offers of big posts and chose Lourdes as his cherished life work.

He died here, after thirty years of selfless service. Then there was Dr. Le Bec, a senior surgeon of St. Joseph's Hospital in Paris. You see the caliber of the men who have run the Medical Bureau. Dr. Marchand and Dr. Vallet followed Le Bec—both of them highly distinguished physicians. Lastly, myself—*pas grand'chose,* not much—but loyal and faithful to the great tradition."

"I don't wonder you're proud of it. But now tell me—what are the exact powers and functions of the Bureau? How does it work?"

"Of course—I knew you would ask that. Here"—he took a well-worn little book from his pocket—"I will read you the official statement."

" 'The Medical Bureau of Lourdes is a medical office officially charged to proceed . . . with the examination of the cases of cure on the day when they occur at Lourdes, and to note those cures which are patent, and which could not be the result of the forces of nature. It is also equipped for the study of healings which have taken place in any other part of the world, provided the name of Lourdes has been invoked.' "

"And is it open all the year round, or just during the summer?"

"Just during the summer, the pilgrimage season, from Easter to the middle of October."

He read further from his little manual: " 'Besides the President, the Bureau is composed of all the doctors who come each year to inscribe themselves in its register and to take part in its labors.' Any medical man is welcomed at the Bureau, whatever his religious opinions or lack of any. He may freely examine the evidence, criticize, and take part in the discussions. A simple identification card is all we require, showing that we have to deal with a reputable physician.

"And as I told you," continued Dr. Leuret, "these doctors are by no means all Catholics. During my time here, Jews, Moslems, Buddhists, Hindus, Protestants of all sects, have been among our colleagues; atheists and unbelievers, too. It's this study of the cures by men of such different beliefs and viewpoints that guarantees our competency and our good faith."

"How do you run as to nationalities?"

"Well, let us see—" He turned to his table of statistics. "In 1953, some fifteen hundred doctors signed the register and took part in the examinations at the Bureau. Two-thirds of them were French; the rest Belgians, Italians, Spaniards, English, Germans, Dutch. Very few Americans—distance, of course, has a lot to do with that. Though oddly enough we have quite a number from Oriental countries, and some from the Near East. Of course it varies each year. The countries near at hand, like Belgium and Italy, naturally send us the most."

"How about age? How do you rate with the younger men, for instance?"

"Very high when they see how carefully we scrutinize the cases. We get always two or three hundred doctors and interns among the younger crowd each year, who come to study the records and assist at the examinations of patients. It's a wonderful laboratory for them. The older men are professors of medical faculties, doctors of both city and country hospitals, surgeons, and specialists of many different kinds. Each is encouraged to give his views and opinions as freely as at any medical congress. We have lively—sometimes impassioned—discussions; but always in a friendly spirit.

"Here," he said, "is a grand opportunity to pool knowledge and to learn from one another; to compare the development of certain methods and therapeutic techniques as practiced in different parts of the world; to rub shoulders with confreres of many types of experience in many lands. Not to mention an opportunity to study practically every known disease—and for each one, usually several cases of his own specialty. It's the greatest polyclinic in the world!

"The alert modern physician appreciates all this, and, more and more, a visit to Lourdes is coming to be known as a valuable professional asset, as well as for some a memorable religious and spiritual experience."

He went on to fill in other details. By the end of that first morning I had a very good idea of the background and practical workings of the Medical Organization.

On the functional side, it's not so complicated, considering the mass of patients they have to deal with, the large numbers of sick who come to Lourdes each year.

According to official statistics, 33,276 came in 1954. Each pilgrimage is accompanied by one or more medical men, and no sick person is accepted without a medical certificate from his home physician, stating his disease, present condition, and progress of the disease at the time he left home. At the Bureau, when a supposed cure is being judged, everything is necessarily based on the accompanying medical certificates.

During the busiest season, several pilgrimages are held simultaneously each week—as for instance during the first week of my stay when 1,000 came from Newcastle, 1,200 from Brussels, and 1,000 from Turin, all at the same time. This means the presence of a number of medical men besides those visiting Lourdes out of personal curiosity or interest in the work there. All doctors are urged to register at the Bureau immediately on arrival.

When a supposed cure occurs, the doctor of the pilgrimage takes the patient to the Medical Bureau at once for examination—and eventually verification of the cure. The patient is thoroughly examined by the doctors who are present at the Bureau at that time and a careful report is drawn up on a special form. There follows an exhaustive and vigorous discussion of the case, around three principal questions: (1) Did the illness really exist? (2) Is there a cure? (3) Can the cure be explained naturally?

A *rapporteur* keeps precise record of all findings. And the patients give their testimony under oath. Note that this first record does not in any way constitute an argument in favor of a miracle. It is simply an initial document and opening of an inquiry. At this first session the patient is given a date and a place in the Bureau files; a study is made of the papers he brought with him on the pilgrimage; first accounts of witnesses are assembled; the patient is put through extensive physical and psychological tests, and the endeavor made to establish with all possible exactness his state before coming to Lourdes and his state at the moment of presenting himself at the Bureau.

At the end of this first session, either the record appears sufficiently significant and is retained for the following year, or it is inconclusive and is immediately discarded. If it is retained, the patient is put under observation; a physician of his own region is named as investigator. The latter will pursue this investigation—and his observation of the patient —for one year. He will gather new documents, will search out witnesses that may have been lacking, will talk with the patient's home physician, with his relatives and neighbors, and will be responsible for presenting the case again the following year, on completion of the inquiry.

The severity of this scrutiny by the Medical Bureau is shown by the fact that, in 1947, seventy-five cures were retained for investigation; only eleven came back the next year and of these only six were ultimately kept. In 1948, eighty-three records were set up at the first hearing; only fifteen came back, and nine were finally kept and sent on for study as possible Miracles. Sometimes cases are held over longer than a year for more complete inquiry, at the request of some physician. All of which explains why a cure is never announced under two years' time, and sometimes longer.

When a case has been retained, the patient under investigation is called to the Bureau again at the end of a year for a second examination, much more rigorous than the first. This time his case is gone over "with a fine-tooth comb." Much more information is now available on him. He is studied, discussed, and often sharply challenged by the group of doctors who are going to risk their professional reputations by signing or refusing to sign the statement certifying his apparent cure.

At the end of the second examination the following questions are formally put to the doctors participating:

1. Did the illness described by the medical record exist at the moment of the patient's pilgrimage to Lourdes?

2. Was the malady suddenly stopped in its course at a time when there was no tendency towards improvement? Which symptoms disappeared at this time?

3. Is there a cure? Can you prove it with certainty? Did the cure take place without medical treatment?

4. Is it necessary to delay a decision?

5. (Finally, the ultimate question): Is there any possible medical explanation of this cure? In the present state of science, can any natural or scientific explanation be given?*

If not, and if after all this careful analysis and investigation the doctors of the Bureau are satisfied that the case appears to be a genuine supernatural cure, it is sent on for further study and judgment by the Medical Commission.

To make scientific competence and precision doubly sure, a Medical Commission was set up which should study cases away from Lourdes, solely on the evidence of medical documents and from a purely technical standpoint. Its seat is in Paris and it has included among its members

* (Ed. Note: For the current questionnaire, see Appendix D, p. 337.)

some of the foremost physicians and surgeons of that city. At first a national Commission, it has now been enlarged to take in doctors and experts of other countries—particularly those nearby (such as Belgium, England and Italy) so that members may be able to attend the Commission meetings.

The list of names of the present Medical Commission shows the distinction and quality of the men who make up this body.

When the Medical Bureau of Lourdes is satisfied as to the genuineness of a cure, or if there is some question in their minds about it, they send the record of that cure—the documents, certificates, results of examinations, X-rays, bacteriological analyses, and everything to do with the case—on to the Medical Commission.

The Commission makes a thorough study of the case, calling in such specialists as may be needed for more extensive observation. The duty of the Commission is not to declare a miracle, but simply and solely to declare (or fail to declare): "We find no natural or scientific explanation of this cure." If they do so declare, the case is then sent on to the Bishop of the cured person's diocese, with the recommendation that a Canonical Commission be appointed to investigate it. It is the Church that decides whether or not it is a miraculous cure.

"As physicians," the President of the Commission told me, "we can only state our conviction as to whether the case is or is not outside natural and scientific law. The theologians have then to determine whether it shall be proclaimed a miracle." And the theologians, as we shall see, are even more strict and conservative than the doctors.

Far from trying to "contrive" a miracle, as critics of the Church sometimes suggest, the Canonical Commissions are so severe on every detail that when a case succeeds in passing their requirements, one may be sure it is indeed extraordinary and outside the laws of nature. Only fifty-one cases in a hundred years have passed this bar and been pronounced Miraculous Cures by the Church. The requirements of the Church are discussed in a separate chapter.

The Medical Commission of Lourdes

Dr. Grenet	*President. Specialist in Children's Diseases, Paris*
Dr. Auvigne	*Surgeon. Specialist Genitourinary Diseases, Nantes*
Dr. Biot	*Endocrinology. 30 Cours Albert Thomas, Lyon*

Dr. Ch. Lancrenon	*General Medicine. 3 Rue de la Trinité, Paris*
Dr. Langeron	*General Medicine. 63 Rue Vaubun, Lille*
Dr. Lanos	*Surgeon. St. Joseph's Hospital, Paris*
Dr. Lhermitte	*Neuropsychiatry. 9 Rue Marboeuf, Paris*
Dr. Mauriac	*General Medicine. 12 Rue Vauban, Bordeaux*
Dr. Merigot de Freigny	*Ophthalmology. St. Joseph's Hospital, Paris*
Dr. Michon	*Surgeon. Urinary Diseases. 40 Rue Barbet, de Jouy, Paris*
Dr. Oberlin	*Surgeon of the Paris Hospitals. 121 Bvd. St. Germain, Paris*
Dr. Pasteau	*General Medicine. Parce, Sarthe*
Dr. Sendrail	*General Medicine. 26 Bvd. Carnot, Toulouse*
Dr. Huc	*Orthopedic Surgeon. 44 Rue Notre Dame des Champs, Paris*

The following international members have been added to the Commission:

Belgium

Dr. G. Van Schuren, *Professor of the University of Louvain*
Dr. Ch. De Gheldere, *Boussu, Tournai*

Germany

Dr. Ernest, *Chief Physician, Hildegardiskrankenhaus, Cologne*
Dr. Meixner, *Chief Physician, Schonmunzah, Schwarzwald*

Great Britain

Dr. Daniel O'Connell, *Charing Cross Hospital, London*
Dr. Dorothy Makepeace, *38 Ashley Gardens, London*

Ireland

Dr. J. Stafford Johnson, *Richmond Hospital, Dublin*
Dr. J. F. Morrin, *Chief Surgeon, St. Vincent's Hospital, Dublin*

Spain

> Dr. Juan G. Queralto, *Professor of Medicine, University of Barcelona*
> Dr. Augustin Garcia Die, *Spanish President of the International Medical Association of Lourdes*

To go on with the medical organization: it is interesting to note the steady growth of interest by doctors. The first year the Medical Bureau was established, five doctors visited it; the second year fifteen; the third year twenty-seven. During the year 1953, 1,556 physicians have signed the Visitors' Book and taken part, many of them, in the examinations and activities at the Bureau. Here are some of the specialties and residences that one finds in the Visitors' Book:

Specialty	*Residence*
Otology	Argentina
Pathology	Edinburgh
Cancer	Paris
Ophthalmology	San Diego, Calif.
Psychiatry	Luxembourg
Stomatology	Casablanca
Cardiology	Wien
Orthopedic surgery	Glasgow
Neurology	Lausanne
General medicine	Amsterdam
Surgeon	Princeton, N.J.
Gynecology	Lille
Pediatrician	Turin
Dermatology	Lisbon
Cancerology	Newcastle
Radiology	Grenoble
General medicine	Calcutta
Genitourinary *spec.*	Rouen
Pharmacology	Louvain
Eye and ear	Dublin
Tropical diseases	Tunis
Diseases of the brain	Bordeaux
Tuberculosis	Toronto
Bacteriologist	Liverpool

Specialty	Residence
General medicine	Brussels
Obstetrics	Aberdeen
Urology	Rome
Skin diseases	Oslo
Cardiology	Geneva
Surgeon	Hongkong
Tropical diseases	Madagascar

What is the attitude of these doctors, when confronted with the facts? How do they react? What do they say?

Some are curious and unbiased; some are honestly stumped, frankly admitting they have no explanation. Some are definitely hostile and declare, with Zola: "Even if I saw a miracle, I wouldn't believe it!" Some are exasperated by the embarrassing problems put before them. Others are incredulous but sincerely interested in searching for the truth, and sometimes are lucky enough to find it—in the presence of an extraordinary cure. But more and more men of worth come to listen and to see for themselves, to study and weigh the evidence presented to them. They soon gain respect for the Lourdes cures when they observe the scientific procedure and strict practices at the Medical Bureau. Many become firm friends and helpers with the work.

One of the younger doctors, who has been coming every year, confided to me: "I don't mind telling you, I had my doubts about this place. But when I first came, Dr. Leuret told me, 'Here, you are a doctor first, a Catholic second. Never forget it!' I certainly never expected to find such merciless rigor in going over the cases. The doctors seem to lean more toward proving that no miracle has occurred than toward trying to find one!" This professional skepticism makes them very solid with the younger generation.

With all their interest and goodwill, however, the visiting doctors are birds of passage. They cannot be counted on for the methodical checking and supervision of cures during the "probationary" year, or for other duties connected with involved and lengthy research. The Bureau is thus dependent on its own means—often very insufficient—to continue its diverse inquiries in the home area of the patients, not only in France but in foreign lands.

Recognizing these limitations, some of the doctors habitually assisting at the Bureau decided to create an International Medical Association to supplement the work of the Bureau and to become, so to say, laboratory workers for it in the field. The extraordinary development of the Association since its creation in 1927 is the best proof of its usefulness and its practical service.

AMIL, as it is affectionately called at Lourdes, is an international organization of doctors banded together to support the work of the Medical Bureau and to help in every way with the medical investigations and the scientific study of cures. It consists of 5,000 doctors from some thirty countries, each of whom pays 200 francs a year as dues; some give much more. This meets the annual budget of the Bureau—one million francs per annum. The Church gives them not one penny; "The Work of Lourdes," the general fund for Lourdes institutions, not one penny either.

"When I was invited here," says Dr. Leuret, "I was told we were to be entirely self-directing, self-supporting. 'You are to be technically autonomous, financially autonomous also.' While sometimes difficult, this has its advantages, too. For me this is a fact of major significance: *The medical work at Lourdes is run by doctors and supported by doctors.* Thus it can never be said that our work is under ecclesiastical domination or for propaganda purposes."

AMIL has two main objects: (1) to support the work of the Medical Bureau; (2) to help organize the pilgrimages and the study of alleged cures, so that the medical side—doctors' certificates, laboratory reports, and so on—shall be scientifically correct and well put together.

Each country, province, and region has an AMIL member in charge. When special research is needed on a case or when some particular type of specialist is wanted, AMIL supplies the technical information and the doctor required. Before the existence of AMIL, records at the Bureau and for the sick going on pilgrimage were sometimes very sketchy. The Association makes the Lourdes medical work scientifically much more exact and has added enormously to the prestige of the Medical Organization.

Growing interest in psychosomatic medicine has also undoubtedly played its part in increasing respect for and interest in the study of Lourdes cures. Last summer the National Psychiatric Association of France—400 doctors meeting in convention at Pau—came over in a body and spent an entire afternoon listening attentively to the accounts of cures and activities by the doctors of the Medical Bureau. Twenty, even fifteen years ago, such a thing would have been unheard of.

Let us not be overoptimistic. A large number of doctors still exist to whom the very name of Lourdes is anathema. But the number is steadily decreasing. In another twenty-five years it may be negligible.

An American Doctor
Analyzes a Lourdes Cure

Every day, patients are examined at the Bureau from nine to twelve in the morning, and from two to four in the afternoon. All doctors who happen to be in Lourdes, either on pilgrimage or on visits of personal interest or curiosity, are invited to take part in the examinations and discussions. I was kindly permitted to be present at a number of these.

The Bureau occupies two entire floors of its present building—ten good-sized rooms, airy and well-equipped. Various Pilgrimages and Associations have contributed a good part of the equipment.

Through wide double doors the patient enters first a waiting room with many benches, where a nurse receives him, registers his name and address, and the name and address of his home physician. This puts the Bureau into immediate contact with the doctor who has been in charge of the person up to this time.

All day long, people are waiting here to see the doctor on duty—mothers with their children; Pilgrimage doctors with some specially interesting case or patient needing attention; paraplegics, diabetics, heart cases, tumors, polio victims. Every sort of malady and agony is studied within these plain gray walls.

A door to the left leads to the official examination room—a large workmanlike place, with benches for forty or fifty doctors, an examination table for the patient, a desk for the presiding doctor and *rapporteur*. Over the desk (somewhat ironically) a plaque with Zola's observation:

"There is no more heroic task than to establish even the smallest of truths." Zola, the arch-enemy of Lourdes.

Behind these formal outer apartments are the X-ray rooms, the office of the President of the Bureau—a comfortable study where the doctors gather for conferences and discussion of the cases—and the library containing many valuable medical works and early Lourdes records. Farther on is a series of rooms equipped for special examinations—gynecological, urological, ear-nose-and-throat, and so on. Downstairs is a room for eye examinations and rooms for developing X-ray films.

X-rays are a vitally important factor in the study and appraisal of alleged cures. A fine Phillips X-ray apparatus given by the Dutch Catholics has enabled the Bureau to make some two thousand fluoroscopic examinations and about as many X-ray pictures within the past five years. The French colony of San Francisco presented splendid electrocardiographic equipment in charge of none other than Bernadette's grand-nephew, Dr. J. M. Soubirous, who is a heart specialist and a thoroughly up-to-date physician.

When a cure occurs, the Pilgrimage doctor, or sometimes a brancardier takes the patient as soon as possible to the Medical Bureau. A preliminary examination is made—then usually a much more detailed one on the following day, when there has been time to assemble all the physicians available.

Even the most coolly detached and skeptical must feel a little of the thrill and excitement that pervades the room when the newly cured patient walks in, followed by a beaming nurse or relative and a group of doctors and professors of Faculties from half a dozen countries—all on the *qui vive* to see for themselves this extraordinary phenomenon: a "miraculous" Lourdes cure!

Often the President will invite one of the visiting physicians to preside over the examination. An American physician, Dr. Smiley Blanton, directed the examination of one of the most famous cures—Charles McDonald. Thirty-two doctors gathered at the Bureau to study this remarkable case. Dr. Blanton afterward read an account of it before a joint session of the American Psychoanalytic and Psychiatric Associations. Here is a summary of the case taken from that account and from Mr. McDonald's own story.

Charles McDonald was born in Dublin on August 12, 1905. He had a healthy childhood. His brothers and sisters were also healthy. At sixteen he left school to work in his father's carpenter business. He was keen on sports and a capable athlete. He married at nineteen and has now three children, girls, all in good health.

His illness began in 1924. He became tired and irritable and had to give up work for several weeks. He resumed work in November but kept losing weight. Then he began to have night sweats and his cough became so aggravated that he consulted Dr. Young of Sandymount, Dublin. Tubercle bacilli were found in his sputum and an X-ray showed active tuberculosis of the lungs.

McDonald was sent to a sanatorium for five weeks, then entered a Dublin hospital (in April, 1925). There he had two hemorrhages from the lungs. He lost thirty pounds in six months.

On July 3, 1925, disobeying medical orders, he set out for Johannesburg, South Africa, where he remained for six months. Here his cough ceased and he regained weight and strength. He took up work in one of the gold mines, working always on the surface, however. For five years his health remained good.

Early in 1931, after a strenuous football match, he felt pain in hips and neck. Soon after, pain began in his left side and in the lower part of his back, especially when he rode his motorcycle. Things got so bad that he could not apply the brakes of his car without feeling a stinging pain in the lower back. In October, 1931, his doctor, after taking a spinal X-ray, said that he had tuberculosis of the twelfth thoracic vertebra.

McDonald was put into a steel corset from the shoulders to the hips, opening so that he could take a sun bath. After three months he was no better. The doctor suggested a bone-graft operation. McDonald refused and decided to return to Dublin. On the voyage he abandoned his brace, finding it too hot and tiring. Back at home he tried to work, but pains on the left side and in the back were so severe that he had to stop. For three months he rested, under no medical care meanwhile.

In June, 1932, he was examined by Dr. Lane of Dublin who diagnosed tuberculous disease of the vertebra and sent him to Dr. Lynch to determine whether the condition of the lungs would permit an operation. Dr. Lynch said no—the lungs were too bad. Once more the young man was put into a steel brace.

In September, 1932, a large abscess developed in the right lumbar region, and another, later, in the left shoulder. The shoulder abscess was aspirated but that in the lumbar area had to be opened, as the pus was too thick. Both these abscesses discharged freely during the spring of 1933.

In June, 1935, McDonald became very ill. He collapsed during a violent fit of vomiting. A week later his body was badly swollen. He consulted still another doctor, O'Connell of Dublin, who diagnosed his trouble as acute nephritis (inflammation of the kidneys). He was taken to Meath Hospital where he remained for thirteen weeks—again under the care of Dr. Lane, also of Dr. Boxwell. Examination of the urine showed albumin, blood cells, and granular and hyalin casts. Any movement caused severe pain especially in his back, and he had to be given frequent sedatives.

In November, 1935, Dr. Boxwell said the patient would have to be sent to a hospital for incurables. The cheerful name of this institution was Hospital for the Dying. McDonald refused, and went home. He called in Dr. O'Connell again. The doctor visited him weekly for three months. The family was now being supported by a small tobacco shop which Mrs. McDonald ran in one part of the house.

The doctor told Mrs. McDonald that he could do little for her husband and that he considered him a hopeless case. Finally, in June, 1936, he said to his patient: "McDonald, I'm sorry—I can do nothing more for you."

It was then that McDonald thought of Lourdes. He had a strong presentiment that he would be cured there. He kept telling his friends that if he went to Lourdes he would certainly come back on his feet. He insisted that his wife should pack for him the suit and clothes in which he would return as a well person.

He joined the Catholic Young Men's Pilgrimage of Ireland, which took place September 4–10, 1936. The journey had to be made on a stretcher, sitting being too painful. "I had been an invalid for over four years," says McDonald, "and for fifteen months before going to Lourdes was confined to bed. Twice I was given the Last Rites and pronounced by more than one doctor to be beyond medical aid. I was unable to sit up for more than four minutes to have the wounds dressed. Pain had nearly driven me mad at times. When the ambulance came to take me to the train, I was placed in a carrying sheet and with infinite care transferred from bed to stretcher and thence to the ambulance."

For admission to the Pilgrimage, he had a certificate from Dr. O'Connell stating that he had Pott's Disease of the twelfth dorsal vertebra, nephritis, and tuberculous arthritis of the left shoulder. Some fifteen X-rays at Meath Hospital established the diagnosis. Dr. Hannigan was in charge of the pilgrimage which included a dozen medical men.

McDonald left Dublin for Lourdes on the night of the third of September, 1936. His wounds were dressed on the fourth of September by Nurse Falvey on the Pilgrimage train. She testified that there was considerable pus draining from the sinuses in his back and shoulder.

He arrived in Lourdes on Saturday, September 5, and his wounds were dressed that day by Dr. Hannigan. At this dressing the doctor noted that McDonald had two large sinuses (draining abscesses) in the lumbar region, a large sinus just below the outer end of the collar bone, and two more in the left shoulder.

On the morning of September 6, he was taken to the baths and carefully lowered by six brancardiers into the pool, lying on a special webbing. His bandages were taken off, and when he came out they were put on again. In this way Lourdes water touched his wounds directly and cleansed them. He was considerably chilled by this bath and felt no benefit from it.

On September 7, he was bathed again. He felt confused and cold but after he was dressed and removed from the piscine to the Grotto where a service was being held, he began, as he said, to feel "the first glow of health."

"It should be remembered," says Dr. Blanton, "that for fifteen months the patient had been in bed, so helpless that he had to use a bedpan, unable to move his hips or shoulders without severe pain. But now, lying on a stretcher in front of the Grotto, he experimented by moving his arm slightly. There was no pain. He loosened the brace strap on his shoulder and raised his shoulders from the pillow—without pain. He thought that perhaps he felt no pain because the shock of the bath had taken his mind off his condition. He waited an hour, and moved his hips again. Once more there was no pain."

"My expectations had become a certainty!" said McDonald jubilantly. "The Blessed Virgin had healed me!" He said that there at the Grotto he "felt more fit than I had ever felt in my life. I knew I could get up and walk." The brancardiers and nurses restrained him.

All that day he was outdoors in front of the Grotto. Back at the hospital in the evening, he told the doctor he was going to get up in the morning. He was forbidden to do so.

Next morning (September 8) when the doctor and nurse were out of the room, McDonald got up and walked to the foot of the bed—the first time he had been on his feet for fifteen months. He said, "My knees would have given way and I would have sunk to the floor had I not held on to the bed." He dressed himself with help from no one and walked without pain.

That day he was taken to the Grotto, not, as usual, on a stretcher but in an invalid chair. "I remained in the chair until after the Blessing of the Sick, in the afternoon. Then I left the chair . . . and walked up the steps into the Rosary Church where I was able to make a complete genuflection and to kneel in one of the benches. On rising some minutes later I repeated my genuflection and walked out of the church down onto the Square, where I resumed my chair for the official photograph of the pilgrims."

This the man who for more than a year had not been able to make the slightest move without agonizing pain, or raise his head and sit up for more than four minutes at a time.

"That night," says McDonald, "I told the doctor he could roll up my stretcher and place it in the guard's van of the train, as I was traveling home as an ordinary passenger. On Wednesday morning I dressed without assistance and when brought to the baths for the third time, walked in, undressed and dressed myself unaided. This I had not done for more than three years.

"I left Lourdes on Wednesday night. Our homeward journey was full of rejoicing. On arriving at Dublin Station I had the supreme pleasure of dispensing with the ambulance which had been so vitally necessary one short week before. I ordered a taxi, thus fulfilling my promise of returning on my feet."

At the time when McDonald left Lourdes it was still not a complete recovery for, according to Dr. Vallet's statement, his wounds were not yet entirely healed and were draining pus. Under these conditions he was not taken to the Medical Bureau for examination. It was on the return trip, before the train arrived in Paris, that his wounds healed. Dr. Hannigan stated as follows:

> I certify, as doctor in charge of the sick in the Irish Pilgrimage, that I examined Mr. Charles McDonald. He presented then: three fistulas of the left shoulder, two fistulas in the lumbar region all of which discharged pus. During the trip going and coming from Lourdes I personally cleaned his wounds. While on the way out, discharge was abundant and the patient had to remain lying on his stretcher.
>
> After the second bath there was a marked improvement and I authorized him to try to walk, which he did with facility. During the return voyage his wounds were dressed in Paris by the nurses. There was only a slight

fluid from one of the lumbar fistulas. All the rest had healed up.

Dr. Hannigan wrote again on August 29, 1937:

> I have seen Mr. McDonald twice since his return from Lourdes. I can declare definitely that there are now no traces of his former illness. Mr. McDonald is a well-balanced, active, healthy man, who can get through his day's work without trouble or undue fatigue. [He had now gone into the insurance business.] All the former sinuses are firmly healed. Personally, I am very glad to be able to testify to this cure, as when I first saw him I regarded this case as hopeless. (Signed, Ch. Hannigan.)

From Dr. Young, 49 Tritonville Road, Sandymount, Dublin, came another certificate:

> I certify that in 1934 I examined Mr. McDonald and found him suffering from active tuberculosis of the left shoulder and a lumbar abscess. I have recently examined Mr. McDonald and found no active signs of his disease and as far as I can see he is completely cured.

From Dr. C. J. O'Connell, 35 Fairview, Strand, Dublin:

> I certify that on September 1, 1937, I examined Mr. Charles McDonald and found the abscesses, two in the lumbar region and three in connection with the shoulder, completely healed. The urine contains neither blood nor albumin. At my first visit in 1934 this patient was suffering from acute nephritis and active tuberculosis of the dorsal vertebrae. He was sent to Meath Hospital under the treatment of Dr. Lane and remained for thirteen weeks, leaving at his own request. Seen by me the day following at his own home, the urine contained albumin and pus. I wrote out the certificate for the Pilgrimage and considered this man's case incurable.

The diagnosis given by Dr. O'Connell on the pilgrimage certificate read: "Pott's Disease, caries, nephritis, and tuberculous shoulder."

The report of an X-ray given on September 9, 1937 by Dr. R. A. Ruyert of St. Kevin's Hospital, Dublin, is as follows:

> The left shoulder joint clearly shows old trouble in the joint between the humerus and scapula which had made definite progress. This trouble exists no longer, the cure having taken place by ankylosis. The left kidney shows foci of disease now completely cicatrized. An examination by injection of uroselectan shows as regards the kidneys that the left kidney is hypertrophied, the pelvis dilated, and its outline changed. The function of this kidney is, however, perfect. The right kidney is slightly dilated but otherwise normal. Both lungs show several tuberculous lesions now healed. There is some thickening of the pleura at left apex. It is difficult to say if the disease is completely cured, but it is certainly inactive. (Signed, Dr. Ruyert.)

As soon as McDonald returned to Dublin he began to walk about half a mile a day. Two weeks later he was able to walk several miles. In December (1936) he began to ride a bicycle. On September 16, 1937 he returned to Lourdes, where Dr. Blanton and other physicians examined him on September 17.

Thirty-two doctors were present at the Medical Bureau during McDonald's examination. In their concluding remarks they made the following statement:

> Charles McDonald has been afflicted with (1) tuberculosis of the left shoulder with three fistulas; (2) tuberculosis of the dorsal spine with two fistulas; (3) chronic nephritis characterized by the presence of pus, blood, albumin. These three conditions were in full evolution at the moment of the pilgrimage to Lourdes, the five fistulas giving off pus.
>
> They were abruptly halted in their evolution on September 7. An immediate functional healing after a bath in the piscine was followed in less than four days by a defi-

nite cicatrization of the five fistulas, of return of normal urinary secretion rid of its infectious germs; cessation of pain, return of partial movements of the left arm and lumbar region.

This healing, obtained without the use of medicaments or of any therapeutic agent whatever is confirmed by one year of excellent health and work. . . . No medical explanation, in the present state of science, can be given; considering the extraordinary rapidity of the healing of these tuberculous affections, judged incurable by the specialists called in to treat him, and whose beginning was noted by general infection, later by bony localizations. This healing is written down as on the margin of the laws of biology.

The signatures of the thirty-two doctors end this statement.

In his report to his American confreres Dr. Blanton concludes:

To summarize, we have a man who seems certainly to have had tuberculosis of the lungs. He also had an infection of the twelfth thoracic vertebra which had destroyed it, and an infection of the shoulder which had practically destroyed the bony structure of the joint. In bed fifteen months, he had to have his wounds dressed twice daily. After the second bath in the piscine he was able to move without pain; he was able to walk that day; within three weeks he was able to walk several miles a day; his sinuses were practically healed in a period of two weeks.

What is the explanation of this healing?—for that it is a healing I am myself convinced. The records seem adequate to support this conclusion and they were made by well-trained and reputable physicians. Furthermore this is not an isolated case but one of approximately ten or twelve that occur at Lourdes yearly, in which the records seem well and honestly made.

We must lay aside as untenable the accusation that these cases are in any way "fixed" or the histories "doctored." There does appear to be at this shrine . . . a sudden quickening of the healing processes, a removal of symptoms, and a feeling of well-being. The percentages of such cures . . . are certainly too great to be laid to coincidence, nor do the details of the cures conform to the laws of recovery as we know them. Even coincidental cures in our hospitals do not, in the space of two or three days, get up and walk without pain after fifteen months of life in bed with continual pain. . . .

The basis of the cures seems to lie in some aspect which has to do with the psychology of the situation. . . . It is my feeling that in this case and in similar cases at Lourdes there is a quickening of the healing process, due to the emotion aroused by the transference to an all-powerful, all-loving Virgin Mother. . . .

I feel that we are justified by what we saw at Lourdes in stating our tentative belief that processes leading in the direction of death were not only halted but reversed, and the libido liberated in this way was put to the use of the individual in the restoration of health. I believe that something does occur which is, as Dr. Vallet has remarked, on the margin of the laws of nature.*

---

* Charles McDonald is in excellent health today—a robust man of forty-nine. He comes to Lourdes frequently, and was there with his daughter shortly before my own visit.

❧ 9 ❧

Lourdes Atmosphere: Psychological Influences

Dr. Blanton thinks that psychological factors have a great deal to do with the cures. This may seem true to some—at least in the matter of creating an atmosphere, opening the way.

The little room at the Bureau where I work on the records looks out on the river Gave on the one side, the pavement along the Esplanade on the other. On both sides pilgrims are walking up and down all day long; families, Sisters, priests, young people, old people. And all these people are praying.

Families come saying their prayers aloud, together; offering their united supplications for some suffering loved one. Sisters lead their groups of little girls or boys, reciting the Rosary. Now and then a distraught father or mother with a compassionate confessor wheel their child toward the Grotto, uttering low, desperate pleas for help. Sometimes a lively procession of students swings along, energetically beseeching; sometimes just some tranquil old priest murmuring his Collect for the day.

At the Statue of Notre Dame, people are on their knees all around; at the statue of Bernadette also; at the Grotto, in front of the piscine, up along the Way of the Cross, on every path and colline. Even the clock chimes *Ave, Ave—Ave Maria!*

All day long, this praying army passionately offers its prayers toward heaven. One would have to be made of stone not to be affected by it. The rhythms get into your blood. You find yourself humming and saying the things *they* say and hum. And if this affects the able-bodied, how much more must it affect the sick—relaxed, receptive, many of them semiconscious, with no positive activities or plans of their own to engage their attention.

Another powerful element in the Lourdes atmosphere, already referred to, is the devotion of its workers: the spirit of dedication and self-giving that permeates the whole place. It is the spirit of the early Christian community, where all give their services and share alike in the daily tasks.

Hundreds—even thousands—of people work hard all winter, save bit by bit, do without, so that they can come to Lourdes for some days or weeks in the summer and work hard there from morning till night. Brancardiers, nurses, nurses' aids give their vacation time this way, year after year; public-school boys, daughters of famous families, teachers, lawyers, scores of clerks and business people.

The girl in the souvenir shop at my hotel works in the shop mornings (comes from England every year) so that she can help at the baths in the afternoons, dressing and undressing roomfuls of wet, frightened women. The girl at the Cook's Travel Agency, who works from nine to six at her job, goes every night to help at the Grotto until midnight. "Every night when I go the Grotto . . ." she would say, her face alight.

One brancardier said: "These few days at Lourdes each August fix me up for the whole year. I *live* for twelve months on what I get here in just one week!"

Two thousand brancardiers are here for the Rosary Pilgrimage alone. Many brancardiers and nurses are Cures of former years. The Cures coming back, strong and well, caring for them, nursing them, give tremendous inspiration and hope to the sick.

The service of these voluntary workers is lavish and untiring. They run up and down flights of stairs, they carry bedpans; sit beside idiot children whose guttural cries never cease. They change fetid dressings, bathe malodorous wounds. It is not their profession—they are not paid for this. They do it not only cheerfully but joyfully, happily. Why? They pull those invalid carriages to and from the Grotto and the hospital twenty times a day. Everybody with a smile—joking, laughing, encouraging. And praying constantly—at the baths, while carrying the patients, dressing and undressing them, while washing and feeding them; at the station, at the Procession—everywhere.

Psychologists today are measuring mental and emotional wave

lengths. If they could measure the wave length of such an atmosphere, surely it would be found to have a powerful effect on the human organism.

Sometimes prayers are answered in a roundabout way.

I asked one of the English doctors who had been coming to Lourdes for several years whether she had ever seen a miracle.

"Not literally—not right under my nose. But in a way I saw one."

"Tell me!"

"A woman came to Lourdes one year with a mongoloid child. You know what a lot of those there are. This one would draw anybody's pity: such a horrible-looking little monster—great pop eyes, enormous head, slobbery mouth—you know, you've seen enough of them around here. And the mother such a dainty little thing—so young and pretty, so utterly wretched. I stood near her at the Grotto several times, and, one day at the Procession, I heard her desperate prayers."

"Were they answered? Was the child cured?"

"The child died. But next year the mother came again to Lourdes, and on a pilgrimage of thanksgiving. For she had another child, a beautiful baby, perfect in every way."

"Wonderful!"

"Yes. But the interesting thing is that she kept praying: 'Oh God, give me a well child, a perfect child!' And that is just what God did. So often people don't watch what they're saying," the doctor added. "They're surprised when they get, quite literally, what they pray for!"

One of the Italian doctors told another interesting story. A young Genoese girl, desperately sick with some strange disease of the spleen, came to Lourdes—but was going home without her cure; if anything, worse than when she arrived.

On the last day of the pilgrimage, a Belgian doctor coming through the ward stopped to have a special look at this girl, Maria. He became very much interested in her case.

"Where are you from, Maria—Genoa? You know," he said suddenly, "there's a doctor very close to you there, who has made a special study of tropical diseases and particularly diseases of the spleen. I sat next to him at a medical meeting last year. His name is Dr. Liebermann. When you go back, go to see him. I'll bet he can help you!"

The doctor in Genoa not only helped her, he cured her. When she was completely well—and had become his office assistant—Dr. Liebermann teased her about it.

"Well now, here's a fine thing. You go all the way to Lourdes and the Blessed Virgin does nothing for you. And you come back home to Genoa and a Jewish doctor makes you well! How do you account for that? It looks very much as though the Blessed Virgin let you down!"

"Don't you say such a thing!" cried Maria indignantly. "It was the Blessed Virgin who brought the Belgian doctor into the ward to tell me about you. That was Her way of curing me. The Blessed Virgin knows what She's about!"

Much of my time was taken up, necessarily, in work on the medical records. Thus I met many of the visiting doctors and heads of pilgrimages. Always something doing around the Bureau. The first day I was there, a young priest from India sat reading at the table beside me, his face alight with pride in "Facts of Lourdes." Another day, a Chinese doctor from Hongkong was poring over the files. Often young French interns on holiday with their wives will spend several days of their precious vacation time laboriously copying out data on some of the most interesting cases. They like to discuss these, even with a layman and a foreigner, and regard my thick notes with respect.

Getting these stories of cures is not a simple process. After you have been given permission from the authorities to use the files, and have selected your chosen case for the day, a big black folder, or dossier, is set in front of you, filled with a great mass of papers, pamphlets, and photostats. A dossier may contain as many as a hundred papers—including doctors' certificates, laboratory reports; testimony of witnesses to the illness and witnesses to the cure; depositions of relatives, neighbors and nurses, of brancardiers and bath attendants (where the baths are involved); hospital charts, surgeons' notations; pilgrimage officers' statements, statements by the patient's employers; detailed reports of the Medical Bureau examinations and conclusions; also the report and conclusions of the Medical Commission; and various other documents, such as personal letters from friends and associates—often the most interesting and significant of all.

If the cure is one of those recognized by the Church as Miraculous, there is an entire second set of notes and findings handed in by the

Canonical Commission—after the Medical Commission has finished with theirs.

Most of the papers are written by hand—the spindly French hand, a good deal harder for Anglo-Saxons than their own. To wade through this mass of material, translating every paper from the French as you go, and with proper punctiliousness as to medical and ecclesiastical terms, means long hours of careful work.

Records all morning, the Procession and the sick all afternoon. If I'm not at the baths or the Grotto, I'm at the hospitals visiting patients, or up on the rampe looking on. The days are filled to overflowing—*and* the nights with the pilgrims running up and down the halls of the hotel, singing and talking till all hours.

And then the constant arriving and departing of thousands of people—by trains, planes, cars and autobuses. Lourdes is a strenuous place. You get very little sleep. Your nerves and emotions are under constant assault: a succession of tragic sights and sounds, each time you set foot in the street.

Sometimes you feel the need of getting away from it all for a while. Then there is the lovely Bearn countryside—where in ten minutes you can lose yourself in green woods and heavenly quiet. Or, you can sit on the terrace of the Café Royal and watch the world go by.

The Royal is at the crossroads of all Lourdes traffic—directly in front of the Boulevard and the entrance to the Domaine. Everybody "falls in" there for a bit of rest and refreshment at the end of a hard day. More cosmopolitan than the Paris boulevards, it is *the* place to study the extraordinary mixture of Lourdes types and nationalities: Spanish women with fans and black lace mantillas, chatting with their Director as they drink their chocolate; Belgian and Dutch farmers enjoying big mugs of beers; country priests sipping lemonade and casting sidelong glances at foreign priests drinking liqueurs; a group of English university students ordering Dubonnet and looking deliciously sophisticated; little French girls and boys gorging ices and *patisseries,* while their parents mop hot faces and drink Cinzano.

The brancardiers unharness. The Directors of the pilgrimages lean back in their chairs and relax over coffee and little cakes. Some of the old priests enjoy a joke and a good cigar with the younger men and perhaps a thimble of cognac in their coffee. You might think all this not quite "correct" in a pilgrimage town. But then you remember that these men have been up since daybreak, working incessantly—both priests and brancardiers. By five o'clock they are tired out and it is only right that they should rest a bit and enjoy themselves before taking up their burdens again.

This is a place too for friendly interchange among the different pilgrimages, and for mutual confidences and stirring tales of Lourdes. Some of the most thrilling stories of cures, some of the most deeply touching accounts of faith reborn and lives remade, have been told me over these cups of coffee at the Royal.

Just a few steps farther on, along the Avenue Bernadette, is the Hospital of the Sept Douleurs. Even here at the café, stretchers and invalid carriages go by all day long; but for a few moments one can forget them, and under these gay awnings relax and recover one's forces.

Autocars swing by, bearing crowds of singing pilgrims to and from the station—the Basques and Italians waving a last goodby to the Dutch and English in the café, with whom they have shared their five pilgrimage days. Traffic is terrific, as the different groups and organizations pour out of the Domaine after the Procession. People overflow from the sidewalk onto the pavement—a solid mass, through which autos and motorbikes weave amid incredible shouting and hooting.

Tour leaders wave their arms and call frantic orders, which nobody can hear. Newsboys run up and down hawking the latest Paris papers. At the corner the candid-camera man is doing a rush business among stout Flemish and British matrons and demure Breton girls in lace caps and gaily decorated aprons. The rug vendor and the watch peddler slip in and out between the tables, importuning in their eternal singsong; the sellers of postcards and the sellers of vanilla double their shrill cries. An Arab chief in full regalia causes a sensation striding along with his picturesque retinue—flowing white robes, gold-thonged headdress, shiny black beard.

Suddenly, through all this hubbub and commotion, a swirl of figures over at the gateway—the mighty roll of the Magnificat. All spring to their feet, rush to the pavement, cross themselves, then laugh and ask questions excitedly. Something is happening. A cure perhaps—a miracle? Then you see them.

Following the long line of stretchers and carriages returning to the hospital comes a jubilant little procession: a group of brancardiers forming a guard of honor for a radiant young girl who walks up the street as if on air. She had been carried down to the Grotto that afternoon on a stretcher, after four years in bed with a tuberculous spine. She is returning on her own two feet, singing and praising God.

Everybody joins in the singing. The Dutch and Spanish women hug each other. The little boys throw their caps in the air and cheer. The waiters smile and bring a double order for everyone. They know the splendid aftermath for *them* in the expansive, heart-warming hour after a miracle.

Was it a miracle, really? Time will tell. But that girl's eyes—!

I recognized one of the "unbelieving" French doctors, standing at the curb quite near me. "Well, what did you think of it? Quite exciting, wasn't it?" I said casually.

"It was—" He suddenly turned and fled into a shop, handkerchief held up to his face. I didn't realize until afterward that he was weeping. Never again did he have anything derisive to say about miracles.

At dinner everybody is talking about it. The Dutch are staying at our hotel. The girl is a member of their pilgrimage. They are all tremendously pleased and proud.

One of their nurses is telling the wonderful story, with personal elaborations:

"So I told our pilgrimage doctor, I said. 'Well sir, you have a miracle!' 'Well, well, we shall see. We don't know about it yet.' 'But it's true!' I insisted. 'I saw it with my own eyes! While I was bathing your patient, whom we had plunged stiff as a board into the bath, I saw her arms and legs *bend,* and she whom we had had to carry—four of us—to put her in the bath, I saw her sit down on the edge of the bath and help us while we put her clothes back on again.' "

"She left her cast and brace at the Grotto," another verified joyfully. "Never any need for *those* again, she said!"

"And how do the other patients feel about it?" I asked; "the ones who didn't get their cure? Are they envious, or disappointed, or anything?"

"Madame, they are enraptured! They are in the seventh heaven. They had all been praying for this girl day and night—she was the worst of our cases. All they can think of is that their prayers were successful, and Suzie will go home *whole* and on her own feet!"

Everyone was electrified—beaming; all round the big dining room, faces alight, eyes shining, broad smiles from the ambulant patients delighted at their comrade's good fortune. This was not just the usual exuberant summer crowd, full of *joie de vivre* and healthy physical energy. The joy in these faces, the spirit in that room, were something different, something to cherish and remember.

"Well do I recollect," mused an old brancardier, "the first miracle

I ever saw. I may live to be a hundred, but I'll never forget *that*—or the thanksgiving Mass that followed in our village church after we went home. People made up quarrels who hadn't spoken to each other for years. Estranged children came back home to their parents. It's—well, a miracle does something to you; brings people back to God."

And does all this come about, as certain scientists tell us, through mere "mass delusion" and "some unusual psychological phenomenon," "a sort of 'explosion' in man's brain cells"? They must be very different cells from those we know in ordinary everyday operation.

After dinner we gather in the hall downstairs with our wraps and candle shades. No one wants to miss the greatest of all Lourdes spectacles—the Torchlight Procession. Even the concierge, seasoned veteran of many summers, softens at the mention of it.

"But yes, madame, I still go sometimes. It is *va-iry* beautiful!"

People are streaming out of the hotels up and down the street. Nurses and brancardiers off duty catch up their candles and fall into line with the rest. Bishops and bank clerks, truckdrivers and duchesses; pilgrimage leaders vainly trying to keep track of their straying flocks: all hurry along to the meeting place. At eight o'clock in the evening every pilgrim's feet are turned in one direction, toward the Domaine.

It is night when we reach the Square, but the whole place is brilliantly illuminated. The churches are lit up, and the statue of Notre Dame de Lourdes and the huge cross on the Pic du Jer. The old castle on the hill shines against the sky. High up on the left the Basilica, outlined in fire.

The crowd, too, soon becomes a serpent of fire, weaving in and out along the steps and parapets; and from this undulating throng, great joyous bursts of singing. Each pilgrim carries a candle protected by a paper shade, and sings with his group.

They sing in different tongues but always the same song: the "Canticle of Bernadette," that tells the story of the little shepherd girl and her visions, each stanza ending with *Ave, Ave, Ave Maria!*

This is the theme-song of Lourdes. It is sung on the pilgrimage trains and at different times during the day at the chapels; and it is *the song* of the Torchlight Procession. It is heard every night at Lourdes, for two hours and longer. It is not "good" music; parts of it are very poor poetry; but it has a haunting quality. One hears it, dropping off to sleep, and again when the chimes ring out first thing in the morning. That simple refrain, slipping up through the mind, can recreate the whole Lourdes scene for me in two minutes.

The groups gather at the Grotto, wind along the rampes in an enormous horseshoe, then to the Esplanade—down one side and up the other. Each person holds his candle. Each group carries its pilgrimage sign, also illuminated: Newcastle . . . Limoges . . . Brussels . . . Oran . . . The tiny flames form larger and larger blocks, till they become a huge wheel of fire.

Seen from across the river, the procession is a scene of eerie beauty. Out of the enveloping darkness shine a myriad lights. The candles burning at the Grotto form a great wall of light, the church ablaze above it.

My favorite place is high up at the rail in front of the Basilica, where I can watch the whole vast panorama and see every part and each pilgrimage as it comes along. French families often stand near me—little boys and girls singing lustily with their fathers and mothers, uncles and grandparents. An astounding sight, that crowd as it comes by—matrons and midinettes, stalwart young men, grizzled veteran pilgrims; a bride in her veil, an old woman in her tattered shawl, each face illumined by the paper-shrouded candle, each pilgrim singing with all his might.

Down the path they wind, pealing forth their hymns and *Aves* under the stars—the hospital doors open; the sick looking out from their rows upon rows of beds and singing too. On any night it is an amazing and wonderful scene. At the time of the great pilgrimages—such as the French National, or the Rosary in October—when as many as sixty thousand people march and sing, it is overwhelming.

Have you ever heard sixty thousand people singing one great hymn together? Have you ever seen sixty thousand faces lighted up not only by candles but with radiant love and devotion? It's something you won't forget—in this bomb-ridden, disillusioned twentieth century.

The marching continues for two hours. At the end, the marchers come together in the Square in one huge block in front of the Rosary Church. Hundreds of pilgrims are massed along the rampes and beside the river too. The Bishop on the steps of the church holds up his hand, and the singing stops. He raises his hand again—and the people burst forth into the majestic chanting of the Credo.

Visitors to Lourdes often say that the singing of the Credo is the most impressive moment of all. An instant before, each pilgrim was singing in his own tongue, the result a confused though not unpleasing jumble. Now, suddenly, everyone is declaring his belief in God in Latin —universal language of the Church.

This ends the day's ceremonies. You may be Catholic, you may be Protestant, you may be an out-and-out-atheist and unbeliever. Whoever you are and wherever you come from, you will never forget the Torchlight Procession at Lourdes.*

* Lest the figures regarding the Torchlight crowds be considered exaggerated, I may add that in 1946 the space along the Esplande and the rampes was scientifically measured and found to have a capacity to hold 100,000 persons.

❧ *10* ❧

The Church and Lourdes

Twin peaks stand guard over Lourdes—on top of one a great Cross, shining day and night; on the other an observatory where groups of scientists pursue their studies. There they stand, exactly opposite each other: Science and Religion, the two great servants of man—and of truth.

For a long time people have wondered whether the gulf between the two would ever be bridged—whether they would ever get together. At Lourdes—by a miracle?—they do. Down there in the valley, the Bureau and the Grotto live side by side, working in thorough harmony; under the aegis of an International Association of 5,000 doctors and of the most conservative ecclesiastical body in the world.

We have seen the change in attitude of the Church after the findings of the Episcopal Commission which vindicated Bernadette, and the official establishment of the Shrine under the direction of the Bishop of Tarbes in 1862. From that time on, Lourdes has won the steadily increasing interest and affection of the Church through the years. Witness the large numbers of churches and organizations dedicated to Our Lady of Lourdes—in cities and countries all over the world, the interest of various pontiffs in the Shrine; the great number of bishops and clergy who prepare and conduct the pilgrimages; the magnificent work of the Hospitallers and their continuous activity in the dioceses.

From having been at first an obscure stepchild, regarded with some hesitation and embarrassment, Lourdes has come to be a beloved daughter; next to Rome, the brightest jewel in the Catholic crown.

From early days the Popes have followed the development of the Shrine and the pilgrimages with an attentive eye. Pope Pius IX, in Bernadette's lifetime, was greatly devoted to Notre Dame de Lourdes. He often visited a small replica of the Grotto which had been built in the Vatican gardens. Under Leo XIII the Sacred Congregation of Rites (July 16, 1890) approved the office of the Feast of the Apparitions of the Immaculate Virgin at the Grotto of Lourdes. In 1900, the Bishop of Tarbes asked permission to erect in the Vatican gardens an exact reproduction of the Grotto. The Holy Father approved, and watched the construction with lively interest.

The present Pope, Pius XII, has been a devoted friend of Lourdes for many years—especially since 1935 when, as Cardinal Pacelli, he was sent by Pius XI as Papal Legate to preside over the three days and nights of prayer which closed at Lourdes the great Jubilee of the Redemption.

On that solemn occasion, when fears of war and prayers for peace reached their climax on the part of the whole Catholic world, the present Pope paid his moving tribute there before the Shrine:

> Oh Lourdes—Holy City! In you is united the enchantment of Nazareth, the sacred charm of Bethlehem, the healing power of Bethesda. How many miracles of the Redeemer have you not seen, renewing themselves here! What marvels of grace have been accomplished within your walls. For more than one Thomas you have become the Upper Room where his eyes have been unsealed. For more than one Saul, the road to Damascus, where he has become Paul.

But it was the wise and much-loved Pius X (recently canonized) who perhaps exercised the most powerful and lasting influence on Lourdes destinies. His portrait stands in the center of the baluster of the Church of the Crypt "as a witness [he wrote] for all time to come of my great devotion to Notre Dame of the Blessed Rosary and a proof of my particular affection for the Sanctuary of Lourdes."

It was he who extended to the Universal Church the Office of the Mass of the Apparition of Notre Dame de Lourdes. He delegated the

Cardinal of Bordeaux to preside in his name at the ceremonies of the fiftieth anniversary of the Lourdes Shrine. He enlarged and improved the Grotto in the Vatican gardens, so that henceforth the slender spire of the Lourdes Basilica would shine near the Dome of St. Peter's. On August 13, 1913, he signed the decree introducing the cause of Bernadette Soubirous for canonization.

It was this great and far-seeing Pope who inaugurated the system of Canonical judgments regarding Lourdes cures; his wise mind that first conceived the idea of "an international board of scholars and physicians who should give the Medical Bureau guarantees that cannot be contested."

In April, 1904, two hundred and fifty Catholic physicians went to Rome to pay homage to the Holy Father, taking with them fifteen persons who had been miraculously cured at Lourdes. The Bishop of Tarbes headed this pilgrimage,* accompanied by representatives of the various sections of Lourdes activities. The physicians were for the most part habitués of the Medical Bureau. Thus the Pope could get an idea of both the institutions and the work of Lourdes.

He was deeply impressed; also he realized the need for discretion and dignity in the conduct and direction of such a place. "The word miracle," he said, "should not be uttered lightly." Safeguards must be thrown round it—precautions must be taken.

In October, Dr. Lapponi, the Pope's physician, advised the President of the Medical Bureau that "in his (the Pope's) judgment it would be well for the Reverend Curia to institute a regular process on the most remarkable cases, especially as to the identity of the persons, on the authentications of the physicians, and the depositions of witnesses who saw the patients before their cure."

Shortly after, the Bishop of Tarbes (in a letter dated Nov. 15, 1906) begged "the Bishops of the Dioceses where people are living, called in popular language *miraculés* of Lourdes, to be good enough to establish, upon canonical inquiry, the reality and the supernatural character of the cures"; adding, "it belongs to ecclesiastical authority to declare whether certain cures should be classed as among miraculous acts . . . it is the Bishops who have the power to recognize and to approve new miracles, after having consulted the canonical commissions . . ."

---

* The name of Lourdes was added to the Tarbes bishopric by Pius X in 1912. It then became the Diocese of Tarbes and Lourdes.

Following these instructions, and the desire formally expressed by the Pope, the Bishops appointed commissions and set them to work investigating alleged cures. In consequence of these investigations twenty-eight cures were declared miraculous by Episcopal ordinance on the eve of the Golden Jubilee of Lourdes (1908). These were cures pronounced by canonical judgments of various Cardinals and Bishops, following upon the inquiries and reports of canonical commissions and the procedure as directed.

This same procedure is in force today.

When the doctors have finished their work and rendered their decision on an alleged cure, if the decision is in the affirmative the case is sent on to the ecclesiastical authorities for consideration by a Canonical Commission. The Canonical Commission is named in each diocese by the Bishop of the Diocese and each case is determined upon separately.

The Commission usually consists of five persons, two of whom must be physicians. The Church requires that two experts or specialists in the disease under discussion shall be included, that "the experts" must enjoy a certain renown in medicine or surgery; furthermore, specialists chosen must be distinguished for the diagnosis and the cure of the maladies which are concerned in the proposed miracle. The report of the experts, briefly written, and clearly supported by arguments, will reply to the following questions:

1. If it is a question of a cure, may the one named as beneficiary be considered as truly cured?

2. Can the event proposed as a miracle be explained by the laws of nature, or can it not?

Benedict XIV enumerates the seven characteristics which must exist whenever there arises a question of a miracle—and these are to be applied by every Canonical Commission studying an alleged supernatural cure at Lourdes:

1. That the malady was a grave one, and impossible or at least difficult to cure.

2. That the cured malady was not in a state of decline to such an extent that it could have declined soon afterward.

3. That no medication had been used, or if there had been, that its inefficacy was certain.

4. That the cure was sudden—instantaneous.

5. That the cure was perfect.

6. That there had not been beforehand a crisis produced by some cause and at its natural hour; in this case one cannot say that the cure was miraculous but natural, wholly or in part.

7. Finally, that after the cure there has been no relapse of the illness.

Dr. Leuret notes that "one can conceive true miracles which do not present one or another of these characteristics. . . . The Church does not deny the possibility of miracles 'less complete,' but she refuses to authenticate them, so strongly does she exact precise characteristics, easy to verify and which exclude all possibility of error."

Certain doctors are astonished at the severe requirements of the Church in accepting as miraculous an extraordinary cure. Dr. Leuret speaks of having been a member of a tribunal charged with investigating an alleged miraculous cure, and having heard one of the doctor-witnesses exclaim: "How is it that I, who am not a very firm believer, see a miracle in this cure, while you—ecclesiastical judges—are more difficult to convince than I?"

The rigorous attitude of the Medical Bureau itself is in line with that of the Church. Monseigneur Théas emphasized it in his address to the General Assembly of AMIL physicians in 1949:

"Your only role is to be true. You have neither to be severe nor indulgent, but only to be exact and to furnish to the Church medical observations which are indisputable—leaving her to judge in each case whether there has or has not been a miracle."

As stated earlier, only fifty-one cases have been declared Miraculous Cures by the Church, during the ninety-seven years of the Shrine. It may be well to mention again that cures of nervous maladies are not considered—nor are cures of hypersensitive patients "whose emotions would be susceptible of provoking 'nervous discharges' which could modify for example their mobility."

In spite of all these precautions, not only lay people but some of the clergy have occasionally been overzealous with premature announcements of "miraculous cures" at Lourdes. In 1924, the Bishop of Tarbes and Lourdes issued a stern warning in this regard:

The haste of certain pilgrims to proclaim "miraculous" certain happenings which have not yet been the object of sufficient scientific study or of official confirmation, is incontestably of a nature to furnish weapons to the enemies of the supernatural and of the Catholic Church. . . .

Inspired no doubt by most honorable intentions, too much haste in naming such happenings as supernatural, far from producing conviction with unbelievers, favors on the contrary attacks of impiety and of bad faith.

It is of utmost importance then, in order to prevent opinion from falling in error, that no act of a cure at Lourdes shall give rise to a religious ceremony or be set forth in the accounts of pilgrimages, before having been rigorously checked and authenticated by the inquiries and official publication of the verbatim proceedings of the Bureau of Medical Verifications of Lourdes.

In disregarding this rule—imperatively dictated by Christian prudence—newspapers and other Catholic publications will expose themselves to an official denial which, to their very great regret, the President of the Medical Bureau and even the Bishop of Tarbes and Lourdes will be obliged to bring upon them. (Signed, Francis Xavier, Bishop of Tarbes and Lourdes.)

It may come as a surprise to many that the Catholic Church, while maintaining the possibility of present-day miracles, does not require its followers to believe in them, and some do not. Bernadette showed no interest in them. The Lady never mentioned them, or gave any indication of the great healings that were to take place at the Shrine. What The Lady wanted was Prayer and Penitence. This is what the Church wants too.

Among Catholic doctors one finds sometimes the strongest conviction, sometimes the most stubborn skepticism. I talked with a number of Catholic doctors who were greatly interested in Lourdes cures but who are still uncertain as to the forces that may produce them. (These of course are definitely in the minority, and by some might not be considered "good Catholics.")

"There are vast areas of knowledge as yet almost completely unexplored," said one Catholic physician. "All we can say now is that such healings are at present *inexplicable.*"

I must add that no one appears to be trying to convince or change the skeptics, or to change the views of doctors of other faiths either.

The declared freedom offered to all hands in the work is a genuine freedom—and very fine.

I have never seen any proselytizing at Lourdes, except that of example. During the months that I was there no one inquired about my faith or suggested that I change it. What impressed me was the sincere and simple faith, the true religion being *lived* all about me. One thought for the thousandth time how much more eloquent preaching is the silent kind—*being* your religion—how profoundly and permanently that impresses.

The Church does practice one open—and very interesting—piece of propaganda, each summer during the pilgrimage season. Up on the hill behind the Sanctuaries, it presents each year a Missionary Exposition—bringing before its masses of Catholic pilgrims (and other interested visitors) the story of Catholic missionary work in faraway lands. A different area is presented each summer. The year I was there, Africa was the continent under discussion; the year before, India and Ceylon.

Photographs, surveys, arts and crafts, exhibits of all sorts of work done by the native Catholics of the various countries are on view; priests and Sisters, with native helpers, give hourly talks and explanations. Every day, several thousand people see these exhibits and hear these talks. They form a colorful supplement to the regular routine of the pilgrims, and bring in quite substantial returns for the missionary cause, if only through the very modestly priced tickets of admission. They bring these thousands of peasant folk into dramatic and vivid touch with people of other lands and with the work of the Church throughout the world.

This national and international unifying work is one of the most interesting aspects of Lourdes, quite aside from the healing and spiritual side. The bringing together of scores of pilgrimages from different provinces and territories of France is in itself a fine, patriotic work. Coming here brings a person in touch not only with people of the different parts of the country itself—its many regions and departments —but with French citizens from many parts of the world: Madagascar, Syria, Morocco, French Guiana, Algeria, Indo-China, and so on.

I have often thought of the amazing way in which the supposedly un-unitable French come together in such complete unity here. Lourdes has united Frenchmen of all types and classes, all shades of religious and political opinion, and during times of greatest intellectual division and irreligion. Here, from the beginning—and even in the strait-laced and snobbish nineteenth century—French people of all social castes, all grades of education, have come together spontaneously, wholeheartedly, in common worship and in common work of love and compassion. Any Hospitallers' mess is a shining example of this, all political discussion being strictly ruled out. Thus, among such passionate individualists, in a nation we are accustomed to think of as a conglomeration of conflicting and irreconcilable views and groups, we find at this one spot an extraordinary sense of unity and the smoothest and most contented teamwork imaginable. And this extends back into the local units when the people all go home.

Lourdes is a great national center. It is a great international center. Not only for the doctors and pilgrims but for the priests and bishops of many countries who meet here too: a perpetual ecumenical conference, enlarging their individual outlook, permitting them to share experiences, discuss problems of their various lands and dioceses; and through them carrying this wider viewpoint back for the better education and enlargement of thousands of parishioners in their homelands.

As hosts, the Lourdes clergy are famous. It takes real genius to make all these various visitors feel at home and so welcome, so much wanted and appreciated, as they all do feel at Lourdes.

One of the nicest things about the place is its democracy and unpretentiousness, notwithstanding all its splendid ceremonies. The humblest little priest from the back of beyond is invited to say Mass. It is always the visiting Bishops—from Liverpool or Turin or Seattle—who lead the processions, not the resident clergy.

"Just imagine, they asked me—me, a little missioner buried in a tiny village in Japan—to say Mass at the Grotto. And I did!" a young Maryknoll Father told me, joyfully.

The Lourdes Bishop says Mass only once a week—at eight o'clock on Saturday mornings, throughout the summer. When he became ill recently, he had himself carried down to lie with the other sick in front of the Grotto. "Now I am one of you!" he said with great content. "I who have lectured and preached to you so often. Now you will teach and instruct me!"

And here a word about this remarkable person, His Excellency the Most Reverend Pietro Maria Théas, The Bishop of Lourdes. He lives in a modest "Chalet Episcopale" on the hill above the Sanctuaries. His waiting room is open to anyone—and is usually full: Sisters, priests, brancardiers, nurses, townspeople. The first day I was there, two Turks, a French sailor, an Egyptian scholar, and three young men from a seminary in West Africa were waiting to see him.

The Bishop is friendly, charming, *simpático*. His unfailing graciousness and kindliness is from the heart. Day after day I watched the tenderness, sensitiveness, with which he greets the sick. Seeing these multitudes as he does—month after month, year after year, it would be understandable if he became, not blasé, but sometimes perhaps just a bit perfunctory in his greeting and feeling for them.

With Monseigneur Théas—never! Each group, each occasion, each new pilgrimage and ceremony, is a new opportunity for him to show his never-ending compassion and concern for their welfare. The healing of their souls and bodies is ever in his mind.

Everything that a great ecclesiastic can be to his Church—a tender father to his "children," both sick and well; a generous and devoted friend to his colleagues; a genial and self-effacing host to his visiting confreres; a magnificent orator and presiding officer at the never-ending succession of celebrations and ceremonies—all this and much more Monseigneur Théas is to the people who surround him in the office he so ably and humbly fills. There is no office quite like it anywhere else in the world.

11

Changes Connected with Cures

The investigation of alleged cures has always been and remains the prime responsibility of the Medical Bureau. Cures still hold an immense fascination for everyone connected in any way with Lourdes. This is all the more intriguing when it is noted that so very few pilgrims to the Shrine have actually witnessed a cure or known a miracle.

Cures were never mentioned by Bernadette at the time of the apparitions. Clearly, they were not intended to be the central feature of Lourdes. History has confirmed this. In recent years, the tiny number of inexplicable cures has led the authorities, both religious and medical, to reconsider the real meaning of Lourdes. They have given their attention to a comprehensive review of the cures in the Archives, the changes in the kinds of sickness seen in pilgrims, the evolution in the work of the doctors, and the theology and science of cures. The result of all this thorough study has highlighted the problems entailed in assessing cures and has focused attention on what the Message of Lourdes holds for people in the twentieth century.

Since 1955, advances in science and in modern theology have altered considerably the way cures are examined, how they are interpreted, and their relevance.

In the 128 years since the apparitions, out of the millions of pilgrims who came to Lourdes, about five hundred thousand were sick. Many of these people claimed to have been cured there. Indeed, many thousands of them were considered extraordinary cures by the medical control, but up to now only sixty-four cures have been proclaimed miraculous by the Church. Fifty-one of these miraculous cures have been mentioned in the original text of this book, twelve of them in detail (one of these was Lydia Brosse, whose cure was declared miraculous after its publication). Since 1955, another thirteen have been added to the official list; of these, only four occurred and were proclaimed miraculous in the past thirty years. Clearly, the incidence of extraordinary cures eventually recognized as miraculous has fallen dramatically.

The full list of miraculous cures in the Archives (see Appendix E) can be divided into two groups: those before, and those after, 1947. In that year, the medical procedures for investigating cures were radically improved. Before 1947: numbers 1–7 were the first cures, in 1858, recognized by Msgr. Laurence, Bishop of Tarbes; numbers 8–40 were those presented by Dr. Boissarie between 1907 and 1913. After 1947: numbers 41–64 (which include one cure from 1946) complete the list, covering the years up to 1978. None has been added since then.

At first glance, it may seem strange that no cures were proclaimed miraculous between 1862 and 1907, 1913 and 1947, or since 1978. Some explanation for this may be found in the enforced inactivity of the Bureau des Constatations Médicales (B.C.M.) during the various wars, as well as in the wide range of ecclesiastical and medical personnel involved in the investigation procedures. In actual fact, many of the thousands of alleged cures were classed as extraordinary by the medical control during these years.

The bleak years between 1862 and 1883 cover the early days, when the Missionary Chaplains of Lourdes were in sole charge. Such records as they presumably kept are not available. At the time, these priests did not recognize the importance of medical advice; it was requested on rare occasions from a very few doctors. The investigation of cures was first put on a proper medical basis in 1883, when Dr. Dunot de Saint Maclou organized and inaugurated the B.C.M. Dr. Boissarie (President, 1892–1917) not only organized more detailed study of the cures, but, more important, he invited the Church authorities to play their part. This led to thirty-three cures, which had been recognized by the B.C.M. as extraordinary, being declared miraculous. Twenty-two of them were proclaimed by eleven French and two Belgian bishops for the Fiftieth Anniversary of Lourdes (1908), and the eleven others by 1913.

The second period when there was a dearth of miraculous cures reflects the suspension of the pilgrimages and of Lourdes's activity during the two world wars, and the rapid succession of five presidents at the B.C.M. from 1919 to 1928. These men were not long enough in office, due to age or infirmity, to become well established. Even after Dr. Vallet became President (1928–47) and supervised the opening of 406 dossiers on alleged cures, only 129 were recognized as extraordinary. Of these, only one cure was proclaimed miraculous, and that was in 1946. Four others had to wait until later.

Dr. Leuret (President, 1947–54) was the President who forged a much closer link between the Medical Bureau and the Bishop of Tarbes and Lourdes for dealing with the control of cures. It was in 1947 that the B.C.M. became the Medical Bureau and the National Medical Committee was established. This Committee was expanded into the International Medical Committee in 1954, but from the time of the first changes in 1947, there was a real jump in the number of cures recognized as extraordinary and eventually declared miraculous. One or the other of these committees examined fifty-six cures judged extraordinary and presented by the Medical Bureau. By 1965, twenty-seven of these were accepted as proved and inexplicable by this second tier of control. The Church proclaimed seventeen of the twenty-seven to be miracles. In the 1970s, two more cures passed all hurdles and were added to the official list of miracles. Since 1978, no cure has been proclaimed miraculous, although one is still awaiting a decision by the Church. Statistics derived from the Archives can be used to show the annual average of extraordinary cures (judged as such by the medical control). Incidence has dropped from fifty-seven per year in 1880–1915, to twelve per year in 1920–39, to less than one per year in 1947–85.

These figures from the Archives reveal that the number of cures accepted as true and extraordinary has diminished at the very time when the professional standards of medical control were being raised. On the other hand, the number recognized by the Church has increased in the second half of the twentieth century, when the relative and the absolute numbers of miraculous cures have never been more significant.

To some extent, the decline in recognized cures must be related to the present types of sick pilgrims, compared with those of forty years ago. The range of their ailments, their requirements, and their approach to life have altered greatly.

In times long past, the majority of sick pilgrims were gravely ill and usually incurable. Doctors then could do little but support them and encourage them to live out their lives with their illnesses as best they could. They could only rarely alter the fatal course of disease, since preventive medicine and specific remedies were virtually nonexistent. Most patients died relatively young; a few made dramatic recoveries. The only contribution the clergy could offer was to encourage the sick to be resigned to their fate and have recourse to God.

Now the whole scene has changed. Not many are dangerously ill, and very few must use wheeled stretchers. Very seriously ill patients prefer to remain at home, where they feel secure, near their own physician and local hospital. There they can continue their modern ongoing treatment (chemotherapy, radiotherapy, etc.), which is not readily or cheaply available to foreigners in Lourdes.

Some diseases, e.g. tuberculosis, are rarely seen; others, e.g. some cancers, are curable by treatment. Patients with other diseases receive palliative treatment with modern medicines, or are equipped with surgical appliances. Although the life expectancy in many of these cases is much reduced, the patients are often fit enough to travel to Lourdes.

Probably the greatest change seen among the sick pilgrims is the hundreds of handicapped people, many in their own wheelchairs. Handicaps may be physical or mental, congenital (Down's Syndrome) or acquired (disability from road accident). These people can often lead a relatively normal life in society, and favor staying in hotels or hostels, rather than in the Accueils, when they are in Lourdes. The chronic sick and disabled also have quite different needs than in former years. The general public is more enlightened, too, regarding health care, and is accustomed to receiving effective therapeutic drugs, excellent surgical procedures, and all the facilities that state medicine can provide. All this is a result of the change in Western Europe from a rather primitive, rural society to a more civilized, urban one.

Small wonder, then, that they look upon the old reception centers, built seventy or more years ago, as old-fashioned, overcrowded, and uncomfortable. The centers were built to house the thirty-five thousand sick pilgrims who came to Lourdes each year many decades ago. Now seventy thousand sick people come; forty-eight thousand of these require hospital beds. Simple arithmetic explains the overcrowding. Today, patients expect the reception centers to meet the highest clinical standards, with modern facilities and an up-to-date staff. They also look for a modest standard of comfort in and en route to Lourdes. They don't expect to have to wait hours in the cold, wind, or rain, whether at the train station, the airport, or in the town. There is now a plan of modernization that is gradually eliminating existing defects and deficiencies. For instance, recent provision of modern ambulances and jumbulances, enclosed passages, transit lounges, etc., have eased the situation of travelers.

The mental outlook of the sick and disabled has changed too. They want to be as independent as possible, to mingle with healthy people, and to learn more about the pilgrimage in order to obtain the maximum benefit from all the services. Many are alone or lonely at home, and come to Lourdes for the community spirit; to be looked after with loving care and to share their plight with others in a similar situation. Their attitude toward illness has changed as well. Most do not seek a cure for themselves, but for someone else. They want to be treated as responsible people who have accepted their ailment and made the necessary adjustments. In Lourdes, they now seek to deepen their relationship with God and to renew their faith and their prayer life. They realize this will give them help for the spirit and the steadfast courage to lead their lives more fully, and feel that only an encounter with God will supply all these fundamental needs. Where better than in Lourdes to seek this closeness to God? The authorities have recognized the importance of these aspirations and have already adapted the spiritual services, enabling the sick to discover a way to live their redemptive role as sick people.

The assessment of cures as medically inexplicable has always been the task of the doctors in Lourdes, and in former decades they did everything but make the final decision upon the miraculous nature of a cure. In fact, they played such an important part in this work that Dr. Boissarie wrote in 1905, "The history of Lourdes was written in its entirety by the doctors." Pope Pius XI, at the Canonization of Bernadette in 1933, said, "If the doctors have need of the Blessed Virgin, the Blessed Virgin has need of the doctors." To fulfill their vital task, the doctors took the initiative to start and build up a strong organization and worked out a well-defined code of practice.

Over the years since Dr. de St. Maclou began the B.C.M., the standards for examination of cures, and for their acceptance as extraordinary and medically inexplicable, have become increasingly exacting. As medical knowledge increased, the field of inexplicability decreased.

Between 1920 and 1975, several changes were made in the wording of the questions to be answered by the Bureau. These were relevant to the accuracy of the assessment, focusing yet more attention on all the circumstances surrounding the cure and its precise nature.

In 1975, the International Medical Committee of Lourdes drew up a new questionnaire (see Appendix D), covering sixteen aspects of a cure, in keeping with modern medicine. Each member of the committee is obliged to give a definite "yes" or "no" answer to each question. With all the professional information thus obtained, it has become much easier for the members to answer a final question: "Taking into consideration the way it was produced and sustained, does the established cure of Mr. X constitute a phenomenon which is contrary to the observation and expectation of medical knowledge, and scientifically inexplicable?"

Since 1975, each bishop has also received the considered opinions of a small group of doctors appointed by him to a diocesan Medical Committee. These doctors review the work of both the Medical Bureau and the International Medical Committee of Lourdes.

Today the code of practice for the full procedure to establish a cure as miraculous (Church) and recognized as inexplicable (doctors) is carried out with maximum expertise. Medical reports are required from the Medical Bureau, the International Medical Committee of Lourdes, and the local diocesan Medical Committee. Then the theologians on the Canonical Committee discuss these reports and advise the bishop, who makes the final decision. Collecting and sifting all the facts necessary to complete the questionnaire on a single case takes time—often several years.

The exacting procedure to establish a cure as extraordinary and medically inexplicable poses some difficulties, because the Church still insists on using the old strict criteria. Despite the utmost professional care taken by the doctors, the practical problems that arise are far greater than those of thirty years ago.

Merely to obtain a full medical history from a patient can be anything but simple in Lourdes. Many pilgrims, more concerned with travel arrangements, arrive in Lourdes with only brief medical certificates from their doctors. It rarely occurs to them that complete records and copies of the original hospital documents might be needed. And it can be a daunting task to extract information from their doctors and witnesses at home. Many doctors refuse to supply this material; they haven't the time or the interest. Some of the witnesses cannot be traced, having changed their addresses or died. With the vast scale of laboratory and X-ray tests now available, it may be impractical to do every conceivable relevant check. It simply is not always possible to provide an exact diagnosis and proof of the disease.

Treatment, too, demands careful consideration, because many patients have already been given some form of therapy. A decision has to be made as to whether it was palliative or curative. Did the medication simply slow down the fatal course of the disease, relieving the distressing symptoms, but without any real hope of curing it? Or was the treatment theoretically curative but quite ineffective in the particular case?

Detection of a "complete" cure is a rarity. Quite often there remains some vestige to show that the original illness existed, e.g. scars, or a bone in a slightly different position. Satisfaction of the requirement that a cure be sudden and without convalescence is not always obvious. It must be remembered that the concept of suddenness applies to the moment of change at the onset of the recovery process. The process itself may take weeks. Time is required for the recalcification of bones once the cancerous process has been abruptly halted, for instance. And some patients need a bit of time to gather their strength after wasting of muscle or marked loss of weight. A few certainly do get up and walk instantly.

Whatever the problems, whatever the actual number of miraculous cures, Lourdes still remains a charismatic center, a place of healing. Cures do abound. People are restored to health from a great variety of less serious illnesses, often with a psychological overlay. These "charismatic cures" have a limited public appeal, which is confined to those immediately involved. Due to the difficulty of defining and proving the circumstances, they could not fulfill all the criteria to be called miraculous by the Church authorities; but the people are cured, the witnesses are inspired with awe and thanksgiving, and God's ongoing mercy is demonstrated in all their lives.

In the mid-nineteenth century the miraculous cures at Lourdes were interpreted as blessings from God. They defied medical science, which was still in its infancy. It was only natural that people put all their faith and hope in God, and virtually none in medicine. Lourdes became known as the Land of Miracles. These miracles served a triple purpose:

healing of incurable diseases; charismatic healing; and a proof of the existence of God. As rationalism and scientific progress began to dominate ways of thought in Western Europe, man tried to explain everything (and every cure) in non-theological terms. Religion was threatened and the Church took on a defensive role. She suppressed thought and ideas (e.g., the Index, anathemas, etc.) and justified the faith by apologetics.

At the beginning of this century, it became evident that if a miracle had an apologetic value, it must also possess a theological one. The extraordinary nature of a cure was seen to be secondary, revealing an important underlying doctrine. Hence the real significance of a miracle was its sign, displaying the merciful love of God for man. Much later, with two world wars and two Vatican councils in the background, and with the staggering advances in medical science, a new cultural world had arisen, with paradoxical results. Now there was nearly infinite confidence in medicine's healing techniques and its ability to help the disabled to take their place in society. This time it was faith and trust in God that were little considered. Yet even at this stage, people had begun to realize that science alone could not supply all the spiritual and physical needs of the whole person.

In this secular age, the Church could and did adopt a new stance. There was no further need to seek proof of God in marvels and miracles. No longer on the defensive, the Church became open to the world, particularly so after the Second Vatican Council. She replaced anathema with dialogue; she put on a human face; and she sought to be aware of everyday problems of ordinary people. In this new approach to people, especially the sick and disabled, the stress was more on healing the soul than healing the body. The concept of healing the person as a whole was in keeping with the message given to Bernadette: "Pray for sinners . . . Penance, Penance, Penance"—a call to personal conversion.

All this is not to say that care of the sick was to be set aside. But they needed more than prayers and blessings. In this field Lourdes set a precedent, and it was the Faith and Light Movement which set the pace. The first groups belonging to this organization had to function in remote, quiet corners of the Domaine, because the Church frowned upon those priests who wanted to give the sacraments to the mentally handicapped, and it was not acceptable for the deformed and the defective to mix with healthy pilgrims. Eventually, however, the Church authorities began to play their part, and developed a "Health Pastoral," with guidelines to help the sick and the handicapped with both physical and spiritual problems. The civil authorities, too, started to take note of the same message, and today enormous thought and expense are lavished upon the very people who not long ago were treated as outcasts of society.

All this practical care bestowed by the Church on the sick and disabled imparts to the general public a much more expressive picture of present-day Christianity than the occasional miracle could achieve. Nevertheless, miraculous cures, few as they may be, are by no means unimportant. There is still a great deal of work for the Medical Bureau to do in assessing alleged cures. Since 1947, seventy-one extraordinary cures have been passed by the doctors in Lourdes. Besides these, it is generally accepted that the number of cures, whether examined by the Medical Bureau or not, is enormous. Perhaps an analogy might be made here: there are only a few people officially recognized by the Church as saints, but the number of saintly people on earth is enormous.

Perhaps the time has come for the Church to rethink her position on what constitutes a miraculous cure, in the light of modern medicine and Vatican II. Her new objectives, and how to reach them, could well be expressed in a more up-to-date manner. She could portray a miraculous cure in a rather different light, enabling it to be seen more clearly as a sign, and not simply as a wonder. This sign could be a reminder to everyone that the Lord is in the midst of the community today, just as He was during His life on earth. The sign could be seen as conveying a call to everyone to remember that the Lord does respond to need, to prayer, and to repentance.

For many, it may well be difficult to be aware of and to appreciate this merciful love of God, even more difficult to see Christ in one's neighbor. Yet these are most evident in Lourdes; it is still as Ruth Cranston described it in 1955. There brotherly love and charity abound. People flock to Lourdes today in the millions (4,400,000 in 1985), not only for or because of the miraculous cures, but to find the Lord, and through Him to find a sense of real peace and security. This, then, is the Message of Lourdes for the world. Maybe it does seem a far cry from the simple reaction of wonder at the time of the first miracles, in 1858, but it is really only a modern interpretation of the message to Bernadette. The Lady said, "Go tell the priests to build a chapel . . . [and] come here in procession."

PART TWO

Middle Years and Some Famous Cases

12

Five Characteristics of Miraculous Healing

Anyone who studies the records and reports on the cures at Lourdes must be impressed with the extreme prudence and care of the doctors of the Medical Bureau and the Medical Commission in judging alleged cures. Far from being in haste to declare a supernatural cure, they seem to turn up every possible argument against it.

No hysterical or neurotic cases are considered for study, either by the Church or by the Bureau. *No case is studied unless some organic change has occurred,* with medical and laboratory documents to prove it. When this has happened—as for example when a tumor has disappeared or bony structure altered—the alleged cure is examined. If the case appears to be a genuine cure, it "goes into the works" of the intricate and meticulously severe scrutiny and time-process required before a Lourdes cure is officially announced.

The doctors of the Medical Bureau list five special characteristics which mark "miraculous" cures* and which differentiate them from natural cures that the physician ordinarily finds among his patients and that medical science can explain:

1. *Absence of a curative agent* (such as drugs or injections, special treatments, etc.).

---

* I am greatly indebted to Dr. Vallet and Dr. Guinier for permission to incorporate substantial portions of the observations in this account; and to Flammarion & Co., publishers of *La Vérité sur Lourdes* by Dr. Vallet.

2. *Instantaneousness.*

3. *Suppression of convalescence.*

4. *Irregularity of the method of healing.*

5. *Function restored without action of the organ—still incapable of accomplishing it.*

Any one of these five could mark a case as outside the borders of the cures ordinarily known to medical scientists—and therefore to be sharply challenged by them.

In regard to Point 1, and any material aid that might help to bring about a sudden cure: the hospitals at Lourdes (or as they are properly called, "refuges" or hostels) give no medical treatment of any kind. And the majority of the sick are chronic invalids who have exhausted all drugs and therapies, during long years in various hospitals and clinics; who have been given up to die by famous surgeons and doctors powerless to save them; and who have come to ask at the Shrine at Lourdes that which has been proved—not once or twice but over and over again —medically impossible.

Thus no one can say, when a cure takes place, that some wonder drug or injection or cortisone or penicillin has been the cause of the sudden bounding back to life. The water of the Grotto is the only material agent used, and that, as we have seen, has no medicinal properties whatever.

2. *Instantaneousness:* this, for the doctors of the Medical Bureau, is the main characteristic by which they identify a miraculous cure. Obviously, instantaneousness is a severe shock to the medical man. It goes against all the basic laws and procedure impressed upon him throughout his medical training.

Dr. Guinier, who worked for four years at the Medical Bureau making an intensive study of Lourdes cases, describes the bafflement they cause the average physician:

> The laws of biology that we have studied have taught us that all the work of organic recuperation requires, to be perfect, *time* and *slowness;* and here all at once these laws are completely set aside. That which ought to have required a month of attentive care, even granting it might be successful, occurs instantly—perfectly, and perma-

nently—without any apparent intervention of any kind. Microbes are annihilated . . . carcinomas vanish, tubercle bacilli exist no more; gangrenous bones are reformed, severed nerves joined together, wounds cicatrized. Sometimes this happens in a few seconds, sometimes a few hours, but so rapidly that we can say that the factor *time* has disappeared, consequently the cure has operated beyond the laws of biology.*

Imagine the state of mind of a doctor suddenly confronted with such things. Here is a young physician just starting out. He has spent four years—maybe eight or ten—learning the rigorous precepts of the science of medicine, studying what he believes to be unalterable biological principles. He has spent hour after hour and year after year drilling all these things into his mind. Scientific law is his alpha and omega. He has been told that any superhuman power higher than science or man's own mind is a myth.

All of a sudden everything he has been taught is overturned. He sees before his own eyes things which his professors and all the learned books and authorities have taught him could never happen. Yet there they are, happening—becoming facts of human experience.

No wonder Lourdes is hard to take; when, for example, the average medical man is brought face to face with a case like that of Elizabeth Delot, instantly cured of cancer.

Mlle. Delot was a teacher in a girls' school at Boulogne. In her late forties she became seriously ill—so ill that she had to give up her work and go into a hospital. X-rays and clinical tests brought the terrible news that she had cancer of the stomach. Besides, bismuth tests showed that there was a block between the stomach and the beginning of the intestine. This meant death by starvation, unless surgery could effect the passage of food.

When the surgeon who performed the operation, Dr. Houzel of Boulogne, saw the condition, he told Miss Delot's attending physician, Dr. Wallois, that the size of the tumor was such that it could not be

---

* According to biology, the healing of the arteries requires forty or fifty days; that of a nerve entirely severed, three or four months, at least, to heal over and recover its lost function; for a broken bone to knit, thirty to sixty days—according to the thickness of the bone and extent of the fracture. The healings at Lourdes require neither time nor slowness for cicatrization and the production of no matter what tissue—bone, muscle, kidney, lung, or whatever.

removed. All he could do was to make an opening from the stomach into the intestine which would permit the food to pass into the lower digestive tract.

This was done, and at first there seemed to be a slight improvement; but after three months the trouble became worse. The original cancer of the stomach had spread to the liver, and the operated opening itself was invaded by cancerous cells. In July the blockage was complete. Eating became impossible for the patient—even liquids were thrown up. Physicians agreed there was nothing ahead but the misery of constant hunger and thirst until death. Mlle. Delot was lost.

In this desperate state she joined the Lourdes Pilgrimage from Arras, arriving at Lourdes on the morning of July 30. She was so exhausted after the journey that they put her into the water at the piscine with extraordinary precautions. Her first sensation was of pain so intense that she cried with all her strength for death to deliver her. She felt "a terrible burning and stabbing" in the stomach and intestine—as if, she said afterward, "they were holding her under a fiendish hammer."

But when the nurses helped her out of the water, the agony gave way to an unaccustomed sense of well-being. A strange feeling of calm and health took possession of her, also an unexpected vigor. She dressed herself without assistance. At the same time she felt a strong sensation of hunger—unknown to her in a long while. Back at the Hostel, she ate some soup and some vegetable purée, without feeling any discomfort. That night she ate some meat, and felt nothing but a renewal of strength. The next day a repetition of the same diet confirmed the cure. The intestine emptied itself normally.

Examining her at the Medical Bureau, the doctors noted the suppleness of the stomach and the part that had been operated on. They observed that the liver was resuming its usual outline. After her return to Boulogne, her home physician reported that "Mlle. Delot eats just like everyone else—meat, vegetables, everything," and that "she experiences no fatigue, and all her organs are in excellent state." New X-rays taken three weeks after her cure showed a complete reversal of the former condition. Eight months later Dr. Houzel wrote to the Bureau that Mlle. Delot, "operated on by me for a malignant tumor of the stomach, today shows all the signs of perfect health. She now leads a very active life, and has resumed her work at the school on a full-time basis."

The following year she returned to Lourdes and was again examined at the Bureau. After minute investigation, eighteen doctors gave the following unanimous report:

> At the time of her first arrival at Lourdes, Mlle. Delot was suffering from (1) a malignant tumor of the pylorus with extension to the operated mouth of the gastrointestinal passage; (2) a spread of the disease to the liver. There has been a proven cure, proven by the disappearance of the tumor, the reestablishment of general health (increase in weight of 18 pounds), the perfect functioning of the pylorus, liver and intestine, and the proof of time. This sudden healing cannot be attributed to natural processes. It goes beyond the portals of our knowledge.

Since her cure Mlle. Delot has remained in excellent health. "It has never ceased to be excellent," she writes, "from the moment when I came out of the piscine full of life, where a few minutes earlier they had plunged me dying. From that day I have entirely forgotten what it is to suffer with one's stomach. I digest anything."

Here was a cure that certainly could not be laid to errors of diagnosis, or autosuggestion, or any of the classic explanations of the medical skeptics.

Another celebrated case was that of Marie-Louise Arnaud, who was instantly cured of disseminated sclerosis while lying on her stretcher in front of the Grotto. This disease, generally called incurable, is caused by patches of inflammation occurring in different portions of the brain or spinal cord. It often begins with weakness in the limbs; later come muscular incoordination and wavering eyesight. The patches spread, and the disease is usually fatal.

With Mlle. Arnaud the first symptoms appeared with pains in the legs, frequent falls for no apparent reason, violent headaches, and inability to use her hands properly. She could not sew or knit, her writing became almost indecipherable, reading more and more difficult.

Two physicians, Dr. Boudet and Dr. Rimbaud of Montpellier (her home town), examined her and returned the same diagnosis: disseminated sclerosis. She rapidly lost weight, could walk only when held up by someone, had frequent attacks of vertigo, and her vision was much involved. No treatment seemed to help, and death appeared certain.

A devout Catholic, and knowing that from the human point of view her case was hopeless, she decided to join the French National Pilgrimage to Lourdes. Dr. Boudet wrote her certificate. She made the journey on a stretcher, attended by a nurse at every moment. After reaching Lourdes, she was so ill that on the second day she was taken only to the Procession in the afternoon. Being carried there on a stretcher increased her giddiness. She seemed to be very near the end.

August 23 was the anniversary of her brother's death. She begged to be taken to the Grotto that morning, wishing to offer up her Communion for him. When the priest mounted the pulpit, he asked that the sick should try to forget their own sufferings for a few minutes, and to pray for the dead. Mlle. Arnaud was much struck by this coincidence, and began to pray earnestly. After she had received the Communion she wept quietly, thinking of the brother she had loved so much, and, as she records, "quiet oblivious of myself and my illness."

Turning her head on her pillow to hide her tears, "I was astonished (she said) to feel quite distinctly the shape of my right slipper resting on my left foot—for sensation had been so completely dulled by my illness. I opened my eyes. Before me, everything was steady (where before everything seemed to oscillate and wobble about). I could see clearly.

"All this happened in a lightning flash, while the Sacred Host was still on my tongue. With my fingers I could say my Rosary; I sat up without falling over to the right, as usually happened. Sensation had returned to my legs and my limbs now seemed to obey my will. . . .

"At twelve o'clock I was back in the hospital. One of the ladies asked me: 'Well, how are you?' 'Cured, I believe,' I replied. The stretcher was set down and I got up and walked. . . . At two o'clock I was taken to the Medical Bureau. That same night I slept the whole time, calmly and peaceably. I had not had such a night for twenty months." Next evening she started on the return journey to Montpellier. She spent most of the night in the train on her feet, helping with the sick.

At the Medical Bureau the doctors could find nothing wrong with her except an absence of the abdominal reflexes and some exaggerations of those of the knee and ankle. Her eyes were perfectly normal. However, with its usual caution, the Bureau did not declare a cure until it had proved itself with time.

The following year Mlle. Arnaud came again to Lourdes, bringing with her another certificate from Dr. Boudet in which he said: "I have seen Mlle. Arnaud on several occasions since her return from Lourdes.

At the present time there is neither vertigo nor loss of consciousness; no headache or pain in the back; no contraction or tremors; no nystagmus [oscillation of the eyeballs]. Writing is easy and normal; no trouble with the sphincters; Babinski's reflex is normal. The ankle and knee remain brisk—the sole remaining sign of the former illness."

Another letter received from Dr. Boudet several years later stated that in spite of a good deal of trouble in her family, Mlle. Arnaud had been able since her cure eight years ago to lead an active life. There had been no return of any of the previous symptoms. Her handwriting just before and just after her cure makes an interesting footnote to her doctor's observation.

These are only two of the long list of cases described in Lourdes medical records, illustrating the instantaneous character of miraculous cures.

3. *Absence of Convalescence* is another characteristic which goes hand in hand with instantaneousness.

The natural cure of an infectious disease usually proceeds slowly and progressively over a certain period, during which the organism gradually gets rid of the unwanted germs and poisons and the various organs gradually get back to normal. Convalescence lasts sometimes for days, sometimes for weeks or months. It requires special treatment, special care, sometimes a more temperate climate, and various other inducements to coax the body back to normal activity.

But those who are cured at Lourdes do not know that in-between period of gradual strengthening and return to health. The instantaneousness appears to suppress the disease at its source. No matter what the affliction, the degree of acuteness or chronic condition, it is *immediately* that all the organic functions—digestion, breathing, circulation and so on—are restored to normal vigor. The function of digestion and assimilation is first to get back in order—to the astonishment of the invalid, amazed at his sudden imperious hunger.

This hunger is a tremendous need of the whole organism for these individuals who have been reduced to the point of death. There is so much to be regained, so many empty spaces to fill, flaccidity to make firm again, injured tissue to repair. Patients have been known to put on two pounds a day at first, and as much as seventy pounds during the year following their cure. "I am hungry!" is the leit-motif of the miraculous cure, says Dr. Vallet, and one of the first symptoms by which it makes itself known.

This was strikingly evident in the case of little Henri Mieuzet, a boy of seven who came to Lourdes dying of a serious digestive ailment.

Henri was a quiet little boy, highly intelligent, but always delicate. From the time he was a year old, he began to suffer from the illness that nearly killed him: enteritis, or inflammation of the intestines, as diagnosed by three doctors—Chevalier, Basser, and finally by Dr. Vannier, who made out Henri's pilgrimage certificate.

The child's sister had died of the same disease. In his case, occasional attacks soon developed into chronic illness. Living in the country, it was sometimes hard for him to follow the prescribed treatments. In spite of the doctor's efforts, the child's health steadily declined. By the time he was seven, he was in a very critical state.

He had now been in bed for two years, refusing almost all food but milk, and in acute pain most of the time. While his brothers ran and shouted outside, he lay helpless and in agony.

Dr. Basser's notations over this two-year period are weekly repetitions of the symptoms: "Severe abdominal pain, night sweats, blood in the stools—of which six or seven a day, extreme anemia, and loss of weight," all pointing to classic tubercular symptoms as well as the immediate digestive miseries.

"At the present moment," (i.e., when leaving for Lourdes) wrote Dr. Vannier, "this child has almost the look of a dying person. He has become very thin, and eats less and less—lately only liquids. He has not left his bed for long months. He weighs only 28 pounds, whereas eighteen months ago he weighed 42 . . . In his present state, and in view of the apparent uselessness of all the remedies and diets tried up to this time, the child seems beyond therapeutic help."

The doctors considered it folly for him to travel, and said it was unlikely he would come back alive.

Henri's parents nevertheless took him to Lourdes—like so many others, as a last desperate hope. During his time there, his condition, far from improving, seemed to grow worse. The trip itself was very hard on him (300 miles in a third-class carriage), and on the night after their arrival his mother thought he was dying. Wheeling him about on his stretcher to the various ceremonies, plunging him into the icy water at the piscine, might certainly have killed a child in his condition.

On Tuesday, the day set for the return journey, the mother cried her heart out as she looked at the wasted little body and admitted despairingly: "He is no better! It has all been for nothing. I know now that he will die!"

He seemed unconscious after they got him into the train. He lay back on his pillows, white and spent.

One of the nurses on the train later wrote the following account to the Medical Bureau:

> The train departed. After taking a last look at the Virgin as we passed above the Grotto, nurses and patients began to recite the Rosary. They could not finish it without real emotion, for it was during our Rosary at the Grotto that the little Saget girl—a Pott's Disease victim—had been cured.
>
> When the recitation was finished, little Henri, motionless on his mattress up to that moment, suddenly sat up and said, "I want to go see the little girl who was cured. I want to see her right now!"
>
> He stepped down on the floor. His mother, stupefied, began to laugh and cry all together. "I want to see the little girl who was cured," insisted Henri. "Now, right away—at once!"
>
> And here he is, standing up, walking, followed by one of the nurses ready to hold him up if need be. "Very well, come," she said soothingly. And he walked the length of the corridor—this child who had not stirred from his mattress for eighteen months.
>
> When he reached the compartment of the little girl he threw his arms around her, and the two children hugged each other joyfully. By this time everybody in the car was in the corridor, laughing and crying with the mother. And giving thanks to the Blessed Virgin who had wrought this double miracle.
>
> After things had quieted down, Henri went back to his own compartment and, for the first time in several years, *he said that he was hungry.* His mother gave him first a little milk, but that was not sufficient. They gave him then a banana, and a bowl of hot chocolate, which went down very well. Two hours later, for supper, he ate two slices of bread and some pâté—a diet certainly not indicated for intestinal disease! Next morning when he woke up he ate three sweet rolls and a cup of black coffee. And then he

was hungry and ate again before he reached his destination.

Henri Mieuzet was cured instantly, with no period of convalescence afterward, nor any interim condition. From the day of his return home he shared the family meals, which were substantial. His digestive functions were entirely normal. It was, said the doctors, "a complete restoration of the entire digestive tract."

Dr. Vannier saw him immediately after his return and at monthly intervals afterward. His notations on these occasions coincide almost identically with the report of Dr. Vallet who visited the boy seven months after his cure:

"The present state of the child is very satisfactory. Splendid appetite. Easy digestion. Stools regular and normal. He eats like anybody else, has no more pain, spends his days running about and playing with his brothers. Since his cure he has gained eight pounds and has grown almost an inch taller. This child is admirably cured.

"It is a cure," Dr. Vannier adds, "profoundly disconcerting to the physician."

"What especially marks this case," says the Medical Bureau report, "is the suddenness with which the symptoms disappeared, and the rapidity of the recovery. The child passed immediately from a state of most serious illness to a state of health full of promise—which has since been amply realized."

Henri Mieuzet has never ceased to have good health from the moment of his cure. He became a student at the Grand Seminary of Rennes, a vigorous young man, of fine abilities.

Another dramatic example of instantaneous cure with no convalescent period following—after a long and desperate illness—was the case of Ernestine Guilloteau.

This girl, aged twenty-four, arrived at Lourdes with a certificate saying that for three years she had suffered from tuberculous peritonitis. The diagnosis was confirmed by five physicians: Charrier, Valla-Brochart of Thouars (her home), Renon, Collon, and Corbin of Niort —a town nearby. The doctors were unanimous in refusing to operate, saying that the unfortunate girl was simply "a compote of decompositions," that all treatment or medication was useless.

She suffered horribly, took no food at all, and was kept going with parenteral injections. Dr. Valla-Brochart's certificate stated that "for two years she has had only a little milk, tea or coffee—often thrown up for the most part." A living skeleton, she weighed 48 pounds on her arrival at Lourdes. She was unconscious most of the time, and death was declared imminent. The Sisters at the hospital showed her mother the cell where she could put the body. But Ernestine was not to need it.

During the passing of the Blessed Sacrament at the Grotto, the morning after her arrival, this living skeleton suddenly raised itself. She got up from her stretcher, walking unaided, and followed the Procession into the Rosary Church. The crowd looked on, dumfounded. Then a resounding Magnificat broke forth.

Ernestine was taken to the Medical Bureau, where fifteen doctors examined her. They found no trace of lesions; the abdomen had become supple, and there was no pain whatever. She was ravenously hungry, and was able to eat and digest any food. Before her cure she had been unable to move without excruciating pain. Now she walked and moved about with perfect ease. She had been in bed for two years, but the muscles and fat were restored with a rapidity that was abnormal.

She returned to Lourdes a year later on a pilgrimage of thanksgiving, having gained 66 pounds. From the moment of her cure she continued to lead a healthy and happy life.

A professor of the University of Paris with whom I discussed this case told me he was acquainted with Ernestine Guilloteau. He and his family are frequent visitors at a guesthouse that she runs at a summer resort in the Vendée. He says she is in wonderful health—"a very attractive and remarkable woman." The name of the guesthouse is Villa Massabieille.

4. *Irregularity of Method* is another marked characteristic of a miraculous cure. With natural cures, a doctor can gauge the effectiveness of such and such a treatment with two persons suffering from the same malady. At Lourdes, no such determination is possible. No one can foretell who will be the fortunate chosen one of this mysterious healing force. We frequently see two patients suffering from the same disease, and having arrived at precisely the same stage in the course of it. One is healed, the other not. Why, nobody knows.

For one person, the first indication of a cure is strong hunger and a sense of well-being; for another, a tearing pain through the whole body. One gets his cure on the very first day of his visit to Lourdes, another not till his second or third visit, when his illness has apparently grown very much worse.

These, the doctors say, are some of the mysteries peculiar to miraculous cures, and marking them as definitely outside scientific law which operates always uniformly, universally, and forever the same under the same conditions.

5. Point five is perhaps the most amazing of all: where a person with a diseased organ—eye, lung, brain, or heart—finds the function natural to that organ working perfectly, though the organ itself remains unchanged, and biologically incapable of performing that function.

We saw one brilliant example of this in the case of Madame Biré, who was blind for many months—the nerves of her eyes were completely atrophied. Yet after that miraculous moment at the Grotto, Madame Biré saw well enough to read the finest print, months before the optic nerves had regained their normal aspect. (And this last a medical impossibility too, said the doctors, for atrophied nerves do not recover.) She was able to see, they said, when organically she had no right to see. She saw with "dead" eyes.

Almost identical was the case of Gerard Baillie* where, again, the examining doctor said: "The child has a chorioretinitis with double optic atrophy. He should not see." But he *did* see.

The case of Guy Leydet was even more spectacular.† Here, a child in a state of complete idiocy for two and a half years suddenly began to think and move and act, with a brain at least partially destroyed, following acute meningo-encephalitis. He was thinking with a brain that "could not think," just as Gerard Baillie was seeing with eyes that "could not see."

How can such things possibly happen? They can't, says medical science. But at Lourdes they do.

These are not pious inventions of religious devotees, seeking to add luster to their cherished faith. These are actual occurrences, observed by physicians of top standing and set down by them in official medical records over their signatures. They are among the most impressive illustrations of some of the characteristics of supernatural or "miraculous" cures.

---

* See page 227ff. for full account of this case.
† See page 242ff. for full account of this case.

The Author Interviews a Miraculous Cure

I myself saw and talked with one well-known Cure whose case illustrates several of these "miraculous" characteristics.

The cures of men had particularly interested me—I suppose because so many people say, "oh yes, the cures at Lourdes—just neurasthenics and a lot of hysterical women!" They forget that some of the greatest cures have been those of Charles McDonald, John Traynor, Abbé Lochet, Abbé Dessailly, and other male pilgrims.

One of the most famous of the male cures, Fernand Legrand, I interviewed in his own home.

Legrand lives in Gisors, a small town not far from Paris. In my travels to visit the Cures, I soon got into the habit of using the little branch omnibus trains that dawdle along the French countryside, stopping every ten or fifteen minutes at some tiny station, spending half a day to go seventy miles, but finally arriving; as I did that day, at the pleasant little town of Gisors.

It was market day. Steep little streets, plodding beasts and vehicles, crowding good-humored people. . . . I made my way through the teeming market place and across the square. I was bound for the shop of the local cobbler who is known as one of the "grand Cures" of Lourdes; twenty-seven years old at the time of his cure, now fifty.

It is a modest little place halfway up the hill, Legrand and his wife smiling a welcome from the doorway: a very small shop, with a narrow house at the back where the family lives. But every year, Fernand

Legrand saves the necessary 18,000 francs ($50) to go to Lourdes and give his services as stretcher-bearer with his diocesan pilgrimage. He has an extraordinarily fine face: the face of an Emerson, the hands of a shoemaker.

"Bonjour, madame! We were waiting for you. Did you have a good journey? Was it cold in the train? Come inside and get warm, and we will talk of Lourdes and the great things that God has done there!"

We sat by the fire in the cheerful little sitting room, and there, with the dog beating a drowsy tom-tom with his tail on the floor beside us and customers coming in every few minutes to claim a pair of boots or slippers, Fernand Legrand told me his story. Here it is, with a few additions from the Lourdes Medical record.

A healthy childhood—no unusual incidents or illnesses. He lived at that time at Vernon, another little town in the same *département,* not far from Gisors. When a husky young fellow of twenty-six, calamity came upon him. He was injured by a shot in a hunting accident. The lower part of his left leg had to be amputated.

"I recovered well from the operation, and soon got used to the artificial leg. But a year later severe pains began in that leg, then numbness which gradually spread up both legs and to the spine, finally to the right arm until I was completely paralyzed." He had spells of high fever; he lost weight rapidly and was in constant pain.

He was hospitalized at the hospital in Clermont. After two years, he was sent back to the hospital in Vernon, labeled *Incurable.* On March 20, 1933, he came under the care of Dr. Decrette of Vernon, who diagnosed his case as polyneuritis, involving particularly the spinal nerves and the cord itself.

All the classic treatments were put to work to combat the disease, but Legrand only grew worse. The arm and both legs were immobilized —a plaster cast for the right leg, splints for the stump of the left leg and right arm. His legs were greatly swollen and became gangrenous. He ate nothing, became thin as a skeleton (except for the legs), and suffered "the tortures of the damned."

The girl to whom he was engaged urged him to go to Lourdes, and he decided to join the Evreux Pilgrimage. Dr. Decrette, writing the certificate for his admission, answered the pilgrimage questionnaires as follows:

1. What is your prognosis—good, serious, or very serious?
   Answer: *Very serious.*

2. Is the disease incurable?
   Answer: *Incurable.*

3. What end do you anticipate for the present disease?
   Answer: *Progressive development of the paralysis, until death.*

Legrand, held rigid in a horizontal position, could make no movement of any kind. Each effort, each disturbance of the bedclothes even, gave him excruciating pain. It took six men to get him from the automobile into the compartment in the train for Lourdes. The journey was a horror.

He arrived at Lourdes on the morning of the tenth of September and was taken to the Sept Douleurs Hospital. That day and night passed as usual, with morphine injections to calm him. In the meantime, Dr. Decrette had arrived to look after his patient. At the Medical Bureau he described the case to the doctors present, with so much earnestness and concern, that the President of the Bureau appointed Dr. Clement of Hyères to go with Dr. Decrette to the hospital and examine Legrand. The two set out at ten-thirty next morning.

Legrand had already been to the Grotto and the baths with the other sick. As Dr. Clement later recounted, "The patient had just returned from the piscine when we got there. When we reached his bed, Decrette asked me to examine him—'but go gently,' he said. 'He suffers very much when anyone touches him. His legs are so swollen he can't budge.' I took a look at the patient, who was all smiles, and said: 'Well, anyhow, he can smile!' 'Yes, you're right,' said Dr. Decrette, adding to Legrand: 'How is this? I've never seen you with an expression like that on your face. How do you feel?' 'I feel very well,' said Legrand."

Meanwhile, Dr. Clement had taken the right leg out of its cast, and the bandages which enveloped it. "Look here," he said to Dr. Decrette, "you told me he had a swollen leg. This one doesn't seem to be swollen, and it is dry."

"Impossible!" said Decrette. Then, as he looked, he gave a quick exclamation. "But—since when?"

"Since just now," said the patient. "Since during my bath in the piscine. All at once I felt a great warmth through all my body, my legs could bend, and I no longer had any pain."

At these words, Dr. Decrette was so moved he could not speak, and it was several minutes before he got himself in hand. He had seen this man in such a horrible condition, every day, for so long. "Tell us what happened," he managed to say finally.

And Legrand told them . . . this same story he told me now, here in his own home, twenty years later.

"I was carried to the Grotto, and then to the piscine on my stretcher, with the other sick. When they dipped me in the water, I felt as though all my arms and legs were being broken to pieces. But then—that strange and heavenly warmth, all through my body. The pain for a moment was agonizing; then I sat up and began helping the brancardiers to dress me. I could move my arms, and bend my legs. Can you imagine that—I could *move!*"

They took him back to the hospital. He was very hungry. They gave him several pieces of bread and a big bowl of *café au lait.* He ate it all and demanded more—*three times,* though he hadn't eaten more than "the size of a nut" in two years!

"When my doctor saw me like that, he began to weep. It was too much for him. They had brought me there in a dying condition. The only thing left for the doctors was to help me die with the least possible suffering. And now they saw me like this!"

The two doctors examined him. They verified that all the swelling of the lower limbs and of the arm had disappeared; that movement was possible, though still limited, that pain no longer existed. The patient could sit up in bed, and—always the special sign of a miraculous cure—he demanded something to eat and ate heartily.

Next day he was examined at the Medical Bureau. Fourteen doctors were present, among them two from the Royal Academy of Medicine of Italy and several from the Paris hospitals. The patient undressed himself like any normal person, and replied good-humoredly to questions during the two hours of interrogation, at the end of which the doctors set down the following conclusions:

1. Fernand Legrand has indeed been afflicted for twenty-six months with polyneuritis (ascending) and myelitis, characterized by symptoms of fever, pain, edema, arthropathy.

2. The above morbid symptoms totally disappeared on September 11, 1934, at ten o'clock in the morning at the moment of his immersion in the piscine of Lourdes.

3. The patient still has muscular atrophies, and some stiffness of the joints and tendons in which we see rapid improvement from hour to

hour. These symptoms are consecutive to the illness, but not constituent of the illness. They should disappear in a relatively short time.

The cure was steadily maintained during the next twelve months. Legrand worked during that time as a practical nurse in the hospital of Vernon, without a single day off on account of indisposition. He returned to Lourdes the following year and came to the Bureau for his second examination. This time eleven doctors confirmed his cure. They found that all stiffness had disappeared, that reflexes of both arms and legs were normal, and the patient had gained eighteen pounds.

"In conclusion (they stated): there has been a definite cure of the illness. No specific medical treatment had been given for more than six months—except certain drugs to keep the heart going, and numerous injections of morphine. In view of the instantaneousness of the cure, it cannot be attributed to natural causes."

The next year when Legrand went back, he went as a stretcher-bearer in the service of other sick people.

"Doesn't your artificial leg make it difficult for you?" I asked him.

He laughed. "Difficult? Madame, you should see me! Since my cure I can run like a rabbit—wooden leg and all. None of them with real legs can get ahead of me!"

He went to Lourdes on his honeymoon trip and has served there every year since his cure, except during the war.

A stretcher-bearer I frequently saw at Lourdes told me that he was one of those who had helped carry Fernand Legrand off the train on his arrival that day, twenty years ago, as a *grand malade*.

"The most terrible case I ever had to carry. That, madame, was truly a miracle!"

Two other stalwart Cures frequently seen at Lourdes are Robert Guyot and Lucien Belhache. Guyot, a worker in the mines of Dourges, suffered for months from an abscessed left kidney. Under the care of three physicians—Drs. Leroy, Dereux, and Sennelart—he was operated on, but instead of improving grew steadily worse.

Severe pain developed in the left leg and he could no longer bend it or stand upon it. The wound failed to heal, his state of weakness increased alarmingly. Transfusion after transfusion was given him, and he received the Last Rites. His condition was so serious, his wife brought linens to the Hospital for the Sisters to use in preparing him for the grave.

He rallied from this crisis, however, and was carried to Lourdes, convinced that no medical aid could save him. He was cured after his third bath in the piscine. That night his wound was completely healed, he could stand erect and walk without difficulty. At the Medical Bureau he was found normal in every way, and has not missed a day's work since his cure.

The cure of Lucien Belhache is interesting because it occurred in a family of complete unbelievers. Lucien's father and mother had been married "outside religion," and none of the five children had ever been inside a church or even baptized. They lived as carefree pagans, in their home city of Toulouse.

Then, when he was twenty-two, Lucien became ill. While working at his aviation plant he suffered a violent fall which sent him rolling along the ground several yards. During the weeks that followed he had severe pain in his spine, and soon a stiffness that prevented his standing erect.

Dr. Verdier, the family physician, diagnosed his troubles as Pott's Disease, or tuberculosis of the spine, brought on through the crushing of the fifth lumbar vertabra. The diagnosis was confirmed by X-rays and the detailed report of a second physician, Dr. Constantin. The doctors wished to put the young man immediately into a spinal jacket. But Lucien's father had read somewhere that at a place called Lourdes several cases of this disease had been cured. He insisted that this "special treatment" should first be tried.

In order to join the pilgrimage, Lucien received religious instruction, and was baptized before the pilgrimage left Toulouse. He was not in a cast when he left home, but so weak and bent over that others had to support him in walking.

After his first bath he felt considerable improvement, but his real cure came at the Procession, when the Blessed Sacrament was raised before him in blessing. At that moment he had "an indefinable sense of well-being"—he knew he was cured. No more stiffness or pain of any kind. He could stand erect and walk freely!

He was examined at the Medical Bureau the following day. The report states: "There remains no stiffness whatever and the suppleness of the spinal column is complete. All movements free and easy; the walk normal. The illness,—attested by doctors' certificates and X-rays—certainly existed. In the present state of science, the cure, in several hours, of caries with disintegration of a vertebral body, has no natural explanation. It awaits confirmation after the required year's testing."

The following year Lucien returned to Lourdes, himself to serve the sick and carry them back and forth between the baths and the Grotto. He was again examined and the doctors present verified that the young Pott's Disease victim of a year ago now enjoyed perfect health. He was working in his father's business of piano repairing, with long motorbike trips around the country; and as a Scout of the Toulouse troop he went on hikes of ten miles with a pack on his back. His cure was definitely confirmed.

In consequence of this cure, the entire Belhache family were baptized and became devoted practicing Christians. Both Lucien and his wife come very year to Lourdes to help with the care of the Toulouse sick, he as brancardier, she as nurse. He now has an important post in the radio department of Air-France. Lucien, now a husky man of fifty-two, was among those who had the honor to "carry the canopy" during the great Rosary Pilgrimage of 1953: the same Pilgrimage where he was healed, thirty years before.

Skeptics are sometimes to be found among the clergy as well as the laity. An interesting example was the Abbé Fiamma of Paris, who suffered from a severe case of varicose veins with ulcerations, and who had little faith in Lourdes cures.

He told his doctor: "My Archbishop wants me to go to Lourdes, but I go without any confidence that I shall be cured."

He arrived on the last day of the pilgrimage and did not bother going to the baths. Then a brancardier friend told him bluntly that he was a fool not to do at least as the others did. Even then the Abbé did not take a complete bath, but immersed his legs only. He felt intense pain—"like thrusting a red-hot iron under the skin."

He was cured—suddenly and permanently.

So was the Abbé Dessailly, afflicted with tuberculosis of the larynx and of both lungs, according to Dr. Pradal of Pau, who stated in his certificate to the Medical Bureau:

"The patient was suffering from tuberculous laryngitis and complete loss of voice. Swallowing was very difficult. He lost 11 pounds in one month. Fever was constantly present, with temperature varying from 100 to 103 degrees. His general condition seemed to indicate a speedy fatal issue."

The diagnosis was corroborated by both X-rays and clinical examination. The sputum contained tubercle bacilli. The X-rays showed that the upper two-thirds of both lungs were affected.

He was kept in bed, as much as possible in the open air, and urged to eat more; but he seemed to be slipping steadily downhill.

Finally he decided to go to Lourdes. Directly after his first bath he showed marked improvement. He recovered his voice; he could dress himself; and was seized with a great desire for food. He gained 40 pounds in the next two months, 68 pounds within six months, and was hale and hearty when he came to Lourdes the following year.

Since his cure he has never coughed, has had no medical treatment whatever. He returned to work at his Seminary and has been able to perform all his duties with perfect freedom.

14

The Cure of a British Soldier
Gunshot Wounds—Paralysis—Epilepsy

Perhaps the most celebrated of all men-cures is John Traynor.

Traynor was a soldier of World War I, seriously wounded in a bayonet charge at Gallipoli. One bullet entered the inner side of his right arm, traveled up to the level of the collarbone, severing the large nerves of the axilla which supply the skin of the arm with sensation and actuate the muscles. The result of this injury was loss of sensation, paralysis, and muscular atrophy. Doctors urged him to have the right arm amputated, "as it would always be useless." He refused.

Several physicians operated on him—Sir Frederick Treves and Major Ross while he was still overseas, Dr. McMurray and Major Montserrat in hospitals in England after his return home—in a series of attempts to suture the severed nerves. All were unsuccessful.

Traynor was discharged from military service and awarded a pension of 100 per cent, the Ministry of Pensions recording that "the right arm is useless and will probably remain so."

He was sent from hospital to hospital—five in all—in well-meaning but futile efforts to relieve his condition. During his last hospitalization his skull was trephined in the hope of helping his epileptic attacks which now averaged three a day. Besides the atrophied arm, both legs were partially paralyzed, there was loss of control of the bladder and rectum. On the skull at the site of the last operation was an opening which revealed the pulsations of the brain; whenever he coughed there was a protrusion of the membrane. In this condition Traynor was discharged from Springfields Hospital and returned to his own home in Liverpool. Here is his account of his condition at this time:

> When I was a little better I was discharged in an ambulance and carried to my own bed . . . I could not walk or stand, and was in a very bad way. I had not moved my right arm for eight years. I was on special home treatment under Dr. Turner, medical referee of the Ministry of Pensions, and Dr. McConnell and Dr. Aiken. My wife received "attendance allowance" for helping and looking after me. I was on a special milk diet ordered by Dr. Turner. After several months in bed the British Red Cross lent me a chair so that I could get out in the fresh air; my wife or my daughter always carried me from my bed to the chair, or from the chair to my bed. I was supplied with an air cushion on account of bed sores at the bottom of my spine. The Ministry of Pensions supplied me with a light special propelling chair.

After some time he was told that on July 24, 1923, he could be admitted to the Hospital for Incurables at Mossley Hill. But Traynor, a devoted Catholic, decided instead that he would go to Lourdes to ask for his cure. Again, in his own words:

> In the month of July, 1923, I was at home, helpless as usual, when a neighbor woman came to the house and spoke of an announcement that had been made in our parish. A Liverpool diocesan pilgrimage was being organized for Lourdes. It would cost thirteen pounds to go. A down payment of one pound would engage a place.
>
> My wife was out in the yard and I called her in. I told her to go upstairs and get a certain box in which we kept a gold sovereign which my brother had given me and which we were treasuring for some special emergency. I told her I was going to give it to Mrs. Cunningham, our neighbor, as a first payment on a ticket to Lourdes. My wife was very disturbed but finally did as I told her and the neighbor went off and made the booking.
>
> Soon one of the priests in charge of the pilgrimage came to see me. "You cannot make the trip," he said.

"You will die on the way—please give it up." I said I had made my first payment and that I was going to Lourdes.

Then came the matter of a medical certificate. We called in several doctors—every one of them said that such a journey would be suicide. The priest came again and begged me to give up the idea. I would not—and finally succeeded in going without a medical certificate. To raise the twelve pounds, the balance due on my ticket, we sold some of our belongings, and my wife even pawned some of her bits of jewelry.

The day of departure came. At the station, in the press of people and confusion of getting all the sick aboard, Traynor missed the first train—the one he was supposed to board. Again the priest tried to persuade him to give it up and go home. Traynor was stubborn. There was another train.

"I said they could put me in the coal tender or anywhere they liked —*but I was going to Lourdes!* By being stubborn about it I won my point."

The journey was a nightmare. Three times they tried to take him off the train, as he seemed to be dying. Each time there was no hospital at the town where they stopped, and the only thing was to keep on.

The Pilgrimage reached Lourdes on July 22—Traynor by then in a terrible condition. He was taken to the Asile Hospital and kept under sedatives. On July 24 he was examined by three physicians—Dr. Azurdia of London, Dr. James Marley of Wallasey, and Dr. Dennis Finn of Liverpool, who issued the following certificate:

This is to certify that on July 24, 1923, we examined Mr. John Traynor, of 121 Grafton Street, Liverpool, and found his condition to be as follows:

1. Epileptic. We ourselves saw several attacks during his journey to Lourdes.

2. The radial, median, and ulnar nerves of the right arm are paralyzed, the hand is *en griffe* (clawlike), there is wrist drop and muscular atrophy.

3. The shoulder and pectoral muscles are atrophied.

4. The trephine opening in the right parietal region is about 2 cm. 5. (That is, slightly under an inch in diameter.) The pulsations of the brain are visible. A metal plate covers the trephine orifice.

5. There is absence of voluntary movements of the legs, with loss of sensibility.

6. Incontinence of urine and feces.

The Pilgrimage was to remain six days at Lourdes. During that time Traynor was desperately ill. He had several hemorrhages as well as epileptic fits. Nevertheless he succeeded in being immersed in the baths nine times. On the morning of the second day, as he was being wheeled to the baths, he was seized with a severe epileptic fit. . . .

"I felt something burst in my chest, and blood flowed freely from my mouth. The doctors in attendance were much alarmed and when I came round—very quickly—they refused to let me go to the baths, saying I would surely collapse. I insisted on being taken, putting the brake on my wheel chair with my usable (left) hand, and refusing to change my mind. The doctors at last gave in, and I was wheeled to the baths and immersed in the water. When taken out of the water my condition was much the same as before, except that some change unknown to me had taken place which marked the end of my epileptic fits. I never had another."

Nothing remarkable occurred between this and his ninth and last immersion. The pain, paralysis, and sleeplessness continued. Once more Traynor tells the story:

We were to leave on the morning of July 27. The afternoon of July 25 came. I seemed to be as bad as ever. A young Frenchman, Felix Douly, came into the ward selling rosaries and medals, and I spent the last few shillings I had on little religious souvenirs for my wife and children. Then it was time to get ready for the baths.

There were many to be bathed and we all wanted to be finished before the afternoon Procession . . . which began at four o'clock. My turn came. When I was in the bath, my paralyzed legs became violently agitated, so much so that I almost emptied the bath. The brancardiers and attendants were terribly alarmed, thinking no doubt that I was in a fit, though I knew it was not so. . . .

I struggled to get to my feet, feeling that I could easily do so, and wondered why everything and everybody seemed to be working against me. [People were holding him down.] When I was taken out of the bath I cried from sheer weakness and exhaustion.

The brancardiers threw my clothes on hurriedly, put me back on the stretcher, and rushed me to the square in front of the Rosary Church to await the Procession. Practically all the other sick were already lined up. I was the third last on the outside, to the right as you face the church.

The Procession came winding its way back, as usual, to the church, and at the end walked the Archbishop of Rheims, carrying the Blessed Sacrament. He blessed the two ahead of me, came to me, made the sign of the cross with the monstrance and moved on to the next. He had just passed by when I realized that a great change had taken place in me. My right arm, which had been dead since 1915, was violently agitated. I burst its bandages and freed the arm.

I had no sudden pain that I can recall and certainly had no vision. I simply realized that something momentous had happened.

I attempted to rise from my stretcher, but the brancardiers were watching me. I suppose I had a bad name for my obstinacy. They held me down and . . . immediately after the final Benediction rushed me back to the Asile. I told them I could walk, and proved it by taking seven steps. I was very tired and in pain. They put me back in bed and gave me a morphia injection.

Drs. Azurdia, Marley and Finn certify that they examined Traynor after his return to the Asile after the Procession. This was to see if he could really walk, as he claimed.

"We find," they certified, "that he has recovered the voluntary use of his legs; the reflexes exist. There is intense venous congestion of both feet, which are very painful. The patient can walk with difficulty."

Traynor was put in a small ward on the ground floor, with brancardiers to watch him and keep him from doing anything foolish. The effect of the morphine began to wear off during the night, but he still had no full realization that he was cured. He was awake most of the night. No lights were on.

"At five-thirty," says Traynor, "I heard the bell of the Basilica begin to ring out the *Ave* . . . I jumped out of bed and knelt on the floor to finish the Rosary I had been saying before I fell into a short sleep. Then, I dashed for the door, pushed aside the two bardcardiers, and ran barefoot out of the Asile. I may say here that I had not walked since 1915 and my weight was down to 8 stone [about 112 pounds].

"Dr. Marley was outside the door. When he saw me run out of the ward he fell back in amazement. Out in the open now, I ran towards the Grotto, which is about two or three hundred yards from the Asile. The brancardiers ran after me but they could not catch up with me. When they reached the Grotto, there I was on my knees, still in my night clothes, praying to Our Lady and thanking her.

"After I had prayed for about twenty minutes, I got up—surprised and not pleased to find a crowd of people gathered round, watching me. They drew aside to let me pass as I walked back toward the Asile. By now the hotels of Lourdes were emptying and an excited crowd had gathered in front of the Asile. I could not understand what they were doing there as I went in to dress. I put my clothes on in a hurry, but kept away from the bed for fear those doctors and brancardiers would tackle me again and treat me as a sick man.

"I went to the washroom to wash and shave. Other men were there before me. I bade them all good morning but none of them answered me—they just looked at me in a scared way. I wondered why.

"It was still pretty early in the morning when a priest, Father Gray, who knew nothing about my cure, entered the ward where I was and asked if anybody there could serve Mass. I answered that I would be glad to, and went off and served his Mass in the chapel of the Asile. It did not seem strange to me that I could do this, after being unable to stand or walk for eight years.

"I went in to breakfast in the dining room of the Asile. The other men drew back, as if they were afraid of me. I could not grasp the situation nor could I understand why people were staring at me so hard." Every time he tried to leave the hospital that day the crowds made a rush for him. He tried taking a carriage, but was obliged to abandon it and retreat back into the Asile. Excitement ran high in Lourdes that day. The priest who had urged Traynor not to come to Lourdes broke down and cried—openly and unashamed.

The Pilgrimage left for home on the nine o'clock train next morning, July 27. Early that day the three doctors again examined Traynor. Their statement recorded that he could walk perfectly; that he had recovered the use and function of his right arm; that he had regained sensation in his legs; and finally, that the opening in his skull had diminished considerably.

As far as Traynor knew, the metal plate in his skull just disappeared. When he took off the last of his bandages on returning from the Grotto on the morning of July 26, he found every one of his sores healed.

He left Lourdes amid scenes of tremendous enthusiasm. The train went up through France with Traynor "still in a daze," but traveling in his seat like any normal person. News of his cure had of course been telegraphed back home. At the station in Liverpool there was a stampede. The police were compelled to draw their batons in order to force a passage for Traynor and his wife to a taxi. Finally, "We drove home," he said, "and I cannot describe the joy of my wife and children."

He was not presented that year to the doctors of the Medical Bureau. The following year, he came to the Bureau bearing a certificate from Dr. McConnell of Liverpool who had been his physician for sixteen months, the time that had elapsed since he left Springfields Hospital. The certificate, dated June 24, 1924, states:

"John Traynor, aged forty-one, living at 121 Grafton Street, suffering from gunshot wounds in the head and chest, and from epilepsy, has been under my care since his discharge from the hospital. There have been no epileptic crises since July, 1923. Signed, Dr. McConnell."

On July 7, 1926, Traynor was examined at the Bureau by the President, Dr. Vallet, by the three physicians who were present when he was cured—Drs. Finn, Azurdia, and Marley—and several others, including Dr. Harrington of Preston and Dr. Moorkens of Antwerp. After the examination the doctors signed the following statement:

> The right hand is slightly *en griffe* and shows a little wasting of the interossei muscles. The right forearm is less than the left by 1 1/2 cm. in circumference (about one-third of an inch). No atrophy of the pectoral or shoulder muscles now exists. All the movements of the wrist are perfect. The trephine opening has been obliterated; with the finger a slight depression only is found in the bone. There have been no epileptic crises since the cure, in 1923.

The official report issued by the Medical Bureau at Lourdes on October 2, 1926, declared that "this extraordinary cure is beyond and above natural causes."

The most striking part of the cure was probably the instantaneous healing of the right arm. The nerves of that arm had been severed for eight years. Four surgical operations had revealed that they were truly severed, and had failed to reunite them. More than a mere suture would be necessary before the arm could feel and move again; the shrunken nerves would need to go through a long process of regeneration. A feat that expert surgery had four times failed to accomplish, and a process that required months of gradual restoration, were achieved instantaneously during that fateful moment when the Blessed Sacrament was raised over John Traynor at Lourdes.

Traynor arrived in Lourdes a veritable wreck—as Dr. Vallet said, "a pathological museum"; paralyzed in the right arm and in both legs. He went back from Lourdes pushing his own wheel chair, arms and legs normal and with a complete cessation of the epileptic fits and other painful troubles with which he had been afflicted.

"I am in the coal and haulage business now," he states in his conclusion: "I have four lorries [trucks], and about a dozen men working for me. I work with them. I lift sacks of coal weighing around 200 pounds with the best of them and I can do any other work that an able-bodied man can do. I go to Lourdes every year and serve as brancardier there."

15

The Uncured: What of Them?

"But what," people ask, "is the actual percentage of cures? Isn't it terribly small—infinitesimal almost—compared with the vast number of sick who come seeking health? What are the vital statistics?"

To answer that question intelligently, we must first take account of the fact that there are several different kinds of Lourdes cures.

1. There is the official Miraculous Cure which is recognized by the Church and a Canonical Commission as well as by the Medical Bureau and the International Medical Commission.

2. There is the cure which is recognized by the Medical Bureau and the Medical Commission as being "inexplicable under scientific and natural laws" but which is not recognized by the Church as a miracle.

3. There are cures—some 1,200 of them—recognized by the Medical Bureau (after repeated examinations at the Bureau) but which have never gone before a Medical or Canonical Commission for lack of sufficient documentation: certificates, clinical reports, X-ray analyses, and so forth.

4. There are large numbers of cures which have for one reason or another received no official recognition but whose beneficiaries are enjoying the bliss of being whole and well after years of agony. These people care not at all whether their cures are recognized as

miracles; they come to Lourdes and give thanks every year, just the same.

Every Pilgrimage has in its local records its own substantial number of verified cures never publicly proclaimed. And scores of people who are cured make no official report of their cure to the Bureau, simply because they dislike publicity.

As indicated under class 3, a large number of actual cures go without official recognition because of insufficient data. Sometimes the evidence from relatives or home physicians is too indefinite and unsatisfactory to declare a cure; sometimes doctors have not kept sufficiently precise records. Other doctors refuse pointblank to furnish X-rays, diagnoses, or biological reports showing the condition of the patient before the journey to Lourdes and the change which occurred there. "If it's Lourdes, we're not interested," they say.

Under these circumstances it is extremely difficult to obtain accurate data and statistics regarding cures. The President of the Medical Bureau told me, in August, 1953: "We have at the Bureau some 1,200 records and files of 'inexplicable' cures for which we have systematic and orderly accounts—many of them with accompanying X-ray and clinical reports, and all with doctors' diagnoses and certificates. We have notations and material concerning some 4,000 cases that are very probably complete and genuine cures. We have insufficient data to record them as cures but the individuals and their families are unquestionably enjoying the blessings and benefits of a genuine cure."

It is probably safe to say that during the hundred years of the Lourdes shrine, at least ten thousand people have been cured there. This may seem a small proportion, in view of the millions who come; but ten such cures—or even one, as Dr. Smiley Blanton said—would have been dumfounding.

The proportion of women in relation to men is easier to gauge, and runs about three to one. But as three times more women than men come to Lourdes, the proportion of cures runs about parallel. One of the interesting facts is the relatively large number of children who are cured; some at Lourdes itself, others at home or in some local sanctuary where a Novena has been held or the name of Notre Dame de Lourdes invoked.

One of the baffling things about Lourdes cures is their extreme variability and unpredictability. Some people are cured at the baths, others at the Procession; some with intense pain, others with no pain at all—only a sense of sudden ineffable well-being.

Some cures happen at once—in the first bath; some not till the eighth or ninth; some when the patient, having given up hope, is about to leave; others after the patient has returned home and renounced the whole experience. Cures have occurred when the patient did not even come to Lourdes but was lotioned at home with Lourdes water. Sometimes a person is not cured at his first pilgrimage but achieves his cure suddenly at the second—or even the third. Persistence often seems to be an important factor.

Strangely enough, religious faith or deservingness on the part of the patient seems to have little to do with it. Tiny children, who believe and know nothing, may be cured, while saintlike persons are left to endure their agonies to the end.

Devotion to the Catholic faith or to the Blessed Virgin apparently is not an essential factor. Some of the most extraordinary cures have happened to people of no religious faith whatever—such as Gargam, Auclair, and Madeleine Guinot. Mlle. Guinot, an advanced tubercular case, was an unbeliever both by education and personal conviction, who came to Lourdes with a sort of bored acquiescence (and her tongue in her cheek), to satisfy her friends. After her cure she became an earnest, practicing Christian.

And there is also the case of Germaine Birsten, a Protestant, in the last stages of Pott's Disease, who was cured at the Procession. A New England Congregational minister's wife, another tuberculosis victim, had the same good fortune; and numbers of others.

Catholics believe that Our Lady of Lourdes performs some of these cures to bring nonbelievers into the Faith. "She knows She *has* me!" said a young priest who, notwithstanding several pilgrimages, had not received his cure.

The Cures are almost invariably simple people—the poor and the humble; people who do not interpose a strong intellect between themselves and the Higher Power. "The Blessed Virgin does not interest herself much in the rich," they say at Lourdes.

But why this apparent favoritism on the part of a compassionate Mother or Divine Creator? Why is George chosen and not Marcel? Why sinful coal heaver but not saintly nun who returns unrelieved of her hellish pain? This is the inscrutable mystery.

A determining factor, in certain cases, may be some inner psychological or moral conflict. Modern psychiatry points to mental and emotional blocks in some people which retard their cure even under ordinary psychotherapy. Some, for example, have firmly accepted the belief that they are incurable; others that their sufferings have come as a just punishment for sin. Conscious moral guilt, too, can stand in the way of a perfect healing.

Modern clergymen and psychiatrists stress the significance of a guilt fixation and urge the patient to get rid of it by frank and full confessions and changed habits. How powerfully it works may be seen in case after case among the health seekers and sufferers who come to Lourdes. "I'm too wicked . . . I don't deserve it . . . I've sinned too much and too long . . . no, it can never be for *me!*"

Conversely, the attitude of expectancy and childlike readiness to accept and to believe appears to open the way, following the injunction laid down long ago: *"Except ye become as little children . . ."* Those who do often enter into the kingdom of health and healing too.

"But it doesn't always happen!" No, and cures by drugs and physical means do not always happen either. We are dealing with that incredibly intricate and mysterious thing, the human organism with its long and complicated evolution—physical, mental, emotional, spiritual; its strains and reactions; interwoven attractions and repulsions, aversions and rejections; of eons to be probed before we can reach even a rudimentary understanding of this great mystery. Meanwhile we can give thanks for the wonderful things that come to pass occasionally now in the midst of our ignorance.

Even when no physical cure takes place, it has been noted time and again that the most important thing that happens at Lourdes is the cure of souls. Those who have to go back, and live on with their physical miseries, seem to get such a spiritual transformation and inspiration that they can go on cheerfully and gratefully.

People come to Lourdes weary and worn out with pain, hardly able to make the journey because of the suffering it involves, bitterly resenting their sickness and wondering why God has thus afflicted them—a burden to themselves and to those who bring them here. And then they arrive at Lourdes Station and are so warmly welcomed, so gently transported and looked after. They arrive at the Hostel and are surrounded with all that lavish care, and love, and devotion—the humblest of them, the despairing and the lost. They arrive at the Shrine, and there at the Grotto in company with hundreds of other sick—many worse off than they—the transforming touch begins to work. They stop thinking about themselves. They begin to think about their neighbor—

the one in the next bed or in the next little carriage. They begin to pray for him, earnestly, repeatedly, when the "big" prayers of the day are said. They begin to long, above everything else, for his cure.

In sum, *they forget themselves.* They become absorbed in love of God and love for fellow man: the two great solvents for all human ills, as Jesus taught. And so their real healing takes place—imperceptibly almost, but none the less actually and dynamically.

Time after time I have been told at Lourdes—by Dr. Leuret, by nurses, brancardiers, even the man who sweeps the paths: "The sick? Oh, madame, they've forgotten about their own cure. They've forgotten why they came here. All they care about is that that man in the next row shall get well . . . 'Don't bother about me—that fellow over there needs you more . . .' 'Never mind, nurse, I can wait.' 'Look after this poor lady in the next carriage—she really needs attention.' "

Naturally the pain comes back again, but not so terribly. It hasn't the same bitter hold on them. Their minds are not centered on it any longer. The mind is elsewhere—absorbed in something new. They have all these other people to think about—the friends they've made, the nurses, the Sisters, and all those who have served them and cared for them so devotedly; the sufferers everywhere in the world who need their prayers.

And when the time comes to go home, though they haven't been physically cured, though it means another long difficult journey with all sorts of sacrifices and miseries, their one cry is: "If only I can come back next year! If only I can come again to Lourdes!"

It would be absurd to suggest that there are *no* disillusioned or disappointed ones. Unquestionably certain people do leave bitterly disappointed and resentful, still longing passionately for the cure they did not obtain. But—and I believe all Lourdes workers will bear me out—these are a handful compared with the vast majority who go away happy and (despite failure to obtain a physical cure) profoundly grateful for the spiritual and psychological lift which is their lasting reward.

"Of the uncured none despair," says an old pilgrim. "All go away filled with hope and a new feeling of strength. The trip to Lourdes is never made in vain."

This was borne out by a man who worked at the desk of the Hospitality. His own crutches stood against the wall behind him. His strong, tanned face was that of a healthy and happy person. Seeing him there interviewing the sick day after day, an American visitor asked him,

"What about this great question of the uncured? Doesn't it spell unmitigated tragedy?"

"No," he answered, "I don't think so. In fact I *know* it doesn't. I often interview patients before they leave. I have never seen a case downcast—not even the worst. The words you usually hear are, 'God's will be done.'"

He gave several examples. As they talked the visitor again noticed the crutches leaning against the wall. What was this man's own story? What was he doing here, serving without pay during the hottest part of the summer—cooped up in this tiny office, besieged by an unending line of people? He ventured to ask the man about himself. Later he got the whole history.*

His name was Lemarchand. He was a native of Brest. He had been crippled from birth, and longed to go to Lourdes where he hoped he might be cured. But he and his sister were alone in the world; they could not afford to make the trip. Finally, a special opportunity came and they were able to join the pilgrimage.

"On our arrival we went directly to the Grotto. My first impression was very deep, and made up both of hope and sadness—sadness at the sight of the sufferers we passed, hope for my cure. . . . Two days later it was time to leave. The farewell was heart-rending. Not that I was disappointed, but it seemed as if I was leaving my home and best friends."

How often one hears that. People have an extraordinary feeling about this place. Always they speak of it as "home," and of their sadness at leaving, even at the end of a few days.

"I could not have believed that I could become so attached to a place in three summer days," said an English visitor. "There was everything hostile to my peace—crowds, heat, dust, weariness; yet I felt such a home for the soul as I had never before experienced."

Lemarchand felt it too, along with so many others. He promised to come back the following year—and did, for eight days.

"I still prayed for my cure," he said, "but on the second day, while I was sitting among the sick during Benediction, I began to feel ashamed of myself. On my right, a blind man sat rigid in his chair; on my left lay a consumptive. I looked around at all the sufferers and then up to the green mountains and higher to the sky. I could see; and I

---

* This story was first published in an article by J. B. McAllister in *Commonweal* magazine. Reprinted by kind permission of the editors.

could move about; I had the free use of my ears and tongue and arms. I had not known sickness or disease—and I was praying for my cure! I started praying for the blind man and the consumptive. Since that moment I have felt that I should think of others and not of myself."

The following year he and his sister came to Lourdes again. The year after that, his sister, a nurse, worked in the baths. He felt useless. Then he decided to offer himself for clerical work. His knowledge of English proved valuable, and his services were readily accepted.

"I felt like a new man. I, even I, was doing something to help the sick!" He returned each summer and worked during his vacation.

"Perhaps it sounds foolish," said Lemarchand, "to speak of the happiness I have found at Lourdes, I who went there to be cured and am still a cripple. But I have found contentment, and my soul has been cured. And, for more persons than anyone knows, Lourdes has done the same thing."

A famous American pilgrim was Fred Snite—"the man in the iron lung." Snite had contracted infantile paralysis in 1935 and was obliged to lie flat in his respirator or "iron lung" from that time on. He was unable to breathe if out of it for more than a few minutes at a time.

Naturally his going to Lourdes created tremendous interest. Newspapermen and photographers followed him, every step of the trip.

What a moment this would have been for a miracle! But that is not the way things happen at Lourdes. Cures are usually given to the obscure, quietly—in secrecy, almost. "The Blessed Virgin is not seeking the newsreels!" say the Lourdais. "She operates without fanfare or publicity."

This millionaire patient came with a humble heart and a submissive spirit. One would have thought maybe She might have made an exception . . . He was not asking for a miracle—only that the best might be done.

Snite's doctors begged him not to bathe in the piscines. To leave the iron lung and go into the cold water was suicide, they said. But Snite insisted. In his diary that day, he wrote:

> Early this afternoon I had another new experience—a bath in the famous Lourdes waters. . . . In that I had to leave the respirator during the bath, I was quite nervous and excited. Everything went smoothly however, and I was so glad I had decided to do it. The water was very cold, but I did not mind it. There was some kind of happi-

ness in connection with it which I am unable to analyze.
. . . All I can say is that I was glad for the opportunity.

He told friends that, as he bathed, a wonderful feeling of peace came over him, a feeling he had never before experienced. Later he had a second bath, and again everything went smoothly. The water hardly seemed cold.

After attending the procession of the Blessed Sacrament he wrote: "Seeing some of the other sick people makes me feel very fortunate."

Snite wrote in his diary: "And so tomorrow is Saturday, the ninth of our stay and Sunday the last day. I have not in any way given up or lost hope. I am praying very, very fervently, and if nothing happens, as I have said before, God certainly knows what is best for Him, for me, and for the world in general."

The entry for June 4 closes with two short sentences: "Our pilgrimage is at an end. God's will be done."

Snite returned to America, still in his iron lung. Everyone thought he would be terribly depressed and disappointed. Had the journey then been entirely futile?

The answer from Snite or from any of his close friends would be an emphatic "No." He referred to Lourdes afterward with deep appreciation and affection—he named one of his daughters Bernadette. Everyone marveled that he could be so cheerful. This final extract from his Lourdes diary may explain his feeling:

"Life here at Lourdes is so wonderful—such a series of unending thrills, that I find it difficult to record my reactions. Everyone is happy. . . . Here there is no talk of war, of politics, of bodies; here life is a prayer. It's no wonder we are happy.

"We are in a place apart from the world—a place halfway to heaven!"†*

---

† This account of Mr. Snite's pilgrimage was taken from the book *After Bernadette* by Don Sharkey, with kind permission of The Bruce Publishing Co.

* Fred Snite died in his sleep in November, 1954, sixteen years after his Lourdes pilgrimage.

16

Cures Away from Lourdes

It's hard enough for the medical man to admit the fact of miraculous cures at Lourdes. But when he is confronted with cures that have taken place hundreds or thousands of miles away, just by calling upon the name of Notre Dame de Lourdes, or by using Lourdes water—that, he says, is really *too* much to ask us to believe!

And yet it happens—not once or twice, but many times. And the Medical Bureau states that "it is also equipped for the study of healings which have taken place in other parts of the world (i.e., outside of the Domaine itself), provided the name of Lourdes has been invoked."

Such cures have occurred in many different corners of the earth— in America, Oceania, Canada, Ceylon. They have occurred after Novenas* to Notre Dame de Lourdes; at Lourdes shrines or replicas of the Grotto; in Lourdes chapels; or at home after the application of Lourdes water. Accounts of such cures fill a substantial portion of the Bureau records, and fascinated me from the beginning.

One of the most spectacular of these cures in the early days was that of Pierre de Rudder, whose case caused a storm of discussion and argument all over Europe. Here was a case that could not by the wildest flight of imagination be attributed to autosuggestion or hysteria, for it had to do, not with nerves or emotions or even altered tissues, but with

---

* A Novena, as all Catholics know, is a nine-day period of prayers and devotions, directed toward some special end.

broken bones that were instantaneously joined together—the leg bones of an adult man.

De Rudder was a Belgian peasant who lived in Jabbeke, near Bruges. His leg had been broken by a falling tree. The break was so bad that, after the fragments of bone were removed, the two bones that remained intact could be seen in the wound over an inch apart. The lower part of the limb, no longer attached to the top, "swung in all directions like a rag."

Eight years later, the shattered bones still refused to knit, and an abscess had formed round them, causing a horrible running sore. Surgeons, one after another, pronounced the case incurable, and Professor Thiart of Brussels, consulted as a last resort, advised amputation of the leg. De Rudder refused. For more than eight years he suffered fearful torture, having to dress the wound several times a day, and dragging himself along on crutches.

Finally he decided to make a pilgrimage to the statue of Notre Dame de Lourdes that had been erected at Oostacker, a town near Ghent. Three men lifted him into the train. Arriving at Ghent, he got into the Oostacker omnibus, and his leg, though well wrapped, discharged so much blood and pus that the driver loudly complained about the drainage to the seat of his vehicle.

At the Oostacker Grotto, Pierre prayed long and earnestly. First he asked forgiveness for all his sins. Then he begged Notre Dame de Lourdes the grace of being able to work and take care of his children, and no longer to live on charity.

As he prayed, all of a sudden he felt a profound movement through his whole body. Hardly realizing what he was doing, he started to walk—without crutches—all around the Grotto. He did this three times. After that he walked to the carriage which was to take him to the station. On arriving at home, he got off the train in normal fashion.

When he examined his leg, he found that the wound had closed. In a few brief minutes at the Grotto the bones had become solidly knit together. His legs were as firm and sound as anybody's. There was no gap left, and his bones had united. He did not even limp, for both his legs were the same length.

The news spread swiftly. Soon the whole of Belgium was in an uproar over this astounding cure. Pierre's doctor, an agnostic, at first refused to believe it—but went to see for himself. He found his patient hard at work digging in the garden. The physician, Dr. Van Hoestenberghe, later wrote to the head of the Medical Bureau:

Pierre is undoubtedly cured. I have seen him many times during the last eight years, and my medical knowledge tells me that such a cure is absolutely inexplicable. Again, he has been cured completely, suddenly, and instantaneously, without any period of convalescence. Not only have the bones been suddenly united, but a portion of bone would seem to have been actually created to take the place of those fragments I myself have seen come out of the wound. But if a miracle, then there is something beyond natural law—a God exists, and surely He must have given some revelation of Himself.

The doctor returned to the faith of his childhood. And so did scores of others in that part of Belgium. The cure had a tremendous effect in the religious life and practice of the entire district. It caused a sensation throughout Europe.

Twenty-eight doctors undertook a study of the case. They made minute inquiries, superintended by both Catholics and unbelievers. They questioned the physicians who had attended de Rudder, the neighbors in Jabbeke who had witnessed the state of the wound on the day of his departure, and the people who had been present at the Grotto. They put de Rudder himself through the strictest possible examination. In the end, they were forced to admit the authenticity of the unprecedented fact: the instantaneous growth of a piece of bone over an inch long, filling up the gap where it was wanting, the whole process following upon a simple prayer. On the leg where it had been broken there remained merely a bluish spot.

Twenty years went by without any weakening of the leg. De Rudder died of pneumonia at the age of seventy-five. An autopsy revealed nothing new regarding the case, except that "the leg was restored as the most skillful of surgeons might have done it, had an operation been possible. And it was done by getting rid of a suppurating wound immediately, and by the instantaneous creation of a bone."

De Rudder's leg bones are preserved at the University of Louvain, but copper models of them were given to Lourdes and may be seen there at the Medical Bureau office.

Dr. Leuret, writing of this case in 1951, says:

There was an instant formation of bony callus, filling the void between the bony extremities. Whence came the bony substance, and notably the calcium salts necessary for the solidity which was immediate? Dr. Le Bec has shown very definitely that, in view of all the conditions, at least fifty days would have been necessary for the formation in question by normal processes. But in the cure performed at the Shrine of Notre Dame de Lourdes, it took barely sixty seconds.

Lourdes shrines have been the scene of cures not only in Europe, and not only to members of the Catholic faith. Some of the most interesting accounts come from the countries of the East.

In 1880, the Georgian Fathers, banished from France, established a convent at Constantinople. There they dedicated an altar to Notre Dame de Lourdes, adorned with a statue like the one at the Lourdes Grotto; and they kept on hand a supply of water sent them from the Spring.

At once miracles began to happen—so many that Cardinal Vanutelli, Apostolic delegate of the Holy See in Turkey, appointed a Commission to examine them. Palsy, epilepsy, and cancer were reported to have vanished instantaneously. A Jew of Orta, and a child who was born clubfooted, as well as many blind people, were suddenly healed. A woman of Pera got rid of a piece of needle for many months lost in her finger, four years before a like event in the case of Celestine Dubois, at Lourdes. Greeks, Armenians, Moslems, and Jews were cured as well as Catholics. Among the crowds about the convent could be seen people of all types—soldiers, pashas, women of every class, dervishes, eunuchs, and Turkish officers.

"And why not?" says a Catholic writer. "Are not all men Her children, and did not Christ come to redeem them all?"

Catholics say it is no wonder that Mary's mercies should be granted to these Eastern peoples, for the Oriental liturgies—Armenian, Maronite, Coptic, and Syrian—glow with praise of Mary. It must have been strange to see these processions, made up of all sorts of people and creeds invoking Her whom the Moslems call Meriem-Ana, or Bikir Meriem, praying for and being granted these amazing cures.

> After the invocation in the chapel at the Virgin's altar,
> (says one of the records) the pilgrims would go into the
> sacristy. There they were sprinkled with holy water and

had the Gospel read to them. They were then blessed, by placing the Holy Gospels on their heads and kissing the cross engraved in the flat part of the book. Afterwards cures were wrought by the drinking of Lourdes water.

Sometimes the Moslem women would unfold handkerchiefs or shirts meant to be worn, in accordance with Turkish custom, by those for whose recovery they were praying. Before beginning their invocations they placed them on the first steps of the altar, and came to fetch them away afterward. They burned from four to five thousand candles in the chapel, and distributed quantities of water and medals gratuitously. From Mesopotamia and Turkestan came requests for it, and—stranger still—from Mecca and Medina, the two holy cities of Islam.

Many years have gone by since that record was written. The little convent of the Georgian Fathers has grown into a huge abbey, but the church and the altar to Notre Dame de Lourdes remain as they were then. Thousands of thanksgiving tablets cover the walls. People of all creeds continue to pour in, declaring that "Our Lady of Lourdes still dispenses her favors."*

Here and now, in our own time, remarkable cures have occurred in cities far away from the Domaine, during special prayers or a Novena made to Our Lady of Lourdes.

One of the most interesting personalities seen at Lourdes every year is Madame Pillot, who lives in the big industrial city of Nancy in northeastern France. To see her today, in her nurse's garb moving vigorously among the sick, one would never guess that she herself was once a desperately sick patient.

At the age of forty-two, Madame Pillot had a tumor of the brain, certified by three physicians—Drs. Malaterre, Lamy, and Guillemin. Both clinical and X-ray reports supported the diagnosis.

The illness began in 1930 and by 1932 had reached an acute stage. Dr. Guillemin writes:

* This account is taken from J. K. Huysmans' *The Crowds of Lourdes*, with kind permission of the publishers Burns, Oates & Washburne, Ltd.

In the winter of 1932–33, the patient had appalling headaches, delirium, periods of aberration, with fixed ideas. She ran up and down the street during the day, and also at night, in nothing but her slip. Often her husband had to search the streets for her. She would wander off, talking to herself deliriously. At other times she would pile onto the bed anything that happened to be at hand— chairs, chests, different objects. Sometimes she had a fixed idea concerning water and wished to throw herself into the canal. Her husband was obliged to restrain her during such moods. I myself have been present on some of these occasions. Morphine alone would calm her.

These crises would be repeated sometimes twice in one night. The shutters had to be locked in her house, for she had tried several times to throw herself out of the window. She could not be left alone for a single minute.

Between these cries, there were flashes of lucidity even more painful for the patient, accompanied as they were by terrible headaches and the realization of the doom that was upon her.

Despite all sorts of treatment and efforts to help her, the condition became steadily worse, and it appeared, as her physician said, "that the approaching end would inevitably take place in an asylum."

But Madame Pillot was cured—after all human efforts had failed, and all the skill of the physicians had proved futile. The Sisters and nurses in the sanatorium where she had been taken began a Novena for her to Notre Dame de Lourdes, praying earnestly for an end to her sufferings. She was cured on the first day of the Novena. Suddenly all pain ceased and, Dr. Guillemin records, "It is a fact that from that day Madame Pillot suffers no more." He adds:

"Her condition has improved remarkably. She has taken up her usual tasks again, and I have seen her do a day's work that few people in sturdy health could accomplish."

She was examined at the Medical Bureau in August, 1933, and again in 1934. In the meantime the Bureau kept in touch with her and received several reports from her home physician who testified to her excellent health. No more headaches, no more crises, or troubles of any sort; good appetite; and never a drug or sedative of any kind, from the moment of her cure. Prior to that, for a long time she had been having massive doses of morphine. "In short," says the Bureau report, "a negative examination, all along the line."

Madame Pillot comes to Lourdes every year as a nurse with the Nancy pilgrimage, always asking for the hardest cases. Last year again she was there, a most attractive woman in splendid health and spirits. She did magnificent Resistance work during World War II, and was awarded the Military Medal.

Other extraordinary cures have occurred through Novenas and invoking the name of Our Lady of Lourdes. Catherine Lapeyre was cured of cancer of the tongue in her own little attic in Toulouse on the last day of a Novena made for her by the Sisters of the Redemption. She had shown no improvement after a visit to Lourdes the previous year. She longed to make a second pilgrimage but hadn't the money for the journey.

"There is no reason why you cannot have your cure right here at home," said the Sisters. And this is exactly what happened.

An English boy, Joseph Duncan-Bothman, was cured of a suppurating ear and complete deafness at his home in Dover, after a Novena to Our Lady of Lourdes. The boy's father, a member of the Senate of Cambridge University and a former Anglican rector, gave an account of the cure to the doctors of the Medical Bureau.

"For ten years my son suffered from otorrhea (a discharge from the outer ear passage), involving almost complete destruction of the middle ear cavity of the left ear, and total deafness. He was treated by many well-known specialists in England and abroad. Finally a celebrated Harley Street physician declared that the inflammation might reach the brain at any moment and cause death. An immediate operation was necessary to save the boy's life. Even if the operation should be successful, the doctor said, permanent deafness was certain."

The father, a Catholic convert especially devoted to Our Lady of Lourdes, wished "to take the case to a Higher Power." He obtained the promise of prayers from religious Communities, to coincide with Novenas he and his son made each night and morning. He applied Lourdes water—"a supply of which I kept always on hand; and we performed daily devotions at a miniature Grotto which I had erected in my garden. We made a vow that if our prayer were heard we would make a pilgrimage to Lourdes and offer our services to the Hospitality there. I had the firmest conviction that Our Lady of Lourdes would grant our prayer."

The Novena ended. On the following Sunday the boy served Mass at the convent of the Augustinians, near Dover. At the Elevation of the Host he felt an acute pain in his left ear, almost unbearable. After Mass he told his father that he could hear as he had not been able to do for years. The running sore had dried up completely.

Next day he was examined by Dr. Murphy of Dover, who certified that his hearing was normal and that the ear condition was perfect in every respect. Shortly after, the boy, with his father and mother, set out on their pilgrimage of thanksgiving to Lourdes.

Dr. Murphy had cautioned them. "Yes, this cure is wonderful. I congratulate you. But don't set your hopes too high. There might be a relapse."

The relapse never came.

Psychotherapists say that a cure can be blocked through the conscious or unconscious opposition of a relative. Often with Lourdes cures the persistent faith of a devoted relative can be the effective means of bringing a cure to pass.

As, for example, in the case of Madame Gardelle. One of the greatest Lourdes cures ever known came to this little brown nut of a farmer woman, tucked away in a tiny country town in the middle of France: Crevant, near the city of Clermont-Ferrand. People who have lived in France know these sturdy peasant women—valiant, hardworking, good as men at their jobs—not unlike our New England pioneer type.

One day Madame Gardelle woke up with a very bad toothache. She had to go to town and have the tooth pulled. So much time stolen from the land—that was bad. But worse was to come. Following the extraction, the abscessed socket of the tooth refused to heal. Instead, the inflammation spread, and a nasty growth appeared on the inside of the mouth. It grew with frightening rapidity. Soon the whole left cheek was infected, and the left eye was threatened.

Dr. Dionis of Clermont-Ferrand operated. A brief improvement followed, but soon the growth began to spread again, involving the eye to a degree where it seemed she might lose it entirely.

She was sent to a clinic, where Dr. Giddard recorded her affliction as "a swollen tumor completely closing the nasal cavity, bathed in a purulent and bloody liquid." A piece of the diseased tissue was sent for examination to the laboratory of Dr. Laroche, who reported: "We have to deal with a malignant tumor beyond the help of surgery."

The patient was then sent to Dr. Dechambre for radiotherapy. Several treatments were given but the condition was in no way improved.

She returned home in a very bad state. Her pain increased daily, she was obliged to take to her bed. (Tragedy for a woman given to the land!) Morphine seemed the only thing that could help her, and the injections became more and more frequent. Her general condition grew quickly worse, strength failed rapidly, and beginning at the left nostril a red mass of tissue extended all over the left side of the face, forcing the eye out of its socket.

The disease was pronounced cancerous; declared incurable, and all treatments useless.

But Madame Gardelle had a niece who possessed an immense faith in Notre Dame de Lourdes. She persuaded the family to make a Novena to obtain the cure of their invalid. The first Novena was in vain; so was the second. But the niece redoubled her prayers, persisted in using compresses of water from the Grotto, and in spite of her aunt's desperate condition, never gave up hope.

The pain had become so great that it was necessary to give the patient eight morphine injections in twenty-four hours. Delirium was constant, and it was feared the end might come at any moment, especially during the days of March 13–16. During those days Madame Gardelle took no nourishment at all—just a few drops of Lourdes water.

Another Novena was begun, the parish priest and all the neighborhood joining in the urgent and earnest prayers. (As they say in Lourdes, "an assault on Heaven.") Unlike the preceding nights, the night of March 17 was calm and the patient slept—a deep sleep. When she awoke on the morning of the eighteenth, the pain had ceased, also the delirium. Madame Gardelle asked for something to eat. They brought her some soup, which she ate with relish.

Suddenly the niece who was straightening the bed noticed something that made her cry out. "Madeleine, Marie, look! Her face—the tumor—*her face!*"

Everybody came hurrying to the bedside stammering, incoherent at what they saw. *The tumor had almost entirely disappeared.* The eye had gone back into its socket and the nostril was free.

The patient's appetite became rapidly keener, her strength returned, her general condition was transformed. A few days later she took up her work again.

All this is set down methodically, paper by paper, in the record of the case at the Medical Bureau. For cancer of the face is a disease whose cure requires indisputable proof.*

Dr. Haddou, the family physician who had followed the case from the beginning, certified that "Madame Celestine Gardell, 54 years old, suffering from facial sarcoma, is today completely cured. The diagnosis made in November, a year ago, after laboratory examination of a piece of the tumor." Dr. Dionis (surgeon) also records that "the cure is complete." Dr. Gildard notes that "the growth in the molar region has disappeared, the skin has regained its normal aspect." Dr. Dechambre writes, six months after the cure: "Madame Gardelle presented herself to me today in a state of apparent perfect health."

In August, Madame Gardelle was examined at the Medical Bureau, where the record concludes:

> The examination permits us to record that the general condition of Madame Gardelle is perfectly normal and her visual apparatus intact. Her face shows, on the left side in the region of the sinus, a scar of 2 to 3 centimeters (about 1 inch) following surgical operation, and a slight depression due to the absence of the molars and premolars. . . . Five doctors have observed the development of a malignant tumor proceeding beyond the help of surgery, and regarding the nature of which there can be no doubt. All declare that the cure is complete. All recognize that this cure, practically instantaneous, is scientifically inexplicable. We can thus attribute it only to a cause beyond the forces of nature.

---

* The instantaneous or even rapid cure of cancer by means of natural causes is impossible. For, as the doctors of the Medical Bureau point out, in this disease not merely the original cancerous organ is involved. The cancerous cells rapidly invade surrounding tissues, the disease gets into the blood and the lymphatic system, and swiftly penetrates the whole organism. It is thus *the entire body,* not merely the initial organ, which in a miraculous cure is instantly healed—an accomplishment medically and biologically impossible.

17

"I Don't Believe It!"

The last resort of the skeptics, both lay and medical, is a flat, "I don't believe it! It's too fantastic. It couldn't happen. It just isn't so."

When I was a young reporter in Asia, people in remote Indian and Chinese villages did not believe in the New York skyline either. They would shake their heads and smile, and say, "But of course such a place does not exist. It is only a picture!"

Nothing I could say would change their conviction. They had never seen such a place. *It was something outside their experience.* Therefore it could not be true.

Thousands of people are like that about Lourdes. They have never seen it. They have never known these things—in their own town or their own experience. So they boldly announce: "Such things do not exist. I don't believe it. You are crazy—it cannot be!"

"In the medical world," says one physician who comes to Lourdes, "people go about denying what they themselves have not had opportunity to see. But things cannot be denied until they have been examined. That is the role of science. For long years doctors refused to study these cures seriously, though to say that something is not true without first having examined the facts, is to commit a grave scientific error."

"Before you enter into a discussion about Lourdes with anybody," says Dr. Smiley Blanton, "it will save lots of time and much useless argument if you find out, first, if the person you are talking to was ever there. More important, did he actually spend some time there? Breezing through Lourdes on a typical tourist schedule is often more misleading than no visit at all. Most critics of Lourdes are people who have never been inside the place. They sit snugly in their offices at home and write learned dissertations about a center they have never seen, and matters of which they know—from direct experience—absolutely nothing."

One thing you quickly notice: the difference in attitude of the rationalist physician *before* he has seen a cure, and *after*. Doctors who have actually seen a cure usually have nothing to say. They are no longer ready with glib explanations. They are completely bowled over.

Their vocabulary changes, too. Before they've seen a cure, they avoid the word miracle. Afterward, they use it freely—almost involuntarily. A miracle has happened within themselves, also. Their scientific cocksureness has been severely shaken.

Much depends on whether "*I* was there," before they will accept the proceedings as "scientific." If some other doctor reports an extraordinary cure, this is apt to be labeled "charlatanism." But if "I saw it with my own eyes," that's a different matter. Then, it's "scientifically accurate."

Here, as everywhere else, the human factor has to be taken into account. A scientist is a human being. However coolly impersonal he may consider himself, however calmly detached and impartial, he is influenced by personal considerations, prejudices—of background, of national and cultural bias—which manifest themselves in his appraisals, both in his professional and personal conversation.

This is very evident in the story of one self-styled "rationalist" doctor in whom a change of view took place after he actually saw a cure, and saw it occur "right there before his eyes."*

Doctor Carrel came to Lourdes in charge of certain patients with the National Pilgrimage. He described himself as "a tolerant skeptic, a positivist—*interested* in Lourdes cures but not *credulous* regarding them." His religious ideas had long since been destroyed, in the course of his scientific studies.

On his first day at Lourdes he was discussing miracles with Dr. B. who was a strong believer as well as a scientist of note. Dr. C. goodnaturedly chaffed Dr. B. about his views, and especially about a supposed "cure" that had occurred that morning.

---

* This story, taken from the book *Voyage to Lourdes* by Alexis Carrel, is reprinted by kind permission of Harper & Brothers.

"Straight autosuggestion, my dear fellow. That good nun had been getting well gradually, right there in her own convent—but she *believed* that her arm would be cured at Lourdes, and so it was."

"What about the cases of Joachime Dehant and Pierre de Rudder?"

"Pious propaganda. Extremely interesting, but not valid. De Rudder's case is obviously incredible. If his story were really authentic, it would be an archetypical miracle—like the signature of God himself. But it is a duty to meet 'facts' of that kind with complete skepticism."

"Yet twenty-eight doctors in good standing examined de Rudder over a period of several years, and testified to the veracity of the testimony and the facts of his cure. Can you throw out their findings so lightly? And who is to decide which doctor's work is 'scientific' and which not?"

"Well," said the other more mildly, "I am the last to discredit any reputable colleague. Certainly there is an incredible power of suggestion in these pilgrimages, and at some sacred shrines, no doubt; but not for organic diseases. If de Rudder's cure were authentic, if it was methodically observed by scientists, I do not see how it could be explained except in terms of the supernatural. But such things must be seen to be believed."

"What kind of a disease would you have to see cured, to convince you that miracles exist?"

"An organic disease: a cancer disappearing, a bone regrown, a congenital dislocation vanishing. If ever I should see such a phenomenon I would willingly throw overboard all the theories and hypotheses in the world. But this is not likely, among the patients I have to do with here."

He spoke of one patient, Marie Bailly, in whom he had become especially interested—a girl in the last stages of tuberculous peritonitis.

"I know her history," he said. "Her whole family died of tuberculosis. She has had tubercular sores, lesions of the lungs, and now, for the past few months, peritonitis diagnosed by both a general practitioner and the well-known Bordeaux surgeon, Bromilloux. Her condition is very grave. She may die right under my nose. If such a case were cured, it would indeed be a miracle. I would never doubt again."

When she actually *was* cured, and he fully realized it, he was completely overwhelmed.

He had examined the girl just an hour before as she lay on her bed in the Sept Douleurs Hospital: noted her white, emaciated face, her racing pulse—150 to the minute, the distended abdomen, her ears and nails already turning blue.

"She may last a few more days, but she is doomed," he told the Sisters. "Her heart is giving out. Death is very near."

A few minutes later, in front of the Grotto, where they had carried her in spite of his protests, he saw an extraordinary change take place: first in her face, which gradually seemed to be losing its ashen hue; then, more amazing still, in her swollen abdomen—which flattened out under the blanket, before his very eyes. Her pulse now was calm and regular. She drank a glass of milk. Her respiration had become completely normal.

The doctor walked back to his hotel, his mind in a tumult. A dying girl was recovering. It was, literally, the resurrection of the dead. *It was a miracle!*

At the hospital that evening he examined her again, along with three other doctors. They confirmed what he already knew: *She was cured.* In the span of a few hours, a girl with a face already turning blue, a distended abdomen, and a fatally racing heart, had been restored to health.

The sweat broke out on his forehead. He felt as though someone had struck him on the head. His own heart began to pump furiously. It was the most momentous thing he had ever seen. It was both frightening and wonderful to see life come pouring back into an organism almost totally destroyed by years of illness. Here was an indisputable fact—yet a fact impossible to reconcile with science: a girl dying with an advanced organic disease, had recovered—was sitting there on her bed, smiling, eating, talking in a firm quiet voice. Radiant.

"And what will you do now?" he asked her.

"I shall join the Sisters of St. Vincent de Paul and nurse the sick!" she said, eyes shining.

He fell silent. He no longer knew what to think or what to say. He had no explanation to offer. He said good night briefly and went out into the street, and so into the Domaine and toward the Sanctuaries.

As he made his way past thousands of fervent, rapt pilgrims, he no longer wanted to smile at their childlike hopes. All he had ever believed was turned upside down. The wildly improbable had become a simple fact. The dying were cured in a few hours—a few minutes. These pilgrimages had a power of their own, and brought results. Above all, they brought humility.

It was disconcerting, to say the least, to have declared after careful examination that a patient would die, and then watch her recover. He might have doubted his own diagnosis, or his own memory, if he had not kept a written record of the case. But there it was—he reviewed it again: her tuberculous family, her own gradual deterioration, all the classic symptoms, and finally the diagnosis of the physicians and surgeons who had had her under their care.

No, there was no doubt of its having been a true case of tuberculous peritonitis. At the hospital that afternoon he had said she was about to die. Now, tonight, he was unable to offer any explanation for the incredible fact that she was alive and appeared to be cured. On the point of death at noon, and well by seven in the evening!

"When one reads about such things," he said to his friend Dr. B. later, "one cannot help suspecting some kind of charlatanism. But here is a cure I have seen with my own eyes. I have seen an apparently chronic invalid restored to health and normal life. These must be recorded, they must be conscientiously studied.

"Of course," he added, "facts are not the whole answer. Such cures cannot be brought about by natural means. Autosuggestion is not the final answer—nor the Lourdes water either, for cures have taken place without it."

What then? Was it in truth the Virgin, or God Himself who works the miracles? He could prove neither the existence or nonexistence of God. He was alone in the night, a solitary human being, wrestling with his doubts and questionings. Was the phenomenon he had seen a new fact in the tangible world of science, or did it belong to the realm of the supernatural? This was the vital point. It was not a question of accepting some abstract theorem. It was a question of accepting facts that might change the conception of life itself.

In his restless searchings for an explanation, for an answer to the tremendous event he had seen, one thing came back to him over and over again: that girl's face, after her cure; the joy that flowed from her, shining out to everybody in the room. They all felt it. Peace and serenity seemed to flood the place.

He had never beheld such joy or peace, following an ordinary cure, in his experience as a physician.

It was not an emotional joy, but a deep and quiet calm, "a profound sense of well-being" which, he remembered now, is recorded many times of Lourdes cures. It is not recorded of natural cures in a hospital, nor of cures by hypnotism or autosuggestion. This in itself would seem to tell something about the cause: the Power from which the cure proceeds.

Doubts and questionings faded away beside this girl's happiness. Intellectual systems no longer seemed to count. In the face of life and death, mere theories were void. One thing he saw clearly: it was not science that nourishes the inner life of man. It was the faith of the soul.

18

Two Famous Cures

One Sunday afternoon I was chatting with one of the doctors at the Bureau—an old-timer who had been coming every year for twenty years to Lourdes to study the cures.

"Tell me," I asked him, "when you look back over the years, the hundreds of cases you've seen, the thousands of patients you've studied, what are some of the most remarkable cures you've witnessed or known about during these years?"

"Oh," he said, "any number. Hard to select. But—well, there was Madame Augault. That was a very remarkable case—fibroid tumor. I lived near her town, Craon. I knew both the surgeons who attended her. I know her parish priest who has known her all her life. So I know from my own personal standpoint that her cure was genuine. But the official medical documents are all here on file, and it is all thoroughly clear medically, too."

This woman had been ill for twelve years, with a tumor of the uterus which had grown to enormous proportions. These growths often weigh ten to twenty pounds. "I don't know how much hers weighed," said the doctor, "but it was tremendous." X-rays confirmed the diagnosis of the family physician, Dr. Faligant, who certified, "Madame Augault is suffering from a voluminous fibroid tumor which produces intestinal compression and a state of intractable constipation."

Because of a heart condition she could not undergo surgery. Two surgeons whom she consulted, Dr. Martin and Dr. Le Basser, both advised against an operation.

Dr. Loiseleur of Laval, who did her X-rays, suggested possible X-ray treatments but Madame Augault decided she could not afford these.* She grew steadily weaker—could take only liquid food and that only two cups a day. Finally, through weakness, even lost her voice. Because of pressure on the intestine, gastric troubles became a major feature of the general condition. Vomiting was continual. The case had reached a desperate and apparently hopeless stage.

As a last resort Madame Augault decided to go to Lourdes. Dr. Faligant strongly opposed this. He told her it was "a last imprudence" and that she would never come back alive. But Madame Augault persisted.

She had a double reason for wanting to make the pilgrimage. She had a neighbor, a retired railroad employee, who was a complete unbeliever and who laughed at the idea of a cure through divine intervention. Especially a cure for such a malignity as Madame Augault's tumor.

"If Madame Augault is cured at Lourdes, I will become a believer myself," he vowed, "and I will walk barefoot through the streets of Craon, carrying a penitential candle!"

Madame Augault heard this, and was deeply stirred. A profound believer, she became more eager for the conversation of her neighbor than for her own cure. "I *must* go," she said. "Perhaps the Blessed Virgin will cure *him!*"

She made the journey on a mattress—at the limit of her strength and very close to death. Four injections were necessary to help her heart during the trip. Dr. Bucquet of Laval, who visited her on the train, told the doctors at the Medical Bureau later that he "had been startled by the dimensions of her abdomen."

Madame Augault arrived at Lourdes on the twentieth of August and was taken to the Hospital of the Sept Douleurs. From the time of her departure from Craon she had taken no nourishment and she took none until evening of the following day.

On the morning of August 21, she was taken to the piscine on a stretcher. During the brief instant of her immersion she felt excruciating pain, but then the pressure in her abdomen seemed to disappear.

---

* Dr. Loiseleur subsequently reported to the Medical Bureau: "In September, 19—, I examined Madame Augault of Craon who came to me from Dr. Faligant. She showed: a fibroid tumor grown into the little basin (of the uterus), and extended over the pubic symphysis by about 8 centimeters (approximately 3 inches)."

She felt no distress—all pain had ceased. Very tired, she was taken back to the hospital. She took no nourishment at noon, either solid or liquid.

Again, at 4 P.M., she was carried on her stretcher to the Procession. Lined up with her companions in misery, she suffered terribly while waiting for the passing of the Blessed Sacrament. But at that precise moment, as the Host was raised above her, sufferings vanished. It seemed that her energies were reborn, and she could get up and walk!

She stayed on her cot, however, said nothing to anyone as to how she felt, and was brought back as usual to the hospital. Arriving there, she began to walk a little. That night she was hungry, but she ate only dry bread—which she had not tasted in four years. The following night was an excellent one.

Next day, August 22, she returned to the piscine. The attendants who had bathed her before observed with amazement that her abdomen was entirely flat and apparently normal. Besides, she had recovered her voice.

After this bath she presented herself at the Medical Bureau where, within a few minutes, some thirty doctors had gathered to investigate this extraordinary cure. Dr. Juge, surgeon of Marseilles, conducted the examination. The official record at the Bureau reads:

> The abdomen, on examination, was found to be perfectly supple. The skin was "pleated," like that of a woman who has had a child. The abdomen is easily depressable and entirely painless. It is thin—no pain on palpation.
>
> The belt which the invalid wore on her arrival at Lourdes is now 20 centimeters (7 inches) too large. The measure of her bloomers belt also shows a decrease of 18 centimeters (from 90 to 72). The coat which she wore shows the marks of the stretching of the buttonholes from the distension of the abdomen. This garment has become much too big and its sides now overlap considerably.

Results of the gynecological examination are given in detail: vagina supple to the touch; neck of uterus easily accessible; volume and consistency normal, etc. The heart was also normal, pulse regular and well marked. Everyone noticed how easily the patient lent herself to the examination.

After some discussion of the doctors' certificates, X-rays and so on, which attested the existence of the tumor over a period of years, the President of the Medical Bureau concludes:

> The cure of Madame Augault, instantaneous and without convalescence as above related, astonished a number of our colleagues who observed it. The day after her deliverance, August 23, she ate without inconvenience the regular diet served at the common table at the Hospital, went up without fatigue the steep steps of the Rosary Church and the hard climb of the Way of Calvary. (A very hilly path of half a mile.) . . . The opinion of the doctors present is that such a cure can find no place in what we are accustomed to observe in our habitual medical practice and is definitely outside the range of biological laws—that is to say, it cannot be attributed to natural processes.
>
> To complete the record, let us add that the cure of Madame Augault has been steadily maintained. Her attending physician informs us that he visited Madame Augault on her return from Lourdes and several times since. He says she feels well, eats well, has normal stools. The heart is normal. She has gained 2 kilos (4 pounds) this week. Within a month she had gained 16 pounds.

Madame Augault continued in excellent health, according to doctors who visited her in 1951.

And the neighbor fulfilled his vow. He walked barefoot through the streets of their little town, carrying a candle like any sincere penitent, and became a firm practicing Christian. Madame Augault's joy was then complete.

In the files of the Medical Bureau are to be found a number of cases headed: "Cured on the train going home" or "Cured on the point of departure." One of the most interesting of these is the case of Lydia Brosse.*

This young woman suffered for years from intestinal tuberculosis and later from tuberculous abscesses on her back and thighs. At the

* For more on Miss Lydia Brosse, see Part Four, Chapter 27, p. 283.

Hospital of St. Raphael in the south of France, she underwent one operation after another to be rid of these abscesses. Instead, she seemed to grow constantly worse. In September, 1930, Dr. Clement, surgeon at St. Raphael, was about to perform additional incisions; but the patient, weary of suffering and at the end of her resources, asked to be admitted to the Rosary Pilgrimage which was about to go to Lourdes.

For her admission to the Pilgrimage Dr. Clement gave her the following certificate: "I, the undersigned, Dr. Clement, Surgeon of the Hospital of St. Raphael, declare that Mlle. Lydia Brosse, suffering from repeated multiple abscesses, affections of bone and skin, and of tubercular nature, is in a condition to be admitted to the hospital at Lourdes." (Signed, Dr. Clement, St. Raphael, September 26, 1930.)

Lydia departed on the Pilgrimage on October 7. By this time she was suffering from a large abscess extending to both buttocks and had to lie on her stomach during the whole journey. She weighed only 78 pounds, and the doctor who helped her to the train declared that the poor girl would never live to reach Toulon, the next station.

The trip to Lourdes was one long agony. Arrived there, she was so exhausted that the nurses felt great concern for her. She was bathed twice in the piscine (October 9 and 10) but on the latter day she was so weak she was merely lotioned with Lourdes water. Her sores discharged abundantly, the dressings having to be renewed twice during the day.

Her suffering was greater than ever that morning, as she recounted. She could not even pray. The nurses were filled with compassion at seeing her getting ready to depart "in the same corpselike condition as when she came."

The train left at 2 P.M. Before arriving at Toulouse, four hours later, she felt suddenly better. She managed to raise herself on her elbows and declared that she no longer felt pain. The nurses took advantage of the interval to change the dressings. The compresses and the cotton were just as soiled as on preceding occasions. They made a new dressing.

At Carcassone, the Sister-nurse brought Dr. de Vernejoul, surgeon of Marseilles and physician of the train, to change the dressing. To their utter amazement, they found the compress only faintly reddish and the wounds almost closed.

At Narbonne, it was seen that the sores were definitely healed; Lydia, on her feet now, could walk about the train. The rest of the journey she accomplished in a sitting position. Hospital orderlies at St.

Raphael had come with ambulance and stretcher to meet the invalid. Open-mouthed, they saw her jump lightly from train to platform and walk along with the greatest ease.

Although it was raining, she insisted on walking—in her slippers—to the Hospital ("So happy I was to *walk!*" she said) and was received by the Superior and the Sisters, who were quite overcome at sight of this "literally resurrected one."

That same day, which was the twelfth of October, Mlle. Brosse was seen again by Dr. Clement. He later certified:

> I, the undersigned, Dr. Clement, surgeon at the Hospital of St. Raphael, declare that I have had under my care since the month of January, 1929, Mlle. Lydia Brosse for repeated abscesses and phlegmons, most of these very voluminous, the inflammation situated mainly in the buttocks and lower part of the abdominal wall. Incised and drained, these purulent collections cicatrized very slowly and much sloughing off of tissue resulted. On October 12, I found complete cicatrization of various incisions previously made, as well as complete disappearance of a voluminous collection of pus in the left buttock. All trace of inflammation has disappeared and Mlle. Brosse has at this moment all the appearances of good health. (Signed, Dr. L. Clement, October 17, 1930).

A letter from another physician at the St. Raphael Hospital, Dr. Chabal, noted that when Mlle. Brosse entered the Hospital (April 12, 1929) she had pus in her urine and very troublesome nasal and intestinal hemorrhages. He described various operations the patient had undergone on account of tuberculous disease of the bones and recalled her condition when she departed for Lourdes. He, too, observed the amazing change in the patient on her return, and confirmed everything Dr. Clement had found: "Her wounds entirely filled up, and she has now only her scars, enormous but healthy—and an increase of weight to 104 pounds."

Dr. Chabal, an agnostic, adds: "Personally, without denying their possibility, I did not believe at all in miraculous cures. I must acknowledge that this cure, in a patient whose case I had followed, astonished me extremely. Certainly the gravest lesions may be healed, when they are tuberculous, as was the case here, but I do not believe that a natural cure can take place with such extreme rapidity."

On October 8, 1931, one year after her cure, Mlle. Brosse again came to Lourdes in the Rosary Pilgrimage, but in a very different condition from the year before. The account of her examination at the Medical Bureau records that she "appeared to be in excellent health," that "there remained no spot in the once diseased areas which was not completely healed," and that she "has gained 48 pounds in the space of one year."

The record describes in detail the various scars which bore witness to the former disease: on the left arm, right arm, right leg, abdomen, in addition to two great scars in the region of the thighs—"the principal wound in evolution at the time of the cure"—and notes that Mlle. Brosse had been anesthetized *twenty times* in vain attempts through surgical means to effect the cure of these abscesses which had miraculously disappeared within a few hours of her visit to Lourdes.

The President of the Bureau, summing up, and calling attention to the testimony of the various eye-witnesses of the cure, on the spot, as well as that of the patient's physicians at home, concludes:

"It is impossible that 'suggestion,' either personal or collective, could force various microbes to neutralize each other and disappear, cause large collections of pus to be absorbed, fill up gaps made by sloughing tissue, and form scars with a rapidity that amazed the surgeon concerned. Such healing surpasses all biological laws."

A nurses' aide who had helped care for Lydia at Lourdes, writing to her Chief of Service, added a few personal details to the case:

> I remember very well this poor log of a human, lying on her stomach for eighteen months, whose back and thighs were freshly cut and whose wounds went all along her hips! Accompanying my friend at the station (for the return journey) I saw the poor invalid going back in the same corpse-like condition in which she came. By the time they reached Narbonne, of course she was well . . . A week later she went to Toulon to assist at the ceremony of Thanksgiving of the Pilgrimage and publicly to thank the Blessed Mother. Since then she has taken service in the Hospital.

The letter goes on to say:

The doctor who had cared for Mlle. Brosse during her nasal hemorrhages (Dr. Chabal) had told the Superior: "Don't bother me any more, the poor girl is reeking with tubercle bacilli, and there is nothing more to be done for her."

I went to St. Raphael to see her. I saw her scars. Naturally the flesh that had been removed by several operations has not come back; but the skin is supple, there is no pain, and the patient moved around in lively fashion on her chair to show us, who had seen her in such agony, how she felt nothing whatever now, and all positions seemed comfortable for her. . . . One of the doctors said that even if she had been cured (by natural processes) she would never have been able to sit down without pain.

I expect to see her again and I will keep you posted on the developments of this remarkable cure. (Signed, G. La Croix, nurses' aid. Juan-les-Pins, Dec. 2, 1930.)

According to last accounts, Lydia Brosse is still well and vigorous. She leads an active life as a practical nurse.

19

Relapses, Frauds, and Conversions

The cure of diseases logically poses the question of their possible recurrence or relapse. Relapses are extremely rare in Lourdes cures—I found less than ten in records covering seventy-five years. They seldom occur; and in such cases, the doctors point out, a relapse after several years, or death by a malady other than the one miraculously cured, cannot be used as an argument against the miracle. It is still not possible to explain the original cure.

Among the exceptional cases may be mentioned that of Madame Rouchel of Metz, cured of lupus (tuberculosis of the skin), but after two years seized again with the same illness. She died in a hospital nine years after her cure at Lourdes.

A case of relapse, interesting from several angles, is that of Elie Auclair. Auclair, an ex-soldier, developed Pott's Disease after his war service. A complete atheist and violent foe of religion, he had married a devout Catholic girl to whom he was deeply attached. But he scoffed at her faith and said he would rid their children of "all that nonsense" just as soon as they were old enough to reason.

Then this terrible illness came upon him. His wife spoke of Lourdes. Auclair hooted at the idea. He, a free-thinker, go to Lourdes! "I forbid you ever to bring a priest to me!" he thundered. "If I know of it, and have strength enough, I will drive him away."

Some time later, he happened to see Paul Merat, a young boy who had been cured of his same malady at Lourdes, a couple of months before. Auclair was deeply impressed. He thought perhaps the Lourdes waters did have some curative quality. He consented to go. Once there, he was moved by the simplicity and faith of those about him. He saw that there was more to it than just some curative water. Wondering at himself, he began to pray.

Two days later, his abscesses had dried up, mobility returned to the spine, his wounds healed. Auclair, who had come to Lourdes on a stretcher, returned home walking and free from pain. Within a month he resumed his work as a blacksmith.

He was a changed man—a radiant Christian, *living* his faith, and overwhelmed by what God had done for him. But he kept saying, "My past is terribly stained. I was an enemy of God. What have I done that He should grant me such grace?"

He was intensely conscious of his black past and his guilt.

In a few months his pain began again. "It is only just that God should try my faith," he said, "since I have been such a great sinner and have denied His existence."

He returned twice to Lourdes—but did not improve. He developed new abscesses and grew worse. He accepted whatever came as God's will, as suffering visited upon him "because of his faults." He "had increased Christ's sufferings on the Cross." He was overwhelmed by his guilt-consciousness; but was ready to accept cheerfully any amount of suffering as retribution for his "evil past." During the last seven months of his life he suffered intolerably but never complained.

"Our Blessed Lady showed me the right road," he said. "That was sufficient. I shall never forget it." He died holding his Lourdes medal and his crucifix, and with an expression of joy on his face.

The question of fraud has been a burning issue at Lourdes from the very beginning. There have been violent attacks by Lourdes adversaries on the veracity of both *miraculés* and witnesses; also accusations that the medical men of France are in secret agreement with the Church in the proclamation of miracles. There have been assertions that the whole story of the cures is just a huge piece of Catholic propaganda.

But many of the certifying doctors are not Catholic, and some have no religious belief whatever: such as Dr. Pellé who certified the cure of Jeanne Fretel, Dr. Chabal who certified the cure of Lydia Brosse, and Dr. Bardol who certified the cure of Marie Borel.

In the end, it comes down to the word of the examining doctors and the doctors in attendance at the patient's homes. Are they telling the truth or are they lying? The integrity and prestige of the doctors in charge of the Medical Bureau, the noted specialists and Chief Surgeons of the Paris Hospitals—Oberlin, Grenet, Mauriac, etc.—can hardly be challenged; nor can one doubt the large and very distinguished membership of AMIL. Five thousand doctors in good standing can't all be fools—or fakes. Nor can they be parties to what would be—were Lourdes *not* "on the level"—one of the most gigantic frauds in history. This would be practically impossible, even if morally conceivable. If a fraud, Lourdes would have blown up long ago instead of increasing in dignity and winning the respect of the medical profession steadily, every year.

The severity of the examining physicians at the Medical Bureau, their tendency to reject rather than accept alleged cures, and to subject each cure to merciless (and year-long) scrutiny, is the best guarantee against any fraudulent cases slipping through.

Attempted frauds against the Medical Bureau are not infrequent; some inspired by vanity, some by greed, some by definite animosity and the desire to injure or destroy.

For example, one day a young girl of about twenty, with a quiet voice and an air of complete innocence, presented herself at the Bureau. "Doctor," she said tremulously, "I believe I have been cured! For three years I have been in bed unable to walk, and since this morning I can walk perfectly! Isn't that wonderful?"

The doctor looked her over. "What was the matter with you, my child?"

"Oh, that I don't know, Doctor."

"Where is your medical certificate?"

"I have none."

"And why not?"

"Oh, I did not think I was going to be cured."

The secretary got out his notebook and the doctors prepared to take the record. . . . Lucie M—twenty-one years old . . . Pilgrimage of the North, etc. . . . Then they began the examination.

For one who had not walked for three years, she had muscles like marble. They told her to take off her shoes. "But why?" the girl objected. "My feet do not hurt!"

They wanted to see the way she planted her feet—which naturally is not the same for a normal person as for one who has been in bed for some time. She planted her feet like one who uses them every day. The doctors told her severely: "You are lying. You have been walking straight along. What is all this trumped-up history?"

Then she broke down, burst into tears, and between sobs told her true story. "You see, Doctor, in the village next to mine, last year, one of my little friends became a *miraculée*. When she came home she was greeted with flowers, triumphal arches, the rector blessed her and the mayor kissed her. I want people to do all that for me, too!"

There are half a dozen Lucies every year. Sometimes they can do real harm to the reputation of the Bureau and to the genuine cures.

Another time, one of the brancardiers came running to the Bureau, his face radiant with joy. "Doctor! What do you think? A magnificent miracle! A boy, deaf and dumb from his birth, and the son of deaf-mutes also. He began to speak at the baths this morning. Isn't that *marvelous?*"

"We shall see. Send him along to me."

Some minutes later the young boy of the supposed miracle walked in. Blond, curly-headed, about fifteen, with rather a childish air, he was escorted by an extraordinary individual of about thirty—black as jet, long whiskers, cavernous jowls—in brief, a person one would not like to meet on a dark street at two in the morning.

"You two are relatives?" asked the doctor.

"Oh, no," said the escort. "I have known the boy only three days." He had asked for help, it seemed, in the train.

"When did he begin to speak?"

"This morning, at the baths."

"And what did he say?"

"He said: 'I fervently thank the Blessed Virgin Mary.' "

"But that is magnificent," said the doctor; "that is not a miracle, that is two miracles. First, he has acquired the gift of speech; second, he has instantly learned grammar!"

The escort saw that he had made a blunder. "But doctor, you must understand—for four years now he has been in an institution for deaf-mutes."

"Well, well! And he could not by chance have learned to speak in that institution?" The doctor turned to the boy. "Now look here, my son, tell me the truth: how long is it since you have been able to talk?"

"Since two years, doctor," said the youngster.

The escort, in considerable confusion, hustled him out of the Bureau. But the two were not through yet. They bought two thousand post cards and spent the rest of the day writing on them: "Souvenir from a deaf-mute miraculously cured at the piscine on this very day." They sold the cards, for ten francs each to gullible pilgrims, the escort pocketing the proceeds—which amounted to about 18,000 francs, (fifty-odd dollars) before the police caught up with them.

The worst type of all frauds is the intentionally malicious. One morning a woman came rushing into the Bureau with disheveled hair and in great excitement, crying: "I am cured—I am cured! Come at once—a real miracle!"

Her malady, the woman declared, had been an anal fistula. Now, thanks to the Blessed Virgin and glorious St. Bernadette, she was "freed-delivered!"

The doctors brought her into the office and began to take the record: personal antecedents, family history, history of the illness, history of the cure. The patient answered all questions readily, even volubly. When she had finished, she rose to leave.

The doctors detained her. "Wait, madame, we have not finished. We must now examine you."

"Examine me—but why?"

"In order to verify your cure, madame."

"And all that I have been telling you—that is for nothing?"

"For nothing, madame, if we do not examine you."

"But I do not wish to be examined."

"Then you should not have come here and made us waste thirty-five minutes. Why *did* you come here?"

"I came to have myself verified."

"Very well, in order to verify a cure we must examine the patient. If you do not consent, we shall tear up the record."

"Then I shall not be verified?"

"No, madame."

After much protesting and objecting, finally she yielded, and the examination took place. Five or six doctors assisted. There was nothing whatever the matter with the woman, and never had been—certainly not of the malady she described. When the doctors asked her to show them where the anal fistula was, she pointed to a little white scar (vestige of an old cyst operation) quite high up on the back and in a spot where certainly no one ever had an anus!

The doctors' annoyance was evident. The President said to her firmly: "Madame, you have lied to us. What *is* all this story?"

She looked much embarrassed, finally said she would tell it "to the Chief of the Bureau, but not to all these people."

The President took her into his office and there, in bits and pieces, the truth came out. She had been purposely sent, by an antireligious organization of one of the big *départments* in the middle of France, to bring back a personal document showing that at the Medical Bureau of Lourdes they recognized miracles *without examining the patients*.

The enemies of Lourdes were clever, but not clever enough. If the Bureau had not acted with its usual severity, if the doctors had said, "Well, madame, we will verify this next year," they would have been immediately involved in a press campaign, perhaps national, which they could never have lived down, whatever proofs they might have produced. The result might have been catastrophic.*

One of the worst frauds against Lourdes was perpetrated by Zola who, by his own confession, in his novel *Lourdes* deliberately altered the facts in accounts of three cures and made their story come out to suit himself—i.e., in death, not health as actually occurred.

"My characters are my own," Zola wrote to Dr. Boissarie grandly. "I shall do whatever I like with them."

But they were *not* his characters. They were living persons— Lourdes characters—whose stories he had purloined and abused; using enough of the truth to leave no doubt as to *who* they were, but changing the ends of the stories so as to make the conclusion entirely false. When his ruse became known, he secretly visited the cured persons and offered them comfortable sums of money to leave Paris and live in a foreign country. They indignantly refused.

On the positive side, a strong impetus to moral living and active religious faith is given by Lourdes cures, both in their immediate circle and farther afield. We find many examples of this among the letters and personal notes filed with case histories.

John Traynor records "a large number of conversions" in Liverpool after his cure. His return, whole and well, made a tremendous

---

* These three stories are taken from official records in the book *Guérisons Miraculeuses Modernes* by Drs. Leuret and Bon and are reproduced by kind permission of the Presses Universitaires of Paris.

impression. And there was the family chauffeur of Marie-Louise Arnaud, so moved by her cure that he was converted and became "a good Christian." There was the atheist neighbor of Madame Augault, who kept his vow and walked through the streets carrying his penitential candle, following her astonishing cure. Mademoiselle Delot, also, tells of her neighbor who, though dying, had refused all religious consolations. She went to visit him.

"Mademoiselle," said the patient, "I saw you before you went to Lourdes, and the contrast I see in you now makes it impossible for me to doubt the power of God, about Whom I never learned much." He asked to be permitted to make his confession and receive the Last Rites and died happy, "in religion."

There was the whole Belhache family, who "had lived as pagans" till the cure of Lucien, and then came into the Church all together; they have been fervent and active Christians ever since. And Elie Auclair, and Gargam, and Madeleine Guinot, and Madame Pouxvieille, and many others. It is safe to say that every Lourdes cure brings a score of converts into active Christian faith—in addition to reviving in their own families a faith that had sometimes lapsed into apathy. Multiply this by ten thousand and you get the nucleus of a substantial religious revival.

A striking aspect of this spiritual renaissance is its impact upon the medical profession. Dr. Vallet wrote in 1944:

> No one can ignore the revival of religious faith during the past forty years; the medical world not excluded. The physician who is of a positive mind has found in the Fact of Lourdes a solid rock on which to reconstruct the shattered temple of his faith. . . . And it is not only a few isolated cases among the doctors who have thus come back to God, but a majority . . . among them some of the greatest names in French medicine, and those you would least expect to find.

He is referring here to a majority of the medical men who have visited Lourdes—some 30,000, he says, since 1890.

> The thing that incited this medical army to come to Lourdes for some of course was a tremendous and quite legitimate curiosity; but for others also . . . the desire (confused and a bit melancholy) to find again the reasons

for belief which their studies and life itself had rendered
dim and obscure—until a state of complete darkness had
been reached.

What confidences have I not heard!—until a recognized confessor could be found to clear the consciences
weighed down by years and years of abandonment, and
lead these wanderers back to spiritual security again.*

And not only the doctors. Evidence for the fact of miracles has a
powerful effect upon the belief of people generally. Whereas miracles
have been, for many, a primary reason for doubting the truth of large
portions of the Bible, proof of their occurrence here and now gives new
foundation for faith in the Scriptures as a whole.

"If miracles occur, then God exists!" is the basic theme of this
revival of religious belief through Lourdes.

---

* From Dr. Vallet's *La Vérité sur Lourdes*, with kind permission of the author and of
Flammarion and Co.

20

The Big Pilgrimages

No story of Lourdes is complete without some account, however brief, of the big pilgrimages, for there is nothing like them anywhere else in the world. They bring anywhere from 20,000 to 100,000 people together in this one place, at this one Shrine, to pray, to give thanks, to meditate . . . to "recollect" in times of joy and gratitude, or after periods of strife and disaster.

The two historic yearly pilgrimages—the French National and the Rosary—have been going on since the very early days of the Shrine—1871 and 1872 respectively; the National under the direction of the Assumptionist Fathers, the Rosary Pilgrimage under the Dominicans. They bring pilgrims from every diocese in France, from French territories, and other countries also. The priests of these Orders organize them locally in the various dioceses.

Then there are special pilgrimages such as that of the French Army—25,000 in 1954; the Men's Pilgrimage—20,000; the Pax Christi—an international pilgrimage of the Catholic Peace Movement; the Pilgrimage of Deported Persons—60,000; and the War Veterans Pilgrimage topping them all with 100,000 soldiers from twenty nations.

The French National (last week of August, each year) brings a large number of sick, usually around 1,200, and is famous for its many cures. The Rosary is a pilgrimage of prayer and devotion. It is the last big event of the year and highly prized by Lourdes devotees.

Each pilgrimage follows the classic pattern: Prayer at the Grotto—

then up along the Way of Calvary. Welcome by the Archbishop; the Baths, the Procession and Blessing of the Sick; prayers at the different altars; visits to the churches and museums, and to the homes of Bernadette; confessions—Masses—the Torchlight. For the well, sometimes excursions to the mountains or the sea (Biarritz is only thirty miles away). For the sick, additional prayers and "recollection," the cherished Communion at the Grotto or at the altar of Bernadette. Finally the farewell—always a time of sadness. Nobody likes to leave Lourdes.

In some of our accounts of Cures we have followed a pilgrim from the time he leaves home until his return: his preparation—prayers and confession; sometimes, through the Hospitallers, meetings with other sick who will be traveling with him. On the train more prayers, hymns, and joyful anticipation. A Lourdes train leaves the home station with a rousing *Magnificat;* the *Ave Maria,* the *Song of Bernadette* and other hymns are heard throughout the length of the train, and at each station along the way.

The departure of the White Train from Paris at the time of the French National Pilgrimage is a remarkable sight. For days in advance, trains filled with pilgrims and invalids have been starting for Lourdes, from the north, south, east and west of France. The White Train carries the *"grands malades,"* the utterly helpless and hopeless cases whom science has declared itself powerless to relieve.*

On the day of departure the Austerlitz Station in Paris looks like a vast hospital. Rows of stretchers are lined up—on them men, women, children, all so white, so wan, so visibly sick unto death as to make one's heart ache. The train, its white pennon flying from the engine, is in readiness; one of the carriages is fitted up as a pharmacy, where the Sisters of the Assumption dispense food and medicine during the journey. The Sisters are at their post.

The priests who direct the pilgrimage move to and fro among the sick, speaking words of comfort. It is wonderful how these patients, practically all of whom belong to the working classes, rise to the occasion. They long to be cured, certainly, but there is no impatience in them; and they enter into the spirit of the pilgrimage with a sense of acceptance and humility which, considering their condition, is infinitely touching.

The Cardinal Archbishop of Paris never fails to visit the *grands*

---

* Parts of this account are from an article in the *Rosary Magazine* of New York with kind permission of the editors.

malades at the station, passing from one to the other, speaking a cheering word.

Then the business of carrying the sick into the trains begins. The brancardiers handle them so gently, so carefully. It is no easy matter to lay the invalids down in their appointed places without adding to their suffering, causing them additional pain. The train is an ordinary one and, though all precautions are taken to make the journey as easy as possible, much unavoidable discomfort must be faced.

All the available places are given to the sick. The volunteer workers—men and women—who look after them snatch a few minutes rest on camp stools they have brought. People who think of the French upper classes as completely light and frivolous would be surprised to find the nobility and wealth of the country largely represented in the plainly dressed women and devoted brancardiers who serve their patients so untiringly. Usually they are standing all day and night.

Most of their charges are actually dying. Several have received the Last Rites, just before leaving home. But whatever their condition, every one of the *grands malades* is a willing traveler and often a cheerful one. It is the onlookers who shed tears as they watch one stretcher after the other carried into the train.

At last all is ready, and, at the end of two hours' hard work, priests, nuns, infirmarians, brancardiers—everyone is at his post. The railway men close the doors, the *Magnificat* goes up with a great shout, and the White Train with its freight of suffering humanity slowly steams out of the station.

Arrived at Lourdes, these sixty thousand people who have poured in from all over France "for the National," with their twelve or fifteen hundred sick drawn up in eager, waiting ranks along the Esplanade, make a never-to-be-forgotten spectacle. Father Robert Hugh Benson tells how they look, seen from the Basilica above, during the Procession:

> The crowd was beyond describing. Here about us was a vast concourse of men; and as far as the eye could reach down the huge oval and far beyond the crowned statue and on either side—stretched an inconceivable "pavement of heads."
>
> Above us too, on every terrace and step, back to the doors of the great Basilica . . . was one seething, sing-

ing mob. A great space was kept open on the level ground beneath us . . . and the inside fringe of this was composed of the sick, in litters, in chairs, standing, sitting, lying, and kneeling . . .

After perhaps half an hour's waiting—during which a constant gust of singing rolled this way and that through the crowd . . . the Procession appeared . . . the singing ceased . . . a priest standing solitary in the great space began to pray aloud in a voice like a silver trumpet . . . the crowd with one passionate voice repeating:

"Lord we adore Thee! Lord we worship Thee. Lord we love Thee. Save us, Jesus, or we perish!"

The Archbishop left the dais—advanced with the monstrance. One after another of these taut quiet figures received the blessing. Overhead the quiet summer air was aquiver with the power of those passionate entreaties, charged with feeling as a thunder cloud with electricity. And then—all of a sudden it came!

I saw a sudden swirl in the mass of heads beneath the church steps, then a great shaking ran through the crowd . . . A cry broke out and it rang through the whole square, waxing in volume as it rang . . . Hands clapped, voices shouted: "A miracle! A miracle!"

Just as suddenly the shaking ceased and the shouting died to a murmur.

The canopy moved on and again the voice of the priest rose high and clear with triumphant thankfulness: *"You are the Resurrection and the Life!"* And again, with entreaty once more—since there still were two thousand sick untouched by that Power, and time pressed—that infinitely moving plea: *"Lord, he whom You love is ill. . . . Lord, that I may see. . . . Lord, that I may hear. . . . Lord, that I may walk!"*

And then again the finger of God flashed down—and again, and again; and each time a sick and broken body sprang from its bed of pain and stood upright. . . . Five times I saw that swirl and rush—the last when the *Te*

Deum pealed forth from the church steps as . . . the Sacrament came home again.*

Yes—there are great cures and grand events at the National. There have been as many as a hundred cures at a single Procession, in the fervent early days.

The military pilgrimages are no less remarkable, though in a different way. Lourdes will never forget the great War Veterans' Pilgrimage, when soldiers of twenty countries—including recent enemies—came together in three days of prayer for peace. Nearly a hundred thousand of them there were—Scots in their kilts, Bretons in their big hats, Belgians, Canadians, Irish, Italians, French, Dutch, and many others, most of them wearing decorations, many of them wounded.

Group by group they marched to the Grotto—a magnificent caravan. The Abbé Bergey—Director of the pilgrimage and himself a famous veteran—made the opening address, asking his comrades to give an example of Christian brotherliness in a world which seemed to have forgotten it. "All of us have fought for our countries. Now we must say to the world that we have had enough of fighting and that the time has come to love one another."

Immediately after the Benediction, four German veterans wearing their decorations entered the Grotto. Two of them took up their position on either side of the altar. Two others, seated near the grille, remained ready to relieve them; and all four began the prayer—continuous and fervent—which throughout the three days of the Pilgrimage would be offered day and night on this spot; the British followed the Germans, then the Irish, the French, the Scotch, the Canadians, the Belgians, the Italians, and so on.

Masses go on continuously at the Grotto. At the end of each service, the soldiers of that group depart to climb the Way of the Cross. A moving sight, this endless defile of men who had climbed their own Calvary many times during the terrible war years, now completely absorbed in the sufferings of their Master.

The Mass for the Dead brings them all together on the steps and Esplanade in front of the Sanctuaries: the great Requiem chant sung by

* From the book *Lourdes* by Robert Hugh Benson, with kind permission of his executors.

a "choir" of one hundred thousand voices. Then the Procession, with its crowds of sick and wounded of many nations.

Many touching glimpses: Thousands of men praying in the different churches and altars. Confessions being heard all day and through the night. Toward midnight of Saturday, 354 priests were counted, up and down the Domaine, hearing confessions in the open air, on the benches of the Esplanade, and along the river. All these sturdy soldiers on their knees, asking forgiveness and praying for help to do better in the future.

Then the grand Pontifical Mass of Sunday—the crowd augmented by people from all over the country. At ten, the bells of the Basilica ring out in joyful welcome. Every inch of space as far as you can see is packed with people.

Down the left rampe comes a dazzling sea of flags—flags of twenty nations, allied and enemy—more than three hundred of them; new flags of proud silken beauty, others in tatters, the companions of stormy days and zero hours. Immediately behind them, the splendid procession of Cardinals and Bishops in their gorgeous red and purple.

And now the veterans—row upon row, line upon line, a slow, majestic, irresistible mass, thousands upon thousands—slowly advance, singing the *Ave Maria* of Lourdes, the "Song of Bernadette."

Slowly they move down the Esplanade, slowly they turn and come to a halt in front of the benches where the mutilated and the "big wounded" are seated: stand before them, heads bowed, in silent recognition. This simple gesture, performed in absolute quiet, brings the vast crowd to tears. This, everyone says afterward, is the real and fitting climax to the Pilgrimage of the War Veterans.

The Pilgrimage of Prisoners and the Deported in 1946 had a somber splendor all its own. Here, 60,000 persons brought their gratitude for the past and their promise of Christian fidelity for the future. In the filth and wretchedness of German concentration camps they had prayed to Notre Dame de Lourdes, and had vowed, these miserable thousands, that "if ever we get out, we will go to Lourdes on a pilgrimage of thanksgiving." Now here they were, fulfilling that pledge.

To accommodate these swarming thousands, the big field at the right of the Domaine was turned into a "Camp of Return"; the different groups finding their place under the old labels: Dachau—Belsen—Buchenwald. Here the companions of the evil days found one another again with joyful cries, or more often embraced without a word, unable to speak. People dart across the path suddenly recognizing friends they had thought dead; handshakes, exclamations, shaky laughter. The Minister of the Armies, Monsieur Michelet—himself an old Dachau "graduate"—throws his arm around his old *copains,* sharing those poignant reminiscences.

From early morning a vast stream of people winds endlessly toward the Camp of Return and to the Sanctuaries. In the Square on the Esplanade an enormous podium has been erected, seventy feet high, with eighteen altars, visible from all parts of the Domaine. In front, on the open space of the Rosary Church, three funeral biers draped with the Tricolor and surmounted by a Cross—homage to those dead in captivity. The living, passing before them, stop, kneel and pray, choked with emotion. Here at night, after the great Torchlight, 60,000 men give forth the death-defying cry: "You are the Resurrection and the Life!"

R. P. Robert, Dominican Religious, escaped from the camp of Rava-Ruskaia, gives the opening address. He recalls to his comrades the memory of the Mass in the camps, where the most indifferent found comfort in a faith reborn—where they had promised Notre Dame de Lourdes if ever they were freed, to come here and thank her. "Today we keep that vow. Free of the German jails, we begin a task perhaps more difficult than the tests of imprisonment: to bring our Christian faith into the difficult life of the postwar years, taking up our big burdens in the confusions of these days."

A spirit of deep quiet and "recollection" pervades the Pilgrimage. From three o'clock in the morning Masses are celebrated at the various altars. All day long the men make their confessions. The body has been freed—now one must free one's soul. Communions follow, one upon the other, without ceasing, while the Grotto and the Basilica are jammed with kneeling people.

At the Procession in the afternoon, a vast reunion of former prisoners and deported. General Giraud, the Prince of Bourbon-Parma, and the other famous personages, are lost in the mass, intent only on joining their thanks with those of their companions of the bitter days, at this fraternal meeting place where all are equal: An endless file of men marching in rows of four on each side, a spectacle of moving grandeur.

Many touching incidents marked this Pilgrimage. On the first morning across the Esplanade came six women—knapsacks and canteens strapped to their shoulders, faces tired but joyous. "They have done thirty-two days *on foot* here to Lourdes, from Chartres," said a brancardier. "Without stopping, they have come to bring their thanks to Notre Dame de Lourdes."

People watched them wonderingly. Impatient to accomplish their mission, they hurry to the Grotto. The brancardier fills in details.

"The Chief of this remarkable caravan, Madame Ayle, is fifty-three; the youngest member, twenty-five. Madame Ayle's husband was shot by the Germans. She was a valiant Resistance worker and an ardent Christian. Deported, she made herself an apostle of Notre Dame de Lourdes to her companions in the concentration camp. They pledged themselves to make this pilgrimage if they should emerge alive from the Nazi hell. You see they have fulfilled their promise."

Another group—unusual visitors for Notre Dame de Lourdes, certainly—were twenty coal miners from Pas-de-Calais, brought by their local curate. A *kermesse* (county fair) which he had successfully organized permitted the little priest to offer this bounty to his old comrades in captivity. All of them were Communists, and thus, in principle, not pilgrims. But this fraternal gesture touched them. It was made with a generous heart, and accepted in the same spirit. After all, a trip to Lourdes, if it is not a pilgrimage, is always a "poem for the eye," not to be refused. Anyhow, a meeting place for former brothers in misery. As to the prayers, processions, Masses, and so on, "We will be tolerant spectators," they said, "not actors."

And yet, once arrived, these independent fellows would not leave their little curé. They followed him everywhere. With him they looked, marveled, listened, sang and—responded to the prayers. Next morning, two of them went to Communion; the following day, six. Lourdes—the Camp of Return.

A pilgrimage of peace and calm—but also of great spiritual strength—is the Rosary; organized by the Dominican Fathers and arriving each year at Lourdes the first week in October. I had the privilege of being present at the 1953 Rosary—40,000 people from all over France—1,200 sick: a spirit of extraordinary quiet and devotion.

I was down at the station from six in the morning, watching the trains come in—twenty-two of them that day, from Lille, Nancy, Grenoble, Bordeaux, Lyon, Avignon, Tours, Nice, Dijon, and many other places; thirteen or fourteen cars in each train—the very sick in the last carriage. One marveled again at the skill with which stretcher cases are handed through the windows—three brancardiers inside the train, four or five outside, receiving the patients with utmost care and gentleness. Tall men are needed to reach up and receive the stretcher.

Then the sick are wheeled out and placed in the big autobuses waiting outside, and carried to the hospitals. They roll off singing the *Ave Maria*. A big moment for them—almost at the Grotto now, after their long, difficult journey.

The Rosary is a pilgrimage of prayer and recollection. There are the usual crowds, the usual processions and Masses and addresses—but with a difference. People on this pilgrimage come primarily because they earnestly seek spiritual strength and sustenance; though as we know, many of the big "cures" have occurred at the Rosary too.

The sick join in all the ceremonies, to a remarkable degree. I remember especially the morning when, lined up on the Esplanade in the form of a huge Cross, they recited the Stations of the Cross in unison. Twelve hundred of them, lying there in the clear October sunshine in their little carriages, the big crowd of the well pilgrims a human wall around them.

Come for the most part from poor homes, some out of drab little sickrooms—prisons of pain for months or years—what these few days at Lourdes must mean to them! What a tremendous impression these great gatherings and processions, these rituals and ceremonies shared together, must make on them: this great Fraternity of the sick and suffering, drawn up there in their little carriages, watching and participating. The sunlight, the great peaks, the towering trees, the beauty of the country-side; the combination of imposing sanctuaries, statues, fields and rivers—beauties of nature and of religion, all around them. It might be almost too much for a sick person.

As I look on, standing quite close to that living Cross, my eye meets that of a sick person, who smiles at me suddenly, spontaneously. Without removing her gaze she starts praying, her eyes still upon me. I am reminded of a thought that has come to me more than once at the Grotto, watching these inert forms, these constantly moving lips: *the sick praying for the well*. Who knows how many prayers have gone up for *me* here; prayers offered by generous sick folk I never saw before, of whose altruism and help I have been totally unconscious—I and hundreds of others who have been the beneficiaries of their earnest and unselfish supplications.

"But yes, madame," said the brancardier to whom I spoke of this. "The gift of the sick to the well, here at Lourdes, is perhaps greater than the gift of the well to the sick. We brancardiers are constantly aware of it!"

Pilgrimages not so large have yet their own significance. A clipping from a recent Lourdes newspaper reminds me of some of them: the Pilgrimage of Italian Farmers, the Pilgrimage of French Railway Workers, the Miners of the North, the Poor of Pau, the German Swiss, the Cadettes of Mary (2,000 young girls from many dioceses); the Pilgrimage of the Deaf and Dumb, the Scouts of Paris, the Young Basques, the English Schools (400 boys, 800 girls), the Children of Bigorre—3,500 of them, come to walk proudly in the Procession. And the Pilgrimage of the Employees of the Hotels and Stores of Lourdes, which seems to me one of the most interesting, as the business people of Lourdes are often censured for their alleged unspiritual qualities. Here, at the beginning of the season, several hundred young men and women are excused from work to come and listen to the Christian counsels of Monseigneur the Rector, to pray at the Grotto, "do" the Way of the Cross, walk in the Procession, make their confession and attend their Mass—to follow the entire pilgrimage program, "with true piety and devotion," according to the Rector.

Many small-group pilgrimages are listed: sixty Ukrainian refugee pilgrims coming from England; thirty-six from Ottawa and Quebec; eighteen pilgrims from Ceylon; one hundred from Bilbao, Spain; thirty-six from Chicago; eighty from Malto; seventeen from Finland; forty-two from Alexandria, Egypt; fifty from Dunkerque: All these arriving during the one week of August 8, 1954.

In addition, that week: the Pilgrimage of the League of Belgian Workers—bringing 3,000, and 500 sick; the Pilgrimage of American Soldiers (only a few, but tremendously enthusiastic); the National Council of Catholic Women of Canada; students from the College of Wald on Lake Constance; 450 students and professors from universities and high schools of the Argentine; 1,800 German Catholics from Cologne, under the direction of the Knights of the Order of Malta.

Finally, the Crusade of the Blind—1,300 of them, from all parts of France, led by their Almoner-General. What can such a pilgrimage have to offer this contingent, for whom miracles have been few and far between? What can this unseeing visit, after a long, hard journey, mean to them? What can the blind get out of a pilgrimage to Lourdes?

They get more out of it than many of us who see. They get the inner shades of meaning and atmosphere more acutely, perhaps, than other people who come here, and receive perhaps more benefit, with their highly sensitive perceptions as they join in the various prayers and ceremonies. They "take in" truly the pervading spirit of the place.

"Life is beautiful for those who have no fear," their preacher, Father Boury, tells them. "For anyone who has *an end* in life, and knows that it is a useful end, life is beautiful. A blind person can have a useful life the same as anybody else—can make of his life a service; so for him too, life is worthwhile."

And they begin their service there and then with the singing of great Gregorian chorals and monastic Offices, an art in which they are specially trained, and a glorious contribution to that day's pilgrimages.

Yes, there is much more to Lourdes than the curing of sick bodies. A new vision for the blind. . . . Girls deciding to replace exiled nuns in the schools. . . . The profound impression on large bodies of organized workers. . . . The great influence on the children who come here by the thousands with their spiritual preceptors. . . . The effect on the doctors and scientists of many lands. In brief: the work of Religion, of spiritual development and rehabilitation in a hundred different guises. Prayer and Penitence, as The Lady said—the greatest work of all.

No pilgrimage has greater popular appeal than the Pilgrimage of the French Army, particularly this last year (1954) when French fortunes were at a crucial point. For three days (June 12 to 14) twenty-five thousand soldiers came to pray for their comrades-in-arms and for the fulfillment of their own hopes and aspirations in a dangerous and uncertain world.

Many officers and military dignitaries accompanied them—the Chief of Staff of the Army, General Blanc; General Jousse, General Badre, General Descours, Commander Potter, and other distinguished personages. The Archbishop of Paris, Cardinal Feltin, *Ordinaire* of the Army, presided. But everyone's attention was focused during those three days on the vast assemblage of youth. As their Almoner said in opening the Pilgrimage:

> Who can look upon this great company of young men,
> some just starting out, some seasoned men of battle, with-
> out profound emotion? Twenty-five thousand young men

from all walks of life, all classes, all outlooks, representing their generation with its qualities, its faults, its hopes, its longings. Twenty-five thousand young men on the threshold of life, ready to take active part in it, to found a family, to accept responsibility, to choose. [These three days at Lourdes, he hoped, would help them] decide now to respond to Christ, to take His message seriously, to pledge their lives today in the interest of tomorrow—to take their generation in hand, to transform the world!

Are you capable of this transformation? Yes. Because you are princes of all the possibilities, because you have not yet the habits that chain and hold down the adults, because your youth brings you into a climate of the new —of discovery and sincerity.

All were deeply conscious of the men fighting 6,000 miles away, in Indo-China, and of the terrific problems that beset their country and the world. "All this," said Monseigneur Théas, in his talk to the men, "imposes on your pilgrimage a gravity and a significance of which you are entirely aware."

He spoke to them of the quality of some of France's military heroes —particularly Marshal Foch who led the Allied armies to victory in 1918. Everyone knows the deep religious faith of this great general, but not all are aware of his intense consciousness of personal weakness and his complete dependence on the Divine Power. We have proof of this in his personal letters.

On April 7, 1918, he wrote to his brother Germain: "Without the special help of God I would find myself *absolutely incapable* of assuming the heavy task which has been imposed upon me." And on June 22, also to his brother: "Your prayers . . . for me, *are all my strength.*"

Marshal Foch did not shift onto others his duty of prayer, however. Twice daily he got down on his knees. "I pray when it is cold, and above all when things get hot." Each day he said his rosary, and each day he invoked the Holy Spirit and recited the *Veni Sancte Spiritus.* In the most tragic hours he begged for guidance from above.

On December 10, 1914 he said to his brother: "During great events we are the instruments of Providence. How else have I been able to make the decisions which alone could carry us to victory. . . . I cannot explain it otherwise. Continue then to pray; pray to the Blessed Virgin for us, and we shall arrive!"

This was also the Monseigneur's message to the young soldiers in the crises and anxieties of today: *"Pray*—never stop praying and hoping and believing; and we shall arrive, no matter what the obstacles."

And they follow his counsel—crowds of them at the Grotto and in the Sanctuaries, all day. On Sunday, from early dawn, they go the Way of the Cross by groups, each group preceded by a great wooden cross carried by two soldiers.

"A service by command?" asked one of the foreign visitors.

"No, monsieur," came the immediate reply, "a free and voluntary service. We have come here on pilgrimage because we ourselves wanted to come, and in complete freedom to act according to our religious convictions!"

The High Mass finds them packed into the Square in front of the Rosary Church—in the first row the sick and wounded, and behind them the great assembly; calm and profoundly attentive. At the Procession in the afternoon, those thousands of young men are on their knees, ardently praying for their sick. At the Torchlight in the evening, they march through the Domaine for hours, singing the *"Ave Maria"* and then the Credo. Unforgettable spectacle for those who witnessed it: all that wonderful youth, proclaiming strong and clear, its Christian faith.

I have told you—a little—of some of the big Pilgrimages. Every one of them might well have been concluded with the words with which Monseigneur Théas closed the 1936 Pilgrimage of the War Veterans:

> Do you know what I was thinking of, just now when we went up and down these paths in this great Procession? I was thinking of that little peasant of our Pyrenees, that little shepherdess without beauty, without credit, without a complicated theology, without human influence, without eloquence—who, on her knees seventy-eight years ago, a few steps from here, received from The Lady, to give them to us, the commands which have made Lourdes.
>
> My friends, if Bernadette had not knelt with her rosary before the Grotto seventy-eight years ago, *you* would not be here. And if she was capable, this poor weak child, with that one arm to mobilize the world; if she was capable of bringing here the princes of the Church, Bishops,

priests, immense crowds, Papal Legates; capable of bringing upon Lourdes innumerable benedictions such as we have just received—she who had only one secret—can we, today, do better than to follow her?

She gave us that secret; she herself said it when her nurse reproached her for not knowing her catechism.

"Eh, yes," she said, "I don't know much, but I know how to say my rosary and to love God with all my heart."

Can we, today, find a better armor?

❧ PART THREE ❧

Recent Cures:
Causes and Conclusions

In contrast with the highly dramatic scenes of the early days when a cure took place, procedure today is much quieter—more conservative and more scientific.

The cured patient comes directly to the Medical Bureau and is examined, unknown to the crowds. If his cure appears to be genuine, the long investigations into the case are set in motion. Today, with all the rigorous medical inquiries and Church procedure, it takes several years before a cure can be definitely and officially declared.

For this reason a person cured as a child may be in his teens before his case is proclaimed as a recognized official cure. Two of the cases recorded (Pascal and Leydet) were very young when their cure took place, but are now fourteen and nineteen years old respectively.

The war years shut Lourdes off from the usual pilgrimages, so that between 1939 and 1946 no cures were recorded, though some occurred and were investigated later. Between the years 1946 and 1954 a number of remarkable cures have taken place. Some of the most notable were interviewed by me—at Lourdes, or in their own homes—and are described in the following pages.

≥ 21 ≤

Three Canonical Cures

Seven o'clock on a crisp autumn evening. . . . The big gates of the Sept Douleurs Hospital are closing for the night. The last stretcher cases have been carried in, the last of the little carriages put away till morning. Nurses going off duty come hurrying out to meet their friends. Brancardiers take off their leather harness, rub their tired shoulders, joke with their pals.

I wait—near the door. Indeed, I have something to wait for. Here she comes, swinging along in her nurse's uniform, a slim girl with big dark eyes and a big smile: Jeanne Fretel, one of the most famous of recent Lourdes cures.*

She has been on duty since six o'clock this morning. Her ward is four flights up. She "does the stairs" each time her patients need something from the kitchen or the office. She has washed, fed, and dressed some twenty to thirty patients—given injections, done dressings all day long; got them ready for the baths, prayed with them, soothed them, encouraged them. She has been interrupted many times by visitors—families of the sick who wanted to see her, to touch her. Yet here she is, fresh and smiling and unfatigued.

Who would think, as she sits opposite me in the hotel restaurant a few minutes later, laughing and chatting over a good meal, that five

---

* *Jeanne Fretel, tuberculous peritonitis, cured at Lourdes, October 8, 1948.*

years ago today this girl herself was carried from the hospital to the Grotto in a dying condition—unconscious, given up. "I didn't even know I was in Lourdes," she said. "I was so far gone, I didn't know anything—till suddenly It Happened."

Jeanne Fretel had never in her life been well. In 1939, her illness became acute. Diagnosis: tuberculous peritonitis with additional meningeal symptoms. She had thirteen operations. Her case history—one of the most complete of all Lourdes cures—contains eighteen pages of fever charts, eighty pages of detailed hospital reports, laboratory analyses, X-ray records, etc.

Jeanne was born May 27, 1914, in the town of Sougeal, near Rennes. She came of simple people. She had her way to make. She was waitress, practical nurse, mother's helper. From childhood her health was precarious. In January, 1938, when she was twenty-four, she was operated on for appendicitis at the Hotel Dieu Hospital in Rennes. This was the beginning of a long series of operations and sufferings.

The abdomen gradually increased in size, became hard and thick, and intensely painful. Surgeons at the Hotel Dieu diagnosed her illness as tuberculous peritonitis, and performed a laparotomy. This brought no improvement; indeed she became worse.

The year 1946 she spent in various sanitoriums, going through more operations. After all this surgery she was extremely tired and weak. She grew very thin. On December 3, 1946, she came back to the Hotel Dieu, as she said, "to die there."

She had not left her bed for one year and was unable to get up. Her temperature was usually around 103-104 degrees. To calm her sufferings, she was given frequent morphine injections. Some time before, she had been granted a pension as an "incurable."

From August, 1948, to October, 1948, (records Dr. Pellé of Hotel Dieu Hospital) the patient became more and more exhausted. She could take only small quantities of liquid. Signs of meningitis appeared. The abdomen was very swollen and painful. Pus flowed abundantly in the stools, also in the vomit, accompanied by black blood. All hope seemed lost.

For the third time in five years, on September 20, 1948, the patient received the Last Rites. It was in full development of tuberculous peritonitis with meningeal symptoms that she departed for Lourdes on October 4, 1948, with the Rosary Pilgrimage. She was completely unconscious when put aboard the train at Rennes. Dr. Hylli of Landisviau, who helped her during the journey, gave her two injections of morphine.

Arriving at Lourdes Tuesday, the fifth of October, she was taken next day to Mass at the Grotto and to the baths; but no improvement could be noticed. On Friday morning, October 8, she was carried, dying, to the Mass for the Sick at the Altar of St. Bernadette. The priest hesitated to give her communion because of her constant vomiting and extreme weakness. But her stretcher-bearer insisted, and he gave her a bit of the consecrated wafer.

"It was then," said Jeanne Fretel later, "that suddenly I felt well and I became aware that I was at Lourdes. They asked me how I felt. I replied that I felt very well. My abdomen was still hard and swollen but I was not suffering at all. They gave me a cup of *café au lait* which I drank gratefully, and which I kept down.

"After Mass, they took me to the Grotto on my stretcher. Arrived there, at the end of some minutes, I had a sensation as if someone took me under the arms to help me sit down. I found myself in a sitting position. I looked around to see who had helped me, but could see no one. As soon as I was seated I had the feeling that the same hands that had helped me to sit down now took my hands to put them on my abdomen. I asked myself what could be happening to me—was I cured, or was I just coming out of a dream? I perceived that my abdomen had become normal. And then I was seized with an extraordinary hunger."

Taken back to the Hospital on her stretcher, she told the Almoner of her ward that she felt very well and no longer had a swollen abdomen. He, too, noticed the change that had taken place. She asked for something to eat. Dr. Gurgan of St. Meen-le-Grand, after examining her, gave the authorization. Food was brought and she ate with very good appetite: veal with purée, and three pieces of bread. She had not enjoyed such a meal in ten years.

"When I had eaten it all, I still was hungry and asked for more. They brought me as much again, and still I wanted more. Then, for dessert, they gave a dish of rice pudding. I felt fine!"

In the afternoon she got up without help, dressed herself, and went to the piscine. . . . "I had not walked for three years, and I walked as well as I walk today. Having arrived at the piscine, I took a bath stand-ing up and with no fatigue." That evening she dined with appetite and at night awoke once, at eleven o'clock only to complain of being hun-gry. After she had eaten, she went to sleep again.

The next day, Saturday, October 9, she was taken on a stretcher to the Medical Bureau where she was examined by five doctors—one of them Dr. Guyon of Nantes. He, not knowing she had walked the day before, said: "Well, if you are cured as you say, get up! Try to walk, and we shall see!"

"They wanted to help me to get up," (Jeanne's story continues) "but I refused all help and began to walk. The doctor, seeing how thin I was—I hardly had legs at all!—came towards me, fearing I might fall; but I held firm. The doctor went quickly to the scales, wanting to weigh me. Even though he went fast, I followed him just as fast, and was weighed: 44 kg. (96 pounds). I was told to return next year."

The journey home was accomplished without fatigue. . . . "On the way home in the train, I was on my feet a long time, tending other patients. The nurse wanted to give me morphine, to calm me. I refused, and was able to rest very well whenever I wanted. At home, I took up my work straightaway. And since my cure at Lourdes I have remained always just as well as I am now. I have never taken even an aspirin since then."

Mlle. Fretel's story is confirmed by the testimony of the numerous physicians who examined her, at Lourdes at the Medical Bureau and at Rennes after her return. The verbatim report of her first examination at the Bureau confirms all the details above cited, and adds: "The abdomi-nal perimeter which before the cure was 1 meter (39 inches) now is 0.m 78 (32 inches). She walked for the first time since October 17, 1945. The abdomen has become flat and supple, not painful to palpa-tion. Everything is perfectly normal except for muscular atrophy of the legs—very natural after such a long period of inactivity."

Her own physician, Dr. Pellé, who had treated her for so long, saw her on the day of her homecoming and at regular intervals thereafter. He declared in his certificate to the Medical Bureau:

> The patient is completely cured, having no longer any
> of the pathological symptoms which she presented. We
> have followed her case regularly and have noted the con-
> tinued improvement of her general state of health. Her

weight, which was 44 kg. (96 pounds), has gone up to 58 kg. (128 pounds). During the first week she gained 1-1/3 pounds each day. Her temperature is normal. Appetite and sleep are very good. From the very next day (of her return) Jeanne Fretel was able to undertake a very active life, which continues without any pathological incident. She has never felt any pain. Every day she gets up at five-thirty, goes to bed at eleven at night. She has the most tiring work in the whole house.

On October 23, 1948, an X-ray was taken at the Hospital Center of Rennes, Dr. Barbot reporting:

No organic lesions discoverable by X-ray study of the intestinal tract. The spasticity observed in preceding examinations and which seemed intense is now normal. The right and transverse colons take the barium washing very well and evacuate slowly.

On October 5, 1949—one year after her cure—Mlle. Fretel came before the doctors of the Medical Bureau for a second examination. Naturally this cure had caused a great stir. Twenty-two doctors were on hand, among them several who had examined her the year before. The examination went on for two hours. At the end the doctors declared their conviction that it was a genuine cure, that "the disease had been abruptly arrested in its course when there was no apparent tendency toward improvement. All morbid symptoms have disappeared. No medical explanation of this cure can be given. It is outside natural law." There follow the signatures of all the physicians.

The Medical Commission at Paris, after studying these various documents, reported (March 12, 1950):

The impressive history of this illness, the importance of the dossier which includes thirty temperature charts (eighteen before the cure, twelve after), the calibre of the doctors who examined the patient, the meticulous details of the daily records during the period from April to October, 1948, the period just before the cure, compels our

long and earnest attention, and leads us to conclude that
this is an inexplicable cure.*

A Canonical Commission confirmed these findings, and on November 20, 1950, Cardinal Roques, Archbishop of Rennes, proclaimed the case of Jeanne Fretel a Miraculous Cure.

An interesting sidelight on this case reveals that the physician in charge, Dr. Pellé, was an agnostic and unbeliever—"hostile" to religion, the Medical Bureau report says. However, it was his precise records and certificates, before and after the cure, that established it as a miraculous case in the eyes of doctors and clergy.

I saw Jeanne Fretel on the evening of October 8, 1953; five years, to the day, after her cure. She comes each year as a nurse with the Rosary Pilgrimage: an attractive, slender young woman, animated, full of life. Sitting opposite me in the hotel after a long day's work at the hospital, she filled in the details of her story.

She had thirteen operations—three on the mouth ("there were great holes in my jaw"), several on the feet, the others on the abdomen. After she became so terribly ill, she was fed with serum only, and was given injections of morphine, four or five every twenty-four hours. Friends offered her the pilgrimage trip to Lourdes, and saw that she got on the train. "But being so far gone, I was not conscious of my departure or the trip or anything." The Dominican Fathers were very good to her. She was in a coma till that Friday morning when, brought to the altar of St. Bernadette in a dying condition, she came away cured.

When she got back home and reported to the hospital, one of the young doctors went running to Dr. Pellé.

"Jeanne Fretel," he gasped. "It is Jeanne Fretel!"

"Poor girl—she is dead?" asked Pellé.

"Come and see!"

When Dr. Pellé saw her he was speechless. He left the room, overcome. Back in a few minutes, he looked at her, the tears running down his cheeks. He spoke to the Sister who was there with them, then gave Jeanne the most rigorous examination. He could hardly believe his own findings, after having seen her so desperately ill for so long. "I

---

* The writer possesses a complete photostat file of the medical record of Jeanne Fretel, with temperature charts, daily hospital records, laboratory analyses, X-ray reports, etc. Eighty pages in all.

have been for Dr. Pellé something terrible—a blow to his scientific self-respect!"

Even now she is incredible to him. Each time she comes to see him, he says: "So! You are feeling sick, *hein?* You aren't feeling so good?"

"But certainly, I am feeling fine! I'm always fine—couldn't be better."

He seems almost disappointed. But it was thanks to his fine records and thorough information on the case that Jeanne was declared a *miraculée.* He rendered her a tremendous service. He had served her devotedly all through her illness, and has always had a great affection for her.

Jeanne is in perfect health now. She works as a practical nurse. It is confining work, and the hours are very long; but this doesn't bother her at all.

At Lourdes, at the Hospital of the Sept Douleurs, she feeds the sick, changes their dressings, gives them all the regular nursing care. The trip from Rennes—6 P.M. to 10 A.M.—is very hard on the sick. Jeanne gives injections all night long, thinking of the time when *she* did that long and painful journey on a stretcher.

The life of a *miraculée* isn't easy, she says. Everyone wants to see you. It's a perpetual assault—on the street, at prayers in church, in the train, everywhere. "Last year I wore a blue sweater for the Pilgrimage. Everyone would point me out. 'You will know her, she's the one with the blue sweater.' So this year I wore a black one. But it's just the same."

Six persons came up and spoke to her during the brief time that I was with her, even at table in the hotel. "I can't refuse them," she said. "I can't refuse *anything,* after what has been done for me."

Her correspondence is tremendous. Letters come from all over the world—from doctors, from sick people, from unbelievers wanting to be reassured. If she sends typewritten replies, people are not satisfied. The letters must be in her own hand. She works far into the night, often writing those letters after her regular day's work is done. She gets invitations to lecture—to go to the ends of the earth—to exhibit herself. Once she had to take part in a film—a church film. "Never again!" She is going to stay at Rennes and do her work—visit the sick, give them consolation when she can.

An attractive, intelligent woman—lots of personality; sensitive insight, keen appreciation of life's values, both spiritual and human. Her great desire: to give her entire life in service to other sick people in gratitude of what has been done for her. "One asks oneself again and again: why was *I* chosen? Many others deserve it far more."

Many people have become believers because of her cure. The Cardinal often sends for her—the doctors too—to talk with skeptics, and sometimes to the dying.

"Were you very scared when you had to go before the Cardinal and the Canonical Commission—and before all those doctors at the Bureau?"

"Terribly!" she nodded vigorously. "All those eyes—and questions fired from all sides. Very confusing." She remembered having given a couple of inaccurate dates—she was so mixed up at the time— referring to the year 1937 instead of 1938. They had pulled her up sharp.

"It sounds more like a criminal investigation than that of a *miraculée,*" I suggested.

"Very severe," said Jeanne.

But then, after all the examinations, inquiries, probings, and recapitulations, finally came the great moment: the solemn *Te Deum* Mass in Rennes Cathedral that Sunday, following the pronouncement by the Canonical Commission and the Archbishop that Jeanne Fretel was a Miraculous Lourdes Cure.

A long road—for the girl who had been carried on a stretcher dying and unconscious to the Grotto at Lourdes—now the radiant creature walking up the aisle in the Cathedral between Bishops and Archbishops, and crowds of lifelong friends to sing "My soul doth magnify the Lord!"

Jeanne Fretel's whole life is a Magnificat.

Two of the most striking "Before and After" pictures at the Medical Bureau are those of Mlle. Gabrielle Clauzel.* The note under the pictures states that this lady comes from Oran, Algeria, that she was instantly cured of a long and almost fatal illness: spondylitis, or inflammation of the spinal vertebrae, with complications involving various organs.

I had the good luck to be at the Medical Bureau and to have a long talk with Mlle. Clauzel when she came for her yearly examination and check-up. Seven doctors were present. Two had known the patient for a

* *Gabrielle Clauzel, rheumatic spondylitis, cured August 15, 1943.*

long time. One, Dr. Zimmerman, was an actual eye-witness at the time of her cure. These doctors and the Oranian parish priest, Father Capparos, told the story.

Dr. Vincent, pilgrimage physician and old friend of the Clauzel family, was the first to speak: "I have known Mlle. Clauzel for many years. Her father, one of the great merchants and industrialists of North Africa, founded the Friends of Notre Dame de Lourdes Society in Oran, and was its first President. Mlle. Clauzel later became President and for years did all the organizing and management of the Oranian pilgrimages. She was a tireless worker—absolutely devoted. Imagine, then, everybody's concern when Mlle. Clauzel became ill—and gravely ill at that. Dr. Maurin was called, and remained her attending physician.

"She was stricken first with articular rheumatism in her left wrist and with great pain along the spinal column. In March, 1938, after much pain on the lower right side, she had an appendicitis operation. Following this, the pain grew more severe, which seemed to indicate that, like all her other troubles, it came from the spinal condition.

"Recovery was slow after the operation. She had much difficulty in walking. To stand upright was painful; the body was bent forward; even a sitting position was extremely tiring. She could not hold her neck straight; her head would always fall forward."

As Mademoiselle Clauzel said, "I felt as though I were crawling, rather than walking. Then in January (1939), I had another acute attack, and could not stand up at all."

The pain now spread over the whole spinal column. After an X-ray on March 1, 1939, Dr. Maurin diagnosed the case as vertabral rheumatism. Dr. Porot of Algiers, called in consultation, agreed. The usual treatment for rheumatic disease was followed: regular doses of salicylate through the mouth and intravenous injections of potassium iodide.

The fine summer weather seemed to bring a slight improvement. To her great joy Mlle. Clauzel was able to go with the Pilgrimage to Lourdes, in August as usual—but this time she had to take part in the various ceremonies from her little carriage, for she could not stand or move by herself. War was declared while she was still in France. When she finally reached home, she seemed for a while somewhat better. But in January, 1940, she had a relapse; and again in November, 1940, she was stricken with a new attack more violent than ever before.

"Mlle. Clauzel then went to bed—where she remained," said Dr. Vincent. "The illness took on a very serious aspect. The patient could not raise herself in bed. The least movement caused terrible suffering.

The principal organs became involved—first the kidneys, then the liver and intestines. Her heart was also seriously affected. She had continual severe headaches and her eyes could hardly bear the light of day.

"Nevertheless, during intervals of calm, she continued to interest herself in the Society of the Friends of Notre Dame de Lourdes. Strangely enough, she never thought of asking for her cure. People had asked for it for her, but she herself just didn't think about it."

"I knew very well," put in Mlle. Clauzel, "that Our Lady of Lourdes could do anything, but so many other things seemed to me more necessary than my cure, I asked for everything else but that!"

She thought she might be helped if the doctors would remove some small, pointed pieces of bone—"parrots' beaks," they called them (the medical term is osteophytes)—that had shown up in the X-ray picture of her spine. She begged Dr. Maurin to perform this operation. He did so, unwillingly, in October, 1941, only because he thought it might help her morale.

Benefit was nil. In June, 1943, a second extraction of parrots' beaks —again without good result. During all this time the disease was steadily growing worse. From the beginning of 1943 Mlle. Clauzel grew very thin. During June this loss of weight became frightening. The patient herself knew that now, only with great difficulty, could she climb back up again the road to health.

In August, they took her to the country, to the family home at Palissy. She suffered at this time from continual vomiting and was unable to take the least bit of food. Her heart was very bad, her pulse frighteningly rapid. Her family feared that the end was near.

She had gone to Palissy on August 6. The week that followed was a terrible one for her. She weighed, at that time, just seventy pounds. On August 11, Dr. Pamart, summoned from Sidi-bel-Abbés nearby, gave his opinion that the patient could not be saved. In the opinion of three physicians, Dr. Vincent among them, her death could be expected at any moment.

Then came the great day of August 15—the feast of the Assumption and the date when, usually, the Oran Pilgrimage was at Lourdes, also her own birthday. This being wartime, the journey was impossible, and the Oran pilgrims had to content themselves with prayers and supplications to Our Lady of Lourdes from a distance. They directed their prayers, especially that year, in behalf of Mlle. Clauzel, their beloved President and leader, who as everyone knew was at death's door.

A Novena on that day was being made to the Blessed Virgin. The

Bishop at Oran and the Abbé Capparos at Santa Cruz were to say a Mass for her. To join with their prayers—though again more for France and for Lourdes than for her own cure—Mlle. Clauzel asked to be taken to Mass at the Palissy village church.

"I thought," she said, "that this Mass would surely be my last, and that very soon I should be leaving everything."

Her family considered her going to Mass absolute madness, for one in her condition. "But, poor girl, it is probably the last thing we can ever do for her," said her sister, weeping. "Let her go." They decided to carry her to the church on a stretcher.

"It was I who helped carry the stretcher," put in young Dr. Zimmerman. "I was a young medical student in the neighborhood at that time. Her brother and I carried her from her home to the church. She weighed almost nothing. We set her down in a corner of the church where we could keep an eye on her."

Some Italian war prisoners had been allowed to come to Mass that morning. The church was full. The Mass lasted an hour and a half—a long time for one in Mlle. Clauzel's condition. "At one point," said Dr. Zimmerman, "she showed signs of agitation. We were anxious, naturally, thinking she had been tired out by the ceremony. In reality, it was the cure which she felt—without daring to believe it."

"Suddenly, in the midst of the ceremony," said Mlle. Clauzel, "I had a sense of profound well-being—not of agitation, but of a wonderful force acting within me, renewing my entire self. I knew that I was cured." She received the Communion. "I wanted to get up at once, and go to the altar, but I remained on my stretcher till the church was cleared. I didn't want to make a scene or create a disturbance of any kind while the war prisoners were there. Later, when they had left, I told my brother what had happened.

"I am cured, I tell you—cured! Help me up."

He thought it was some temporary exaltation—begged her to be prudent and let him carry her home.

"But she insisted," said Dr. Zimmerman, and he and her brother helped her from the stretcher.

"Let me go now," she said calmly. "I can walk."

"And—she walked!" said the young doctor. "She who had not set foot on the floor for three years!"

She walked to the altar and offered her thanksgiving. "It seemed to me," she said, "that I *flew*—that my feet did not touch the ground."

She went home, dressed herself, ate lunch with the family. And what a lunch! Hors d'oeuvres, ham, *pâté,* vegetables, three cutlets, and a slice of cake—she who had hardly eaten anything for months—had not even lifted her head. It had caused her the most cruel agony just to have the nurse help her into a fresh nightgown. She suffered so much that they would wash one side of her face one day, the other the next day.

Now, when they told her doctor she was cured, that she was actually walking: "Yes, but can she raise her head? I'll believe it when I see her raise her head!" Even in the days when she had been able to walk, at the beginning of her illness, she had carried her head downward because of the terrible pain it caused her to raise it.

The parish priest, Father Capparos, now took up the tale. "Never will I forget that Sunday. We had all been praying for her. There was a special Mass at Santa Cruz too, that day. I had just got back home and was sitting down to luncheon. Suddenly, a telephone call. 'Mademoiselle Clauzel is cured! Do you hear, Father? Mademoiselle Clauzel is cured!' " He couldn't believe it. But he notified the Bishop, as was his duty.

"Get a report from Dr. Maurin," said the Bishop. "See what he has to say."

They got the report—also reports from Dr. Pamart and Dr. Porot, other specialists who had been in attendance. Reports, X-rays, the pieces of bone that had been removed from the spine—all were collected, and eventually sent to Lourdes.

The cure was steadily maintained. Mlle. Clauzel gained weight—three pounds a week, until she reached 116 pounds. Her strength returned rapidly. Her energy and the way she moved about astonished her family, who had watched her dying for many months. Ten months after her cure, during a long procession of the *Fête-Dieu,* she carried the heavy banner of the Children of Mary. On August 15, 1944, one year after her cure, she herself carried a stretcher—one of those which supported a large statue of the Virgin.

"No work frightens her," said Dr. Vincent. "Every morning she helps at one of the big Oranian clinics. She has twice given her blood for urgent transfusions. No, there can be no doubt of the permanency of this cure!"

"And now to the official medical record," said Dr. Leuret, producing a thick dossier. "Mademoiselle Clauzel presented herself at the Medical Bureau of Lourdes on April 19, 1945—her first opportunity after wartime obstacles. Testimonies of several witnesses, besides her own, established the facts of the illness and the cure. A full report from

Dr. Maurin was read, describing the illness and the present excellent state of his former patient. X-rays and 'parrots' beaks' were examined, following upon a lengthy examination of the patient herself. Her spine, and all the organs that had been affected, were found to be in healthy and normal condition."

At a second examination, held December 12, 1945, further documentation from Dr. Maurin, and new X-rays of the vertebral column were studied. The twelve doctors present closed their report with the following statement: "We note the complete functional cure of Mlle. Clauzel, maintained for two years without relapse; it has produced in this one-time invalid a renewal of her being which makes her appear twenty years younger."

The Canonical Commission later appointed to study this cure called attention to the various extraordinary characteristics which placed it above and beyond the laws of nature: (1.) Absence of special medication which might explain the cure. (2.) Instantaneousness of the cure. (3.) Absence of all convalescence. Mlle. Clauzel, who on the morning of August 15 was still in a desperate condition, on the evening of that day and during the following days gave the impression of being a person in perfect health. Her diet, following her inability to tolerate food of any kind, gave proof of the perfect cure of the functional malady of the organs which at that time were seriously affected—especially the stomach and the liver.

> This, however (the Commission stated) cannot be called a mere "functional" cure. It must be emphasized that the illness from which Mlle. Clauzel suffered was *an organic illness*—rheumatic spondylitis with compression of the spinal roots, which, like all organic illness, has as a consequence functional troubles more or less serious— very serious in this case, since they brought the invalid to the edge of the grave. The cure of these functional troubles before the cure of the organic cause (vertebral deformation, osteophytes) which produced them, makes the case all the more remarkable.

The most impressive evidence, however, is still to be found in those two photographs—"Before and After." When she went to Mass that August morning, she weighed 71 pounds; at the Bureau the day I saw her, 142.

"And you have never suffered since?" asked Dr. Leuret.

"Never! My health has been perfect—never an ache or a pain since that wonderful moment ten years ago today. There was no delay—no convalescence—nothing! In that instant I was well, and have been every minute of my life since."

Since 1945, at the end of the war, Mlle. Clauzel has come to Lourdes every year. It is she who helps Father Capparos to organize the Oran Pilgrimage—nine hundred pilgrims, many sick patients, brancardiers, nurses, doctors, and priests. She begins in February to get ready for the Pilgrimage in summer: rooms, transportation, all the details. At home she fills a very demanding post in a local clinic. A happy, healthy woman—the picture of good nature and well-being. As usual, with *miraculées*—no pretense, no pride or vainglory. Simplicity, humility, naturalness.

"What did you think," I asked her, "that first minute when it happened—when you *knew* you were cured? What was the first thing that came into your mind?"

Mlle. Clauzel gave her rich, hearty laugh. "Oh, madame, you are going to be disappointed! Nothing seraphic or uplifting. I thought, So! So I have to go on working! I can't have that good rest in heaven I was hoping for!"

Mlle. Clauzel, among those who know her and see her often, has a reputation for great good sense, good judgment, solid character—the very opposite of a neurotic or hysterical temperament: Far from self-suggesting or anticipating a cure, she had gone to Mass that morning expecting only death, and that this was to be her last attendance in any church. Suddenly she gets up, goes to the altar, and walks about the rest of the day, eats and acts like a normal person.

How explain that sudden energy and suppleness of limbs? An hour before, and for many months, she was unable to stand, or to lie in any but one position. How explain eating that meal, which should have "finished" a person so long condemned to fasting? All the digestive troubles from which Mlle. Clauzel suffered, and all the pain that she had endured, disappeared at the same time and with the same suddenness. She led henceforth the life of a well and active woman.

The Catholic Church considered that the circumstances surrounding this cure left no doubt as to the cause. In an Episcopal Proclamation made at Oran, March 18, 1948, the Bishop of Oran declared:

"We judge that in view of all the circumstances this healing is miraculous and must be attributed to a special intervention of God through the intercession of Notre Dame de Lourdes." (Signed, Bertrand Lacaste, Bishop of Oran.)

Certainly no one would call Colonel Pellegrin hysterical or easily suggestible. Solid, substantial soldier, fifty-one years old, veteran of many military campaigns in Africa and Indo-China as well as World Wars I and II, he was never wounded, never sick a day in his life until this illness that struck him down.*

At home in Toulon, all of a sudden one day (December 19, 1948) he felt severe pain in his right side, under the rib cage. A few weeks later, he entered the Maritime Hospital at Toulon. The doctors at first thought he might have a bit of pleurisy; they made various punctures. No improvement—in fact, the pain grew worse. Eventually the attending physician, Dr. Pierre, operated on a red spot in the painful area, "to find out what was going on." The wound did not heal. The patient had considerable fever, and increasing discharge from the wound, which finally became purulent. Diagnosis: abscess of the liver, with chronic fistula.

Colonel Pellegrin was in bed an entire year. Never ill before, he took it hard. He suffered constantly and ran a high fever. Despite various therapies, the wound refused to heal. It had to be dressed two or three times a day. The patient lost weight, was in a very depleted state and thoroughly discouraged.

"Lying in bed—drinking slops like an old woman!" said he disgustedly.

"He had always been so strong—so healthy," said Madame Pellegrin, when they were telling me the story at Lourdes last summer— "and then, just a shadow!"

"How did you happen to go to Lourdes?" I asked him. "What gave you the idea?"

"I was always a believer. All my family were believers—practicing Christians. But it was my own idea, going to Lourdes. I must admit that it came partly from an experience with our eldest child, years ago.

"We were living in Damascus at the time. The boy was only five. He was hit by infantile paralysis of the left side—couldn't move either his arm or leg. We were told that this would probably be for life and

* *Colonel Paul Pellegrin, chronic fistula resulting from abscess of the liver, cured at Lourdes, October 3, 1950.*

would get worse instead of better. My wife begged the Sisters at Damascus to make a Novena to Notre Dame de Lourdes for the boy. On the last day of the Novena the child moved his arm. You may imagine our delight. Gradually the use of both arm and leg returned. While the condition is not absolutely perfect, you would have to know the young man very well and look at him very closely to discover any imperfection.

"So," continued the Colonel, "when my own illness persisted in such a discouraging fashion, and remembering what had happened with the boy, I thought: well, I will go to Lourdes and pray for my cure. Maybe Our Lady will take pity on me.

"We arrived at Lourdes on the second of October. The first day, nothing happened. On the third of October I went to the piscine for my second bath. Then something extraordinary occurred."

His wound was still being dressed several times a day and was discharging abundantly. When he got back to the hotel after this second bath in Lourdes water, he told his wife: "You had better put a new dressing on the wound—they took everything off at the piscine."

He took off his coat and shirt. His wife came with the bandages. Then, when she saw the wound, she cried, "But it's *closed!* Paul! You've been *cured!*"

"I am not ashamed to tell you, madame, we threw our arms around each other and wept!"

"He had been ill for so long," his wife put in. "If you had seen him when he came to Lourdes—so thin and weak! He weighed only a hundred pounds. Now he weighs one hundred and forty."

They had made no great fuss about the matter—no sensational disclosures. They went home quietly. There, the Colonel showed himself to his own Dr. Pierre. The doctor gave a long whistle of astonishment when he saw the wound.

"Well!" he said. "Our Lady of Lourdes did better by you than your doctors did. You don't need dressings any more."

He'd been ill for so long, at first he couldn't believe it. When the skin grew over the wound and formed a permanent scar, he saw that it was truly a genuine cure.

He presented himself at the Medical Bureau (October, 1951) after the regulation interval of a year had gone by, bringing his medical reports—X-rays, and certificates from his doctors and from the hospitals and laboratories that had served him: reports from Dr. Paul Berny, Dr. Roger Bureau, and Dr. Charles Arnoux, in addition to those by Dr.

Pierre; thirty pages of hospital charts, the fever charts especially being impressive. High fever had been one of his greatest difficulties.

The Medical Bureau report on the case reads:

> Pellegrin, Paul. Chronic fistula since 1949. Cured October 3, 1950. Seen first at Bureau October 10, 1951. At the time of his cure, the patient had been going three times a week to the hospital for dressings, the flow of pus being abundant and resisting all therapies. In October, 1950, he departed for Lourdes, with his fistula continuing very active.
>
> The patient, after his second bath at the piscine, observed the complete disappearance of the fistula which had given a purulent discharge sufficiently abundant to necessitate dressings two and sometimes three a day. He did not at first feel sure of a cure. But the nature of the scar and the continued absence of drainage led him to present himself at the Medical Bureau.

The physicians then present examined the scar, which was about three inches long, supple to the touch, and entirely painless, and noted that for one year it had remained healed. The patient was in excellent health. He was requested to return for further examination the following year. At the second inquiry (October 8, 1952) the twenty-nine doctors present considered that "while the cause of this fistula and the abscess related to it are unprecise, the practically instantaneous closing of a suppurating fistula which had lasted eighteen months, makes the case deserving of being retained as an extraordinary occurrence."

The Medical Commission, after a full investigation, confirmed the findings, and declared itself "of opinion that the case should be submitted to Ecclesiastical authority." On December 7, 1953, the Archbishop of Toulon proclaimed it a Miraculous Cure.

Colonel Pellegrin comes to Lourdes every year; serves as one of the *commissionaires* from Toulon, who keep order, direct the crowds, assist the brancardiers in policing the Processions, and help bathe people at the piscine.

"Naturally everyone who has been cured wants to be of some service to Lourdes," says the Colonel.

I used to see him running up and down the Esplanade carrying chairs and benches, helping with the sick, doing all sorts of odd jobs.

One would never know he was top brass, with a chestful of decorations. A solid, well-set-up, splendid specimen of a man—the picture of health; fresh-faced, ruddy, quiet, friendly. Modest, like all the Cures. He has never known a day's illness since his miracle.

22

Cures of Children

Particularly appealing are the cures of children, and particularly interesting, since many of them are too young to be influenced either by
religious faith or by suggestion—the favorite explanation by skeptics
regarding Lourdes cures. A long list of children's cures is found in
Lourdes records. One of the best known in recent years is that of Gerard Baillie.*

Gerard, a boy of eight, lived at the Institute for Blind Children at
Arras, in the north of France. He had not had the use of his eyes since
the age of two, and recognized people only by their voices. It was pitiful
to see him, an energetic, otherwise normal child, groping his way about
like a hesitating little old man, staring at his parents and friends with
blank unseeing eyes.

He had lost his sight after an operation; a degeneration of the inner
tunics of the eye had progressed until the optic nerves in both eyes were
completely atrophied. This, as every doctor knows, means blindness.

His parents brought him to the institution at Arras with the following certificate from Dr. Biziaut, an oculist of Dunkerque: "Double optic atrophy. Blindness—*incurable.*" (Underlined by Dr. Biziaut.)

Another physician, Dr. Viton of Arras, examined the boy and declared on January 26, 1945: "I, the undersigned, certify that I have
today examined Gerard Baille, aged seven and a half years. He is af-

* *Gerard Baillie, chorioretinitis (bilateral) and double optic atrophy—an "incurable" disease
—cured at Lourdes, September 27, 1947.*

flicted with bilateral chorioretinitis, double optic atrophy; blindness—incurable."

For five years Gerard had crept about among the other sightless children at the Arras Institute—feeling his way, fumbling, hesitating, often falling. His mother was heartbroken. She prayed earnestly and constantly that he "might be restored to a normal life." We must be careful what we pray for. Sometimes we are taken precisely at our word.

In September, 1947, a month after Dr. Biziaut had again pronounced the case incurable, his mother brought Gerard to Lourdes, as a member of their diocesan pilgrimage. Nothing happened at the first bath, or at the Procession. But the day after their arrival, while they were walking down the path of the Way of the Cross, all at once the child began to pick up pieces of wood from the ground and to offer them to his mother. Looking up into her face, he cried delightedly, "Oh mamma, how beautiful you are!"

The mother, completely overcome, rushed him back to the hostel. The next day, after his second bath at the piscine, she noticed that he really did see better. He remarked upon the curtains at the baths which, the day before, he had not seen at all.

That same day, September 27, she took him to be examined at the Medical Bureau. The seven doctors present recorded the case as follows:

> The child has an external strabismus (squint) in the left eye. He sees two fingers at a distance of one meter (slightly over a yard), does not see at two meters. He shows a slight vertical nystagmus (oscillation of the eyeballs) more accentuated when tired. He reacts weakly to light. In walking around the room he guided himself by the edge of the table and ran against the chairs, which indicates a considerable limitation in the visual field. The next day, September 28, 1947, seen at the Hospital of the Sept Douleurs, he ran around the room without bumping into the beds, went into the hallway, ran to the elevator, could tell whether it was going up or coming down, and saw the elevator button. He recognized different colors and several objects near at hand.

They took him to an oculist at Tarbes—Dr. Camps, graduate of the National School of Ophthalmology of the Quinze-Vingts, Paris. He examined the boy at length, and declared:

"This child has a bilateral chorioretinitis, with double optic atrophy. He cannot—or should not—see." Yet he saw—not very well, it is true; nevertheless he saw.

Coming back in the car on the road to Lourdes, he saw the mountains with a fresh snowfall on the peaks, and described their beauty. He saw other cars along the road, described their different stylings, and kept urging, "Let's pass them!"

The Bureau appointed two physicians in the boy's neighborhood—Drs. Domesant of Dunkerque and Dhellmes of Lille—to continue the study of the case and to make a report at the end of a year.

Naturally Gerard left the Institute for Blind Children, and began attending a boy's school at Dunkerque, where he proceeded to make an excellent record. He went to school alone, crossing several big highways at the busiest hours of the day. The tremendous changes that had come about for him can best be shown by two letters.

On September 4, 1948, Dr. Leuret, President of the Medical Bureau of Lourdes, wrote to the Directress of the Institute for Blind Children at Arras, asking various questions regarding Gerard's vision before and after his coming to Lourdes:

> In particular, could he get about alone? Could he see an object at some distance away? What was the exact diagnosis for which he was being treated at your institute? During the two and a half years that he spent there was he examined by ophthalmologists—by whom and how many times? When he came back from Lourdes did you find a change in his vision? Did you make any tests to determine whether he could see clearly? Who made the decision that he should leave the Institute?

The reply from Sister Agnes, Directress of the Institute—a very fine letter—is given here only in part:

> We didn't see Gerard immediately before his departure for Lourdes in September, 1947, because he was on vacation with his family. But when he left us in July he was

what he had always been during his stay here: a blind person.

He was absolutely incapable of going about alone. When he came and went, indoors, he bumped into obstacles. No, he was not capable of seeing an object at any distance. He could not take a paper bag of candy offered to him, because he did not *see* it. (And if a child could see anything, he could certainly see candy!) On one occasion a whole roomful of deaf children was moved to compassion when he tried to find his shoes under his bed—his hesitation, his searching with both hands, his big eyes raised and fixed in the *opposite* direction.

When he returned from Lourdes, however, there could be no doubt in our minds: Gerard was no longer the little blind boy who had left us in July. He had regained his sight. He ran about the house freely, from one room to another, remarking on the dimensions of the apartment, making a world of discoveries, admiring the beauty of the little girls' courtyard which he had crossed so many times before without seeing anything.

We put him through a number of tests: to recognize objects by vision alone, without touching them: spectacles, thimble, scissors, penknife, ribbons, watch (of which we changed the hands at his direction); to locate a person in an unfamiliar room, moving from one area to another; to enumerate what he saw from a window, etc.

There is also the definite fact that the child is able to follow a normal school curriculum. This certainly would have been quite impossible last July.

She stated further that she hadn't the diagnosis of the ailment for which the boy was sent to the Institute; that during his stay there he was seen by no ophthalmologists at the Institute. His parents took him to Dr. Biziaut at Dunkerque, she said, referring to Dr. Biziaut's certificate which she enclosed with her reply.

In a later account, Sister Agnes related more fully the story of Gerard's visit to the Institute after his return from Lourdes:

Gerard arrived with his mother. When I came into the parlor he ran and threw his arms around my neck without a moment's hesitation, and kissed me. Then he looked at me—at my white headdress which he had never seen, touched the tip of my nose with an affectionate little gesture, then hugged me again.

To express in words anything so wonderful as the recovery of sight is impossible for him—being so young in years and younger still in experience. He expresses it as best he can. When, one by one, the Sisters come in, he gives their names as they greet him. He knew them all by their voices, though he had never seen them. "Ah," he said to one of them, "you have spectacles. I never knew you wore spectacles!"

His comrades gather round him. He wanted to embrace them all. Some of them blushed for joy, others smiled, some wept. Nothing so touching as those tears in those unseeing eyes.

So many questions. "So you really *see*, Gerard? What is it like—to see?" Evidently it is too difficult for him to put into words. This meeting of the children with their little "miraculous" friend is filled with emotion, both for them and for the onlookers.

A letter from another teacher, one year after his cure, states: "I have had the pleasure of having Gerard Baillie among my pupils during this entire school year of 1948–49. He is a good scholar and a good friend, and attends his classes regularly."

These letters and accounts from personal friends, written in their own hand, seem to me almost as important as the medical documents.

On July 14, 1948, Gerard was examined for the second time at the Medical Bureau. Dr. Smith, an oculist of Glasgow, made the examination. He repeated the diagnosis of Dr. Camps: "This child has chorioretinitis with double optic atrophy. He ought not to see." But, like Madame Biré, he saw.

The doctors, in their record of the second examination, noted:

The boy keeps up with his classes normally. He goes everywhere by himself. He goes unaccompanied from his home to the school—though this involves half an hour's walk and he has to cross four big avenues where numerous cars pass. It is very evident that Gerard sees. At a distance, and without touching them, he can name various objects placed on a desk: a watch, a fountain pen, a bell, a pencil, a crucifix, etc. He copied letters on a white page, he did small sums in arithmetic, he could see the hands of a watch and the Red Cross insignia of the Lourdes physicians. He could tell colors.

The ophthalmological examination shows that pupillary reactions to light are normal. He counts fingers twenty-five centimeters (about eight feet) away. The left eye is crossed. The back of the eye shows the papillae atrophied at both left and right, though incompletely. (Whereas in 1947 atrophy was complete.) Degeneration of the retina and of the choroid (middle membrane), with a little pigmentary degeneration.

Dr. Leuret and seven other physicians signed the statement. The case was sent on to the Medical Commission which reported on it at its session in Paris on April 1, 1949: "The case of a child afflicted with blindness, with choroiditis, atrophy and discoloration of the papillae. He was cured along the Chemin du Croix in 1947. The examination shows that this child, who was completely blind, now possesses sufficient vision, with re-colored papillae."

A year later, the Medical Commission pronounced the cure "inexplicable under natural law" and voted unanimously to recommend its being referred to a Canonical Commission.

The Canonical Commission refused to consider it a miracle because it was not instantaneous and because vision was still not perfect, though sufficient for the boy to lead a normal life. (Which was what his mother had prayed for—*and all she had asked.*)

However, the doctors of the Medical Bureau and of the Medical Commission are firmly of the opinion that the cure of Gerard Baillie is "beyond the laws of nature" and may therefore rationally be considered to have taken place under supernatural influence.

"His infirmity," they declared, "was technically incurable. Yet at Lourdes, in a few hours, and with no treatment whatsoever, *he saw.*" One doctor testified that in his entire experience as an eye specialist he had never known of a case like it: the recovery of vision and recoloring of the papillae following two years' atrophy of the optic nerve.

The cure has been in effect now for six years, and Gerard comes to Lourdes every year with his North-of-France Pilgrimage. He is now a nice-looking boy of fifteen, wears glasses—his vision is 6—10—which he says is a whole lot better than being blind. According to him and his mother, Our Lady of Lourdes certainly did perform a miracle.

Still more dramatic was the cure of Francis Pascal,* whom I recently visited at his own home.

Francis lives at Beaucaire, close to Avignon and the famous Palace of the Popes. He was born October 3, 1934, and was a happy, normal child until December, 1937, when he became seriously ill.

He was seized with a high fever. Water streamed from his eyes, which became acutely sensitive to light. A general stiffness set in throughout his body, and he was subject to constant vomiting. Signs of meningitis increased. His temperature went up to 104 degrees.

Finally the supreme blow: absolute blindness and complete paralysis of both arms and legs.

The child's parents nearly went out of their minds. They were poor people, small winegrowers in their region—but they did everything they could for him. They had him examined by five doctors—Dr. Darde of Beaucaire, Julian of Tarascon, Barre of Avignon, Dufoix fils of Nîmes, Polge, an oculist at Arles (all nearby cities). He was under Dr. Darde's constant care. In March, 1938, a lumbar puncture was made in the spine, and an analysis of the spinal fluid at the laboratory of Dr. Lesbros in Avignon confirmed the diagnosis of meningitis.

In May, Dr. Polge wrote: "Following upon a meningitis the child Pascal was brought to me. He is paralyzed and no longer sees. The ophthalmological examination on the third of May shows: the pupils react very little to the light; a light passed before the eyes was never followed, nor any other object presented. At the back of the eyes, the veins congested and there is a certain degree of optic pallor. Prognosis: 'Very reserved.' "

The doctors in charge saw the child regularly until June, 1938. By this time the paralysis of the arms and legs was complete; sight nil.

In June, Dr. Darde considered the case hopeless, and stopped all treatment. The parents were desperate. Every possible therapy had been tried. As a last hope, they decided to take Francis to Lourdes, with

* *Francis Pascal, paralysis and complete blindness following upon infectious meningitis, cured at Lourdes, August 31, 1938.*

the Pilgrimage of Aix-en-Provence. In the train, the blind child, completely helpless in his little carriage, drew the sympathy of everyone.

To get him admitted to the pilgrimage, Dr. Darde, on July 19, made out the following certificate: "I, the undersigned, declare that Francis Pascal, aged four years, has been under my care for residuals of meningitis—with complete paralysis of the lower limbs. The lesions noted above have not changed during four months, and appear not to have been affected in any way by treatment." (Signed, Dr. Darde.)

Dr. Roman added to this report: "As physician on the Pilgrimage train, I can confirm the certificate of my confrere of Beaucaire. The child traveled in a recumbent position. He saw neither light nor objects presented to him."

The Pilgrimage of Aix arrived at Lourdes on August 23. Francis was utterly helpless at the time. At the Grotto, his mother prayed the Blessed Virgin to "heal him or let him die!" She could not bear to have him go on living in his present condition.

She carried him to the piscine. He was plunged into the water. The child cried out. His mother thought he had been seized with a convulsion. She kept hoping and praying.

"I had faith, madame—I had faith!"

On August 26, he was brought again to the bath. The water had no apparent effect. But a few minutes later something extraordinary happened. The mother was carrying him across the Esplanade, back to the Hospital. Suddenly the child spoke.

"Mama, Mama—look! The lady wheeling the little carriage— it's a tricycle. Mama, look—isn't it pretty?" He moved a finger, pointing toward a nurse who was wheeling a tricycle across the Square.

His mother raced with him back to the Hospital, half fainting with excitement. He *saw!* He moved his finger!

From this moment his sight came back—he became interested in objects around him. Before he left Lourdes, he began to move the arms and legs hitherto paralyzed. After his return to Beaucaire he began to walk—"teetering a bit at first," his mother said, "but after a little, quite normally."

On August 28, Dr. Darde saw the boy again, to his utter amazement, *walking*. The doctor later wrote the following report to the Medical Bureau:

> I, the undersigned, declare that I have had under my
> care, from December 18, 1937, to June 14, 1938, the

young Francis Pascal, aged four years. This child, who was seen in consultation with Drs. Julian of Tarascon, Barre of Avignon, Dufoix fils of Nîmes, Polge of Arles, has been suffering from lymphocytic meningitis (analysis by Dr. Lebros of Avignon). At the end of July the patient was paralyzed in all four members. Visual acuity was nil. The child did not perceive even light and could not distinguish between day and night. An examination by Dr. Polge in May, 1938, was completely unfavorable.

About August 20, this child was to be taken to Lourdes with the Aix Pilgrimage. I was called to re-examine him. The condition recorded in June remained exactly the same: paralysis of the four limbs, vision nil. Returning from Lourdes (August 28), Madame Pascal brought the child to me, leading him by the hand. *He was walking.* I recorded the disappearance of the paralysis and the return of vision. The gait was normal except for a slight degree of unsteadiness.

From that date the improvement has been maintained. This new condition came about after immersion in the piscine at Lourdes. Medically, one cannot explain such a result. (Signed, Dr. Darde, November 9, 1938.)

Dr. Julian sent a similar certificate, adding that the condition of the child before going to Lourdes had been extremely serious.

Because of the war, Francis' case could not be brought before the Medical Bureau until 1946—at which time he was described by the doctors as a "sturdy boy, tall and well-muscled, who rides a bicycle and goes to his classes at school in normal fashion."

From the examination of the documents submitted to us (the Bureau report continues), it is evident that the boy suffered from an organic illness of infectious origin, involving the meninges and the spinal cord. The ocular lesions and the spinal-fluid analysis permit us to confirm the organic nature of the disease. The replies to the official five questions regarding a cure are as follows:

1. The illness certainly existed. It consisted of meningomyelitis with choked disk, flaccid paralysis of the lower

limbs and stiffness of the upper limbs. Cerebellar disturbance.

2. There was abrupt cessation of symptoms at a time when the development of the malady left no hope of a tendency toward improvement. The child could distinguish a tricycle the day of his second bath, and on return home he walked.

3. There has been a definite cure, confirmed by the complete recovery of vision, of the ability to walk, and of all other functions.

4. No question of delay regarding a conclusion on this cure. It dates from ten years ago.

5. No explanation can be given medically for the instantaneous disappearance of the malady and its symptoms.

There follow the signatures of eleven physicians and finally that of Dr. Auguste Vallet, President of the Medical Bureau at that time. The document is dated October 2, 1946.

Further, in a postscript: "Patient re-examined in 1947. This child is in perfect health. Normal vision. Walk normal. Reflexes normal." (Signed, Dr. François Leuret, President [1947] of the Medical Bureau of Lourdes.)

The patient has been seen several times since then. The report is always the same. Francis comes each year to Lourdes on a pilgrimage of gratitude, serves as stretcher-bearer, and is seen regularly at the Bureau. He is now a fine, healthy boy of nineteen, with perfect eyesight, perfect use of his once paralyzed limbs.

"He can read until midnight, and be on the run for hours!" says his mother. "On his feet all day at Beaucaire with the vines, or carrying the stretchers all day at Lourdes—it's all one to Francis. One would never know he's been sick a day of his life!"

Last October, I paid him a visit in his own home.

It was a blustery autumn afternoon, pouring rain. I drove the fifteen miles from Avignon to Beaucaire—a little town of 10,000 population. At the house in the Rue Camille Desmoulins they were waiting for me—smiling faces, kindliness, hospitality: Francis, his father and mother, his aunt, and his little brother who had just come home in his raincoat, dripping, from school.

The mother had a big pot of coffee ready and we sat drinking it in the living room and talking and laughing, while the rain streamed down the windowpane.

"What's it like, for a young man who has been cured at Lourdes, in this day and age?" I asked Francis. "Your friends—do they tease you? Do they make it difficult?"

"Not much. Once in a while, just one or two, you know."

"And these young people—do they believe in Lourdes and the miracles?"

"Most of them do. Even the ones who say they don't, do—really. People in a little town like this believe in them more than people in cities," said Francis. "Maybe that's why God favors them with more miracles."

"The people around here have been very good to Francis," said his mother. "They always give him a wonderful welcome."

"How could they help it?" asked the aunt. "Lots of them remember what he looked like when he went off to Lourdes—blind, and stiff as a board, not able to move hand or foot, poor baby!"

"Every year, now, he carries the banner for the Aix pilgrimage," added the father proudly. "Everybody says Francis must be the one to carry the banner!"

"And the girls? Does it make any difference with the young ladies, this being a *miraculé?*"

Francis blushed. "Plenty of time for that," he said.

"He has to begin to earn his living first," said the father; "get himself established."

"What is he going to be?" I wondered if, perhaps, he might enter Religion, like so many of the *miraculés?*

"He is going to be a winegrower, like the rest of the people of his religion," said his father. "He prefers the outdoor life."

"But Francis is a great reader," said his mother. "How that boy reads and writes! Many journalists came, after the cure. And Francis has lots of correspondents wanting letters from him, or just his signature."

"Oh, there's not so much of that now," Francis said deprecatingly. An attractive, unassuming boy—well brought up; good with his younger brother who obviously worships him. A close affectionate family circle, pleasant to be with. Much the same atmosphere as in a Pennsylvania farm or a ranch in Texas or Montana.

Similar problems, too. Father Pascal told me they sell their wine for twenty-eight francs a liter. The buyer in town pays a hundred. Many middlemen, slim profits, taxes. Everything is very dear. During the war they had a bad time. Food was very expensive. Were they occupied territory? Oh yes! Germans were quartered in the house. No, the Germans weren't bad to them—saw them only morning and night, coming and going . . .

A warm, friendly afternoon, long to be remembered: the cozy little room, the comfortable armchairs, Aunt Melanie's luscious tartlets, the hot strong coffee, the farm animals close by . . .

"We are peasants, madame," Father Pascal said again proudly.

They take their boy's cure simply, deeply grateful, but with no unction or sanctimony.

I was sorry to have to leave them—waving to me from the doorway. Francis took me under a big umbrella to the car.

"Come back again, madame! Anything we can do for Lourdes, you know—well, it's never enough."

His is one of the famous cures—recognized by the Medical Commission and by the Church.

The first medical examination took place at Lourdes on October 2, 1946, with eleven physicians present; the second was in July, 1947, when fifteen physicians confirmed the original conclusion. Again, on September 1, 1948, the case was once more discussed with twenty doctors approving the conclusions previously reached, and declaring that "the cure of Francis Pascal, humanly inexplicable and in effect for ten years, is beyond the realm of natural law."

The Canonical Commission appointed to investigate the case on behalf of the Church referred to the abundance of witness (five doctors who attended the child) and "the exceptional number of proofs attesting the existence of the illness and its absolute care, humanly inexplicable."

The Commission stressed that "it was a serious illness, organic, refractory to all treatment, considered a hopeless case. The cure—which suddenly, after a second bath in the piscine of Lourdes—was perfect, and still is, after ten years, and cannot be attributed to any natural cause."

The Church, in distinguishing between this cure and that of Gerard

Baillie,* declared that the Pascal cure was instantaneous and perfect, and therefore pronounced it a Miraculous Cure. On May 31, 1949, the Archbishop of Aix-en-Provence issued the following Proclamation:

> In view of the various medical certificates appearing in the dossier, especially those of Dr. Darde, dated July 19, 1938, November 9, 1938, June 5, 1939; and that of Dr. Julian, dated December 6, 1938:
>
> In view of the verbatim reports of the Medical Bureau of Lourdes, dated October 2, 1946 and September 1, 1948:
>
> In view of the reports of the Canonical Commission constituted by us under date of December 10 and 17, 1948:
>
> The Holy Name of God being invoked: by virtue of the authority conferred upon us by the Holy Council of Trent, and while subordinating our decision to the authority of the Sovereign Pontiff:
>
> We judge and declare that the cure of Francis Pascal, which occurred at Lourdes on August 26, 1938, is miraculous and must be attributed to a special intervention of the Most Blessed Virgin Mary Immaculate, Mother of God.
>
> Proclaimed at Aix, May 31, 1949, on the fete of the Most Blessed Virgin Mary Mediatrix of all grace.
>
> Charles,
> Archbishop of Aix, Arles and Embrun

From Avignon to Montmarte is a long jump—but the two young men were not so different; not in the essentials, anyhow.

I came upon the case of Yves Joucaut† while prowling through Lourdes histories, and pounced on it; the cure of a Parisian is so unusual, but there it was: "Yves Joucau, seven years old. Pott's Disease, cervical abscessed. Cured at the National Pilgrimage of 1933." I carefully noted the address.

* It is interesting to compare these two cases (Baillie and Pascal) which illustrate the severe requirements of the Church in proclaiming a miracle.

† *Yves Joucau, Pott's Disease, cervical, abscessed, cured at Lourdes, August, 1933.*

It would be amazing if a family were still living in the same place after twenty years, in Paris or anywhere, these days. But there they were, the Joucau family—still living in the same pleasant little apartment in the same modest street not far from the Place Clichy. Madame Joucau, an attractive, slender woman with dark eyes, was quite willing to tell me about her son's cure. She got out some pictures of the pathetic little boy in his plaster cast.

"He was just seven when he was taken ill, madame. Until that time he had always been perfectly well. First he had a growth behind the ear which soon became the size of an egg. Our family doctor, Dr. Cauhapé, had us take him to a specialist, who made an incision. Other doctors later said this should never have been done.

"The child did not improve; on the contrary, he rapidly grew worse. His head began to bend to the side. I would say to him, twenty times a day, 'Lift your head, dear!' He would lift it, but in five minutes it would drop back again. He had no appetite—he became very thin and weak. Of course my husband and I were frantic with anxiety. We had no money to spend for expensive treatments. Were we really going to lose our boy?

"We took him to the clinic at the hospital. And there the terrible truth came out. X-rays showed tuberculosis of the spine—several bones in the neck had already degenerated. They put him in a plaster cast. They told us he had Pott's Disease. He might be in the cast for two or three years—or he might become completely paralyzed.

"Well, madame, you may imagine! Our only child—our son! The doctors promised absolutely nothing, simply looked embarrassed and kept repeating: 'It is very serious, madame—we regret to say, *very* serious.'

"We decided to take him to Lourdes. One of the Sisters of the Assumption made out the papers and got him admitted to the National Pilgrimage in August.

"The day after we arrived at Lourdes he was bathed at the piscine, his plaster cast and all, but only up to the waist. Nothing happened. But after the Procession that day, back at the hostel, he began to move around, said he felt well, wanted to play, to eat, doing things he hadn't done for months! He began to move about, inside his cast. Well, you may imagine—we were in heaven right then, his father and I!

"We went home. The bones and tissues resumed their normal place. We had another X-ray made. Everything normal! The boy has been gloriously well from that day to this. What can we say—except

eternal thanksgiving to Notre Dame de Lourdes? And the little Bernadette too—I have always felt that she had something to do with it."

On February 4, 1934, Dr. Cauhapé—intern of the Departmental
Hospital of the Seine—sent the following certificate to the Medical
Bureau at Lourdes:

> I, the undersigned, Dr. Cauhapé, certify that I ex-
> amined the child Yves Joucau twice during June, 1933,
> for localized pain behind the ear, and sent the young pa-
> tient to Dr. Nectoux, specialist residing at ———. At the
> time the child departed for Lourdes, the wound was in a
> suppurating condition and he was in a plaster cast.
>
> I saw the child during the past few days. All lesions
> have disappeared and an X-ray examination on January
> 22 shows an entirely normal condition of the vertebral
> column. (Signed, Dr. Cauhapé, 83 Avenue de Clichy,
> Paris.)

Another certificate was furnished by the Paris Hospital where the
child had been treated:

> *République Française. Administration Générale de l'Assis-
> tance Publique a Paris. Hôpital Bretonne Consultation de
> Chirurgie—Dr. Deveuf.* Dr. Leveuf, extern of the Paris
> Hospital, certifies that the child Yves Joucau, in July
> 1933, had ostetitis (inflammation of the bone) of the cer-
> vical column, abscessed, as shown by successive X-rays. In
> December, 1933, the X-rays no longer showed any le-
> sions and the clinical aspect of the child is normal.

Today, twenty years later, Yves Joucau is a vigorous, attractive,
healthy young man, working in the electrical services of the Govern-
ment. He takes part in all kinds of sports—football, swimming, tennis,
etc. "He is hardly ever home," said his mother. "Always out with his
friends at some game or other, after work."

However, he stayed home on the occasion of my visit, and we
spent a very agreeable evening in their cozy little apartment. Madame
Joucau's mother was English. She was born a Protestant and became a
Catholic when she married. They are devoted to Lourdes—as the fami-

lies of the Cures always are. They go back every year with the National Pilgrimage.

We went through scrapbooks and albums of photographs showing Yves as a boy, and then as the young man of today: in his bathing suit, or with his tennis racquet, or on his bicycle at the finish of the local bicycle race. The same friendly, simple sort of visit as with the Pascal family. Paris instead of Beaucaire—but the hospitality and kindness just the same.

One of the delightful features of this work was going into French homes, getting in touch with French people again—hearing their stories, sitting with them round the lamp in the evening, listening to music, looking over the old snapshots, talking about similar homes and families in America. International relations would certainly improve if more people, all over the world, could drop in on each other in these little homes of an evening.

UNIQUE IN THE ANNALS OF LOURDES, said the newspaper headlines. THE CURE OF A CHILD WHO WAS AN IDIOT. PARALYZED IN ARMS AND LEGS.*

Today this child is sane and whole. I myself saw him well and happy, running off with his friends to play football.

Guy Leydet was a normal child till the age of five. Then he was stricken with acute meningo-encephalitis—a brain disease that can wreck a nervous system. He came out of it alive, but paralyzed in both arms and legs, and subject to frequent convulsions and epileptic fits. Worst of all, in a state of progressive mental breakdown which ended in complete idiocy.

"He didn't even recognize us," his mother told me. "He couldn't speak at all; he had lost all his happy little vocabulary that he had before his illness." He could not even call his mother—only uttered guttural sounds like those made by congenital idiots.

He forgot how to eat, and had to be fed, as he no longer was able to carry the food to his mouth. Thus he had degenerated even lower than an animal. He dirtied himself with no consciousness of what he was doing. And this condition had lasted for nearly two years.

His parents all but ruined themselves financially in their effort to

---

* Guy Leydet, infantile encephalopathy, with idiocy, quadriplegic, cured at Lourdes, October 6, 1946.

cure him. They tried every treatment and therapy that offered the slightest hope—all in vain. The doctors told them it was useless and pronounced the dread word: "Incurable."

"Then (like thousands of others after exhausting all human possibilities)—we thought of Lourdes."

They arrived at Lourdes that bright fall morning with the child still in the same horrible state. How many idiot children have I seen thus arriving!—slobbering mouth, vacant eyes, incessant gibberish cries. Suppose, like many others, he should live like this for years and years!

Numb with anguish, they wheeled him to the piscine. "Notre Dame de Lourdes was our last desperate hope!"

I often think, as I write the stories of these cures, how casually we take them—we who read about them, we who set them down. "Now that was a rather interesting cure," we say; or "Let me tell you about this one—it made a stir." Casual, even a bit blasé, sometimes.

If we stop to think about it, any single one of these cures is staggering. Suppose it was your child who had become that slobbering idiot—your mother who had gone stone-blind or had cancer of the face. Suppose it was *you* and your husband or wife who went up to that mysterious fountain, carrying all you hold dear in the world—with all your trembling hopes and fears wrapped in that agonizing little bundle. How do you think *you'd* feel when something happened suddenly such as happened to Guy Leydet? I think the heavens would open, and—believer or unbeliever—you would sing glory to God!

They took him to the piscine. The father waited outside, on his knees, praying with the rest of the crowd. Inside the baths, compassionate nurses dipped the rigid little boy into the water. His mother stood near, fearing another convulsion—ready to grab him when he came out. They handed him back to her.

Then suddenly, sensationally, it happened.

Guy Leydet opened his eyes, looked about him with an *intelligent* glance, reached his arms toward his mother and in a clear, childish voice cried, "Mama!" He then began to count his fingers, naming them over, as French children do.

Wild with joy, his mother snatched him up and ran with him out of the piscine to find his father. "He said 'Mama!'" she gasped. "He said 'Mama!'"

The father, longing to believe but skeptical, cautioned her against too much hope. "We have hoped so many times," he reminded, "only to be disappointed."

But in the days that followed they knew that this time it was true. The child's mind was rapidly reawakening. He began to talk. He moved his arms and legs perfectly. They called in their doctor, who gazed in stupefaction at his former patient, admitting he could not understand it at all. "Well—try to re-educate him," he said, still incredulous.

So the happy parents began to teach their boy all over again. It was easy. Within one year he recovered his normal mentality, could read and write and even draw a bit, as well as walk and play vigorously like other children.

On September 26, 1947—one year after his cure—he was examined by forty doctors at the Medical Bureau. Dr. Dailly, a children's specialist of Paris, for two hours put him through all the classic tests by which a physician judges the state of a child's mental development. At the end of his examination, the doctor announced simply: "This child is normal."

The case provoked long and heated discussion at the Medical Bureau. This was not a case of simple mental backwardness, as Dr. Leuret emphasized, but of total idiocy. And of quadriplegic paralysis which had resisted all treatment over a period of many months, and was given up by the attending physicians as definitely incurable. It was this idiot child, who had not spoken for two years, nor shown the least sign of intelligence, nor moved his arms or legs, who on that morning of October 6, in the piscine, suddenly opened his eyes, stretched his hitherto motionless arms toward his mother and said, "Mama!" Since that moment, he has been in perfect health and full possession of his faculties. If this was not an instantaneous Lourdes cure, what was it?

The doctors nodded—or shrugged their shoulders, still unconvinced. One major question tantalized them all.

"With what brain does this child think?" Dr. M—— of Bordeaux put it bluntly. "What brain was he using when he stood up and suddenly called his mother and began to count his fingers, after two years of insensibility? Was it with a new brain, was it with a brain partially destroyed after an acute meningo-encephalitis?"

Another said: "Either he must be thinking with his brain such as it was when he was an idiot, and therefore—like Gerard Baillie seeing with eyes that could not see—he was thinking with a brain that could not think; or, he had been given an entirely new brain. In any case, the fact is absolutely contrary to all natural laws."

In the end, the forty doctors at the Bureau unanimously declared that the child had been supernaturally cured. One of the most eminent among them, Professor Lelong of Paris, clinched the matter by declaring finally:

"If there is a single one among you who has ever once in his whole career seen the cure of such a case—a postencephalitic idiot—I will pledge myself never again to sign a Lourdes dossier!"

He had no takers.

I visited Guy Leydet at his home in St. Etienne. He is now a tall, nice-looking lad of fourteen; very good in his classes, especially in English, geography, and history. I saw his notebooks—beautifully kept, almost no mistakes; fine, accurate drawings.

Guy came in from school, rosy-cheeked and the picture of health, dressed in red pull-over and tweed plus-fours, running up five flights of stairs to their apartment, so as to get back down again quickly to play with his pals.

His father is a professor in a local business college. His mother, a charming and very pretty woman, says they want to send the boy to England next year on an exchange basis with an English boy who would come to them. "He is crazy about learning English," she said, laughing, "and doing very well at it. They teach a lot by ear, and with records. He hasn't chosen his career yet, but I rather think it will be teaching."

I went into the details of the case with her, from the very beginning. After agonizing years—"heartrending," she called them—Notre Dame de Lourdes had had compassion on them. All three of them go every year to Lourdes on a pilgrimage of thanksgiving.

"No, the case was not proclaimed a miracle or a formal 'published' cure, because of lack of the necessary medical documents. The doctors who attended the boy before his visit to Lourdes have absolutely refused to submit any records or certificates. 'Lourdes! We're not interested!' is all they will say."

So, while there is ample evidence of the genuineness of the cure—testimony of neighbors, therapists, nurses, attendants at the piscine—it cannot be officially proclaimed.

"What do we care about that?" says the mother. "We have our boy —happy and well. Our *Te Deums* are sung right here at home, every day!"

I discussed this case with the President of the Medical Commission in Paris. He too was very much interested in Guy Leydet. He approved my including the account of his cure in my collection of Lourdes histories.

"It shows," he said, "how strict are the requirements of the doctors of the Medical Bureau and the Commission. It also shows what amazing things can and do happen at Lourdes: cures which cannot be officially and formally recognized but which have transformed the lives of families and brought joy and health where before there was anguish, despair, and only one prospect: death."

23

Celebrated Cures
of Women

The young are not the only privileged ones among the cures at Lourdes. The old also are favored by the mysterious power which appears to act sometimes after the Sacred Name is invoked. Witness the cure of Sister Marie-Marguerite.*

Sister Marie-Marguerite, born April 13, 1872, was a nun at the convent of the Poor Clares at Rennes. She did all the shopping, errands, outside interviews, and running about for her Community. She was constantly on her feet.

She began to suffer from recurring heart attacks. Later she had a fall, followed by severe pain in the left kidney. Her condition grew steadily worse until 1936, when Dr. Branchard diagnosed her case as an abscess in the left kidney, inoperable because of the state of the heart.

During the same year, an edema (fluid in the tissues) of the legs also appeared, producing great swelling and discomfort: a condition popularly referred to as dropsy. Despite various treatments, the illness made dangerous progress and in the opinion of the doctors was "galloping" toward a fatal end. Sores on the legs discharged abundantly, and aggravated the Sister's sufferings. The heart crises increased. Staying in bed became impossible, and she had to remain sitting up day and night

---

* *Sister Marie-Marguerite, abscess of left kidney and edema of the legs, cured January 22, 1937, during a Novena to Our Lady of Lourdes.*

in an armchair. This terrible condition had lasted for months. It could not go on much longer.

On January 20, the entire Community began a Novena to Our Lady of Lourdes to ask for her cure. Prayers were continued in the chapel all day and all night, in perpetual vigil.

"On the morning of January 22," says Sister Marie-Marguerite, "suddenly I had an impulse to go to the altar at the second Mass." Moved by what seemed to her "a superhuman force," and "in spite of atrocious suffering, bathed in a cold sweat," she dragged herself from her chair. She managed to get to the chapel.

All of a sudden she found herself on her feet—without any support —a feeling of great tranquility flooding her whole being.

"Over my whole body I felt a gentle pressure. It seemed to me that a hand, both gentle and powerful at the same time, passed over my legs —which I felt had suddenly become deflated. New life flowed through them. The bandages, all at once too big, fell to the floor."

As soon as Mass ended, she went back to her room, walking with no difficulty, and was thrilled to find that the edema had disappeared. She put on her shoes, which she had not been able to wear for more than a year, went downstairs, and walked about all day, without feeling the slightest fatigue or the least tax on her heart. Next day she took up her duties again, and has remained well ever since.

In the official records, besides the report of the Sister herself, we find the testimony of the Abbess of the Order, that of the two Sisters who took care of the patient, also the deposition of the physician (Dr. Philouze), who for two years had seen her weekly and who was present the day after her cure. All gave their testimony under oath. To this was added the report of 1945 by three doctors under the Presidency of the Medical Bureau of Lourdes; their formal investigation of the case included the following note:

"Sister Marie-Marguerite, following upon renal and cardiac symptoms from 1924 to 1934, suffered from acute inflammation of the kidney complicated by a generalized edema. This edema of the legs was aggravated by vesicles (blisters) which broke and discharged serous fluid. The Sister was cured suddenly on January 22, 1937, during a Novena to Notre Dame de Lourdes."

This was another cure which came to the attention of the medical and ecclesiastical authorities during wartime. A Commission of doctors appointed by the Cardinal Archbishop of Rennes examined Sister

Marie-Marguerite in November, 1945, and reported that her state of health was excellent—heart normal, no pain in the kidneys, no edema, no painful condition of any sort. All trace of the disease had disappeared. The Sister immediately took up her arduous duties which, in spite of her advanced age, she was able to continue without any recurrence of her former trouble.

Because of the instantaneousness and absence of the convalescence in this case, the Archbishop declared that this cure could not be explained by natural causes. On May 26, 1946, he declared it to be a Miraculous Cure.

For the doctors, a particularly interesting thing about this cure was the immediate and complete disappearance of the large quantity of fluid (several liters) which had been present in the legs and was the cause of their tremendous swelling, plus the fact that no unusual amount of liquid was sloughed off through the normal channels. The Sister thought that the edema must have vanished through the sores on her legs and fallen onto the ground "in a lake." However, not a drop of fluid was discovered on the floor, and the linen was dry and clean, according to assurance given under oath at the Medical Bureau.

All this was astounding, the doctors said, "a material impossibility" —and yet a fact. The President of the Medical Bureau wrote a long article about it.

A Jewish physician, Dr. Koster, neurologist of Amsterdam, gave a report of this case in a paper before the Netherlands Psychiatric and Neurological Association on March 22, 1952. In his paper Dr. Koster paid tribute to the physicians and to the methods of the Lourdes Medical Bureau. He said he was greatly impressed by the way in which information was most carefully and scrupulously gathered before any decisions were finally reached with regard to the cures at Lourdes.

Dr. Koster said he had become interested in Lourdes through the writings of Dr. Carrel. "I asked myself, Why should I not take Carrel's word about Lourdes as much as I would take it about the tissue of the heart of a chicken?* It was on the strength of his statements that I went to the Bureau to see for myself. I was not disappointed."

At last accounts Sister Marie-Marguerite was still in excellent health. I have never met her but I know a number of people who know

---

* Referring to Dr. Carrel's famous experiments in connection with the heart.

her—among them Jeanne Fretel who lives in Rennes and who reported in autumn, 1953, that she was alive and well, and still "very active."

Everyone in Lourdes knows Mlle. Lacommère, the receptionist at the Bureau—brisk, helpful, efficient. She has helped me time and again, especially on one particular morning.

When I went into the Bureau that day, in the outer room sat a smiling little woman, middle-aged, modestly dressed and attractive, waiting for the doctors. I recognized her immediately from her picture, which I knew well. This was Madame Gestas,* one of the famous Cures of the past few years, and an official *miraculée*.

"Talk to her!" whispered Mlle. Lacommère. "I have told her about your book. Go on, she will be happy to talk with you."

Just then the doctors came in and proceeded with the examination—more exactly speaking, the yearly check-up which the Cures usually report for when they come with their local Pilgrimage.

Everybody filed into the examination room: seven doctors, two medical students. I was allowed to go in too.

A secretary turned the pages of the records. "When were you cured, madame?"

"August 22, 1947—seven years ago today!" She had come every year since then for her check-up, and to nurse the sick with the Bordeaux Pilgrimage. She undressed, lay down on the examination table.

Dr. Leuret began with a brief summary of the case, record book in hand. "Madame Jeanne Gestas, adhesive peritonitis. Patient of Dr. George and Dr. Dubourg of Bordeaux."

The doctor glanced benignly over his spectacles at the ex-patient. "Madame Gestas was fifty years old when she came to Lourdes for the cure which human aid had failed to give her. She had suffered for years from gastric and intestinal troubles, and had intense pain when taking even the smallest amount of food." He went on to give a résumé of the Bureau record.

In 1943 the case had been diagnosed as stomach ulcer, verified by X-rays. In December of that year the patient was operated on by Dr. Dubourg, the operation involving a large gastrectomy. But this had

---

* *Madame Jeanne Gestas, adhesive peritonitis, cured August 22, 1947, on Second Pilgrimage to Lourdes.*

brought no improvement. Two more surgeries were performed (May, 1944, and January, 1946).

The third operation brought to light a web of adhesions so close-knit that on incision they would not permit a view of the abdominal organs. The operation was a lengthy one and the patient afterward remained in a prolonged state of shock, followed by pulmonary congestion and high temperature. For days her life was seriously in danger.

She had been obliged months before to give up all work, had become terribly thin, and her weight fell to ninety pounds. After this third operation her condition became even worse. She had constant and violent spells of vomiting, and excruciating intestinal pain. In May, 1946, an especially severe crisis necessitated continuous aspiration for forty-eight hours. A fourth operation was considered but was put off because of the precarious condition of the patient. She suffered from frequent fainting fits after meals, vertigo in the street, and other morbid symptoms.

In August, 1946, she made her first pilgrimage to Lourdes. She came back definitely improved, as her surgeon Dr. Dubourg set down in his own record: "There is a definite amelioration . . . but the symptoms persist which indicate the existence of adhesive peritonitis at the subumbilical level. The general condition, while better, is still bad." The poor woman remained a victim of the same old agonies: digestive troubles, excessive constipation, and vertigo. She was very near despair.

On August 21, 1947, she went a second time to Lourdes with the National Pilgrimage. On Friday, August 22, while taking her bath in the piscine, she felt intense pain—"as though the whole intestine was being torn out." The pain ceased when she left the bath. She did not present herself at the Medical Bureau at this time but her nurses recorded that she took a light lunch at noon. On the morning of the twenty-third, she awoke with a sense of complete well-being. That day she ate anything she wanted, and had no trouble with her digestion.

Since her cure she follows a normal life, has no more pain, has regular stools, and can take up her work again. Seen on September 3, 1947, by her regular physician, Dr. George of Bordeaux, the latter noted that "she is completely transformed, suffers no more, and has regained a generally excellent condition."

The dossier contains certificates from Dr. George, Dr. Dubourg, and from the X-ray laboratory of Dr. Roger Guichard.

Madame Gestas was seen at the Medical Bureau in August, 1948, and each succeeding year. The cure is permanent. After her last examination, she talked to me for over an hour.

"This is a wonderful day for me, madame—I was cured just seven years ago today!" she said with a radiant smile. "I had been ill for four years—desperately ill; but I'd had this trouble really for twelve years. I was operated on three times. After the last operation, the doctor, when he came back next day, said to the nurse: 'She is dead?' "

He had expected her to die momentarily. Indeed, after the first operation he had told her husband there was no hope. *"Elle est perdue! She is lost!"* he said.

Now, she spoke of her first pilgrimage, in 1946. "At that time I had very little faith. I was *against* religion." A Sister at Bordeaux talked to her, helped to build up her faith. On that first pilgrimage she made some hesitant but sincere efforts.

"I made my prayer at the Grotto. I talked to the Blessed Virgin, very simply but very earnestly. I told her what she knew already, that I had not been much of a Christian. I promised her that from now on I would go to Mass, receive the Communion, and try to be a good practicing Christian."

She kept her vow. It was hard, because her husband was a complete unbeliever. But she persisted. In 1947 she came back again to Lourdes.

"At the first bath I had a most agonizing pain, as though my whole insides were being torn out! I thought I was dying—and hoped I was. But when I got back to the Asile I felt better—ate something. I hadn't been able to eat for months—vomited everything." On the following day she ate more, ate things that usually would have caused her absolute anguish: beans, grapes, pears, peaches. She began to realize that something wonderful had happened to her.

"The Blessed Virgin had heard my prayer!"

She thought that she should go to the Medical Bureau to report her cure. The nurse at the hostel said no; if it was a real cure, it should be checked by the doctor at home. She had a comfortable trip back to Bordeaux, eating anything she pleased.

She had to smile at her husband's astonishment upon her return, when he saw her eating anything, walking, and doing everything like any healthy person.

"But I'm *cured!*" she told him jubilantly.

"Tu penses!" (The French equivalent for "You're telling me!") He came home each day expecting to see her ill again.

"And what did your doctor say?" I asked.

"Oh, at first he thought it was only temporary and that all the old troubles would return. But he was very happy when the cure held. No one was happier than he—except me!"

From the day of her cure to now she has been "absolutely well—feeling wonderful." She does all the housekeeping, cooking, and sewing for her family of seven—doesn't mind all the hard work. She comes every year to Lourdes to help with the sick—asks God to help her to understand why she was cured and what He wants her to do with the rest of her life.

One of her griefs is the irreligion of her family. Her husband and son don't believe at all in these things. *She* may come to Lourdes, go to Mass, do anything she likes. But for *them,* all that is nonsense. They make no attempt to account for her cure. "You believe in the Virgin—good. But don't ask us to have anything to do with that."

She leads her own life, goes to Mass, has her own friends who are believers, tries to help a bit with the poor and suffering, and thanks God daily for what has happened to her. A simple, smiling little woman, very modest and unpretentious, in spite of all the newspaper publicity and fuss that has surged around her.

On the occasion of Madame Gestas' visit to the Bureau in 1948, twenty-three doctors examined her and recorded the following conclusions: "From the clinical point of view we find no pathological symptoms, either physical or functional. The liver is a little low and the edge a bit hooked. Spleen not felt. No gas. No pains. Good abdominal wall. Heart normal, pulse normal. Functional amelioration giving impression of complete cure."

The Medical Commission two years later declared that time had confirmed this cure, that all the peritoneal lesions which for four years had tortured the patient had completely disappeared: that the case appeared to them beyond the laws of nature and "inexplicable."

The records were sent on to the Archbishop of Bordeaux for judgment by a Canonical Commission. On July 13, 1952, the cure was proclaimed according to the Canons of the Church as well as by the medical profession, and Jeanne Gestas took her place among the fifty-one official Miraculous Cures of Lourdes.

Madame Rose Martin—cancer of the uterus—
cured at Lourdes, July 3, 1947.

People who say that Lourdes cures consist of "a few neurotics who shed their nervous troubles under strong religious suggestion" get a shock when confronted with a pronouncement like the above taken out of an official medical report.

The first reaction is apt to be: "I don't believe it!" But twenty-two leading physicians and surgeons of Paris hospitals believed it, after rigorous examination of Madame Martin, a yearly check-up since her cure, the study of X-rays, surgeons' certificates and those of her local hospital.

I heard the story from Madame Martin herself, in her apartment at Nice not long ago. Here it is, as given in the report by her physician to the Medical Bureau at Lourdes.

From November, 1945, Madame Rose Martin showed symptoms of cancer of the uterus. In February, 1946, a hysterectomy was performed—she was operated on by Dr. Barraya of the Pasteur Hospital at Nice. Laboratory tests made evident a cancerous growth on the neck of the uterus.

Later complications necessitated two or more operations. In April, 1947, the patient was examined again, for digestive troubles: painful rectal crises, no bowel evacuation without enema, and a growth in the rectum the size of a small orange. One could feel this growth by abdominal palpation.

The unfortunate woman grew rapidly worse. She was confined to her bed for some months, continued to have constant vaginal discharges, no stools without enemas, and matter thus evacuated contained fetid debris.

The surgeons treating the case reported that the original cancer had spread to the rectum. They could offer no hope. Her pain was so great they had to give repeated injections of morphine.

On June 30, 1947, Madame Martin was taken to Lourdes in a grave condition. But after the third bath at the piscine (July 3, 1947) she asked to be bathed standing up, though for months past, to stand on her feet had been absolutely impossible for her. That same evening she got up alone, went to the toilet where she produced a normal stool, for the first time without enema. From that moment, never thereafter did she have any fetid or pathological evacuation. She felt no more pain, and had a "ferocious" appetite.

After her return to Nice, she was seen regularly by the doctor who had treated her—her home physician, Dr. Fay. He certified the complete disappearance of the rectal growth, besides the disappearance of functional symptoms. From the date of her cure there was total absence of pain, no vaginal discharge, daily stool, and steady gain in weight (34 pounds in ten months). "Housekeeper for a large family, she leads a very active and arduous life, but apparently thrives on it," added the doctor.

On July 6, 1948, one year after her cure, Rose Martin was examined at the Medical Bureau at Lourdes by a roomful of doctors. Her general condition was pronounced excellent. She had put on fifty pounds. A proctoscopy made by Dr. Leuret showed that the rectum was absolutely normal; the uterus and other organs were normal also. She has been periodically examined since then by Dr. Fay, who finds her in a flourishing state of health.

The case was sent to the Medical Commission—along with surgeons' certificates, X-ray and laboratory reports, and the complete hospital record. The Commission, at its meeting on February 27, 1949, "after a reading and discussion of the report by Dr. Oberlin on the case of Rose Martin, declares, in agreement with the *rapporteur,* that this case has no natural or scientific explanation, and unanimously considers that it should be submitted for examination by a Canonical Commission."

It was so ordered and on May 3, 1949, Monseigneur Rémond, Bishop of Nice, proclaimed Rose Martin a Miraculous Cure.

I had the good luck to hear Madame Martin's story from her own lips. I found her in her kitchen, cooking vegetables for the midday soup: a sturdy nice-looking woman of fifty, very energetic. Evidently she had been a very pretty girl.

In June, 1947, the doctors had given her three months to live. "I suffered the pains of hell, madame! My husband had to learn to give injections. I couldn't stand it at night, until the doctor came. I had more than 5,000 injections of morphine."

The Sisters down the street—Sisters of the Misericordia—took care of her. How good they were! They came eight times a day—think of that, *eight* times every day!—washed her, dressed her, combed her hair. They would never take any money. "No, no—use that for your own needs, madame. Put all that into getting well."

It was the Sisters who had said she must go to Lourdes, and who made all the arrangements. Her husband went with her. The doctor thought she would never make it. She weighed 70 pounds when she left on the Pilgrimage. Now she weighs 154. When the Sisters saw her come back *cured,* they were overcome with happiness. The doctor didn't want her to go, but she had a presentiment that she would be cured at Lourdes. She insisted on making the effort.

At the moment of her cure, she felt "something moving, inside—through my whole being. Not painful—not tearing—but *moving.*" "It was your cure, madame," said the Sister who took care of her. "You will see, Madame Martin," they had kept telling her, "you will have your cure!"

The faith of the Sisters—how much it means to the patients! How often one is heard to say: "It was a *réligieuse* who took care of me—it was a Sister who came to see me. She talked to me—because of her I decided to go. I owe everything to those Sisters!"

Today Madame Martin is in the best of health. She does the family washing, cooking, cleaning and "feels fine"; she has felt absolutely well from the moment of her cure.

I talked with her physician, Dr. Fay. "Was there any doubt about its being cancer?"

"None whatever. You have seen the laboratory reports and hospital records. She had cancer, she was operated for cancer, but not cured by us doctors. On the contrary, the malignancy spread. This was a dying woman. Only after the bath at the piscine did she get well. She was cured at Lourdes—of cancer!"*

We have had a brief glance at some of the outstanding Lourdes Cures of recent years. Within the scope of the present book it is not possible to go into greater detail. I have given some idea of the documents and data available for on-the-spot study—though it must be remembered, all these papers and records are in French.

As I think about them—the Cures I talked with personally, and those I know most about—certain similarities, family likenesses one might call them, stand out very distinctly. While there is wide variety in the circumstances attending their cures, certain very definite likenesses appear in the people. When you have talked with eight or ten of them you begin to notice these common characteristics.

First, they are simple creatures: "Of the people," practically all of them. Not one that I heard of came from a rich or impressive family.

Second, they seem to be immune to illness after their cure: don't get sick at all, even with common colds or ordinary digestive troubles. They are in excellent health at all times.

* I have in my possession the complete medical record of this case: doctors' certificates, reports of the Medical Commission, of medical examinations, X-ray and laboratory reports, hospital records from Civil Hospital at Nice, from nurses in attendance, etc. Dr. Oberlin, surgeon of the Paris Hospitals and former President of the Commission, made the official investigation and wrote the history of the cure.

Then—they are completely disinterested. They don't want any money, presents, or anything. Their desire is just to *give,* in gratitude for what has been done for them. They won't take money for any sort of help they may bestow.

Finally, they are calm. Though this tremendous thing has happened to them, though they have been bombarded by newspapers and well-meaning friends, they are never in a state of excitement. They come, most of them, from small towns, simple homes, where a great event like this might very easily turn a person's head. I have never seen a Lourdes Cure whose head was turned. They talk about their cure naturally, quietly, without commotion. They have, every one of them, a poise that comes from an inner dignity and the desire to be worthy of the great thing they have experienced.

I have never seen a Lourdes Cure flustered or upset. They are modest, but not unctuous; not a trace of sanctimoniousness or sentimentality in any one of them. They are happy people. They laugh a lot. They have fun.

But most unusual quality of all: they have no pride. Like Bernadette, their vanity seems "quite inaccessible." Let me add quickly, they are not plaster saints. They are human beings with human failings which no doubt are known to their families and friends, just as other people's are. But they are humble to the very bottom of their hearts—and they are pure hearts, with no selfish or ulterior motive.

"Every day," said Madame Gestas, "I ask God to show me *why* this great thing has happened to me and what He wants me to do with the life that He has saved."

Madame Gestas keeps house for seven people. Rose Martin is housekeeper for five. Jeanne Fretel is a nurse. Francis Pascal is a vinegrower, Fernand a cobbler, Colonel Pellegrin a soldier.

None of these people is sitting round looking pious, or setting himself up as something special, profiting in any way (as they easily might) from their spectacular experience. They are doing an honest, man-sized job, wherever they happen to be. Not one of them is having an easy life, or would want it.

Whatever one may consider is the real source of their cure, however skeptical or "credulous" one may be regarding The Lady whom Bernadette so ardently believed in, there is no slightest doubt that a transcendental influence has laid its hand upon these people and has blessed them—not merely for a few moments with a physical cure, but for a lifetime, with deep joy, serenity, and peace. I count it a privilege to have known any one of them.

24

Causes and Conclusions

And over and again, the crucial question: What is behind it all? What is the origin, the cause of all these cures? How do you explain them? More important, how does the medical profession explain them? If they are not miracles—that is, produced by some supernatural power, what are they? What power does produce them, and how?

We have seen the fallacy of many of the favorite theories: *The water,* which has no curative properties, either chemical or radioactive; *the climate,* some special quality in the atmosphere—but there is none. Lourdes has only the agreeable mountain air of many Pyrenees cities.

Errors of diagnosis—this occurs naturally and immediately to a physician. And in the early years, when the system of medical examinations and verifications was less severe, this might justifiably have been brought forward as an explanation of certain cures. Errors certainly occur in every doctor's practice. But today, pilgrimage certificates for patients coming to Lourdes are required to be exact, supported by case histories, clinical data, and doctors' day-by-day notations, which leave little loophole for mistaken diagnoses. A very substantial number of Lourdes cures, as shown in the accounts in these pages, are backed by "Before-and-After" X-rays, hospital charts, and biological analyses. These documents do not lie. They show, objectively and unmistakably, the condition of the patient before and after the alleged cure.

Again, as Dr. Blanton has observed, the percentage of these cures are certainly too great to be laid to coincidence. Doctors today are more apt to consider psychological causes as a probable explanation for such cures.

Emotional shock . . . suggestion . . . psychic factors . . . these are among the most popular of the tentative "solutions." People often speak of the "abnormal emotionalism and suggestibility" of the patients. That such a condition can bring about improvement or sudden cure of neurotics has been observed in various hospitals as well as at places of pilgrimage.

But in many Lourdes cures this element has been lacking: in the cures of the incredulous, of unbelievers, and of young children; in cures that have occurred at home, or on the return journey after all hope was given up; in cures elsewhere than at the baths or at the Processions in Lourdes; and in cures that have occurred after two or more pilgrimages.

Some people insist that miraculous cures are produced by "chants and incantations" that stimulate the patient into a state of exaltation: "That generous breath," as Zolo says, "which emanates from the crowds in the acute climax of faith."

As I have repeatedly stressed, the atmosphere of constant prayer and faith must certainly have a tremendous effect upon sick and receptive persons. Undoubtedly suggestion is a powerful force. But can one contend (as Dr. Guinier asks) "that suggestion thus created can awaken vital energies asleep for months and years, and cause to disappear *instantly* local vascular troubles, muscular atrophy, and articular stiffness which disease brought about?

"Is it possible that 'suggestion,' either personal or collective, could force various microorganisms to neutralize each other and disappear, large collections of pus to be absorbed, gaps made by sloughing tissue to be filled up, scars to form in a few hours or minutes which ordinarily require months or years? (As in the case of Lydia Brosse.)

"Experience proves," Dr. Guinier continues, "that therapeutic suggestion has never been able to cure, either rapidly or slowly, organic lesions.* The regeneration of tissues diseased for a long time or destroyed can only be accomplished by the multiplication of cells, engendered by pre-existing elements and adding to themselves new cells; thus

---

* Bernheim, chief of the Nancy school of therapists who specialized in suggestion, officially stated that "suggestion cannot do away with a lesion, set a dislocated limb, or restore destroyed substance; neither does it kill microbes or cicatrize tuberculous wounds." He declares: "Suggestion is a means which acts only with nervous or functional troubles; it has no effect on organic diseases." He thus places most Lourdes cures outside the reach of suggestive influence. For the cures at Lourdes are chiefly of organic diseases.

succeeding in re-forming skin, muscles, fat, bones. . . . In such a succession of physiological operations *time* is indispensable. No organ rebuilds itself outside of the conditions of time necessary to the growth of tissues." No moral shaking or nervous crisis, he adds, can alter this fact or produce an instant creation of cells.

Dr. Vallet makes another interesting point on this question of suggestion. "If," he says, "as certain schools contend, Lourdes is the prime rendezvous for nervous and hysterical patients only, and if we have means of suggestion unlimited in their power, why are not more nervous patients cured here? How is it that our cures reckon especially affections of the lungs and organic lesions, caries, tumors, cancer, diabetes, diseases in which suggestion plays no part?

"When a cure of cancer or tuberculosis in the last stages occurs, as it has numbers of times, at the passing of the Blessed Sacrament, there are at the same time in front of the Basilica hundreds of patients suffering from nervous afflictions. Why do they not get up?"

Some of the National Pilgrimages have been the occasion of very remarkable cures. He describes one of the most memorable:

"Thousands of spectators. Fifteen hundred sick in long double rows on the Esplanade—a large number of instantaneous cures. Among the sick who then arose from their stretchers and followed the Procession were Fanny Pepper, a consumptive in the last stages; Helene Duval, tubercular peritonitis; Philimene Albrecht, Pott's Disease; Josephine Grosset, tuberculous peritonitis; Irma Jacquart, cerebral affection complicated by paralysis; Felicie Serreau, another peritonitis victim; J. Lacome, Pott's Disease. . . .

"Now such diseases cannot be cured by suggestion. On the other hand, nervous diseases could disappear under this irresistible impulse. In this double row of litters that filled the Esplanade that day there were fully three hundred nervous patients. *Why did they not get up?*

"The secret of our cures is not to be found in the water in our pools. It is not to be found in the religious excitement which surrounds us at Lourdes. Wherein, then, does lie the secret?"

Many people ascribe it to *prayer.* One of the great experts on tissue building puts forward his own conviction on this point. Dr. Carrel writes:

Certain spiritual activities may cause anatomical as well
as functional modifications of the tissues and organs.
These organic phenomena are observed in various cir-

cumstances—among them being the state of prayer. Prayer should be understood not as a mere mechanical recitation of formulas, but as . . . an absorption of consciousness in a principle both permeating and transcending our world.

Our present conception of the influences of prayer upon pathological lesions is based upon the observation of patients who have been cured instantaneously of various affections such as peritoneal or bone tuberculosis, abscesses, osteitis, suppurating wounds, lupus, cancer, etc. . . . In a few seconds, a few minutes, at the most a few hours, wounds are cicatrized, pathological symptoms disappear, appetite returns . . . The miracle is characterized by an extreme acceleration of the processes of organic repair . . . The only condition indispensable for the occurrence of the phenomena is Prayer. The patient does not need himself to pray or to have any religious faith; but someone around him must be in a state of prayer.

Such facts are of profound significance. They show *the reality of certain relations of still unknown nature between psychological and organic processes. They prove the objective importance of spiritual activities* which hygienists, physicians, educators, and sociologists have almost always neglected to study. They open to man a new world.

Elsewhere Carrel stated his conviction that "the power of prayer is the greatest power in the world." Another great scientist, Charles Steinmetz of General Electric, asked by his colleagues what was the most important line of research for them to follow from here on, answered without a moment's hesitation: "Prayer. Find out about prayer!"

Dr. Vallet does not agree completely with the prayer theory as interpreted by Carrel, or with prayer as a complete and final explanation of miraculous cures, capable in itself of releasing the process of healing. Prayer is necessary for healing to be obtained, yes, says Vallet, "but it is not sufficient . . . *it is necessary that God agree to it,* and ratify the execution by His own intentions!"

And here we find ourselves confronted by that knotty problem that has plagued theologians and philosophers from time immemorial: the Will of God.

Vallet writes again:

> These cures are not the result of accident but of an all-powerful will which hears this prayer and whom nothing resists—neither sickness nor death . . . And this will is none other than the will of God. The healings at Lourdes, so varied in their conditions, so different in their method of realization, proceed nevertheless from one unique antecedent: the imploring of God. These cures being obtained, it is He who heals.*

The Church declares the cause of these cures to be "a special intervention of the Blessed Virgin Mary Immaculate Mother of God" or "a special intervention of God through the intercession of Notre Dame de Lourdes." Such a declaration is made in every proclamation by the Church of a Miraculous Cure.

Many Catholic doctors, such as Vallet and Leuret, agree with this. Other doctors say that there are phases and functions of human personality of which we have as yet very little knowledge—they prefer to wait before pronouncing judgment. Orthodox medical men of today tend to believe that these mysterious cures are due to errors of diagnosis in some cases, in others to psychological therapy of one kind or another.

Dr. Blanton suggests that the cause of the cures may be a transference by the patient to the Virgin Mary—a complete surrender to the power and compassion of the Blessed Mother, who, he feels, has the power and the will to intercede for him with the Creator Himself. Dr. Blanton puts an interesting argument for this viewpoint, stressing the influence of mother-worship on the race, the cohesiveness of the group at Lourdes around this worship, and so on. "It is only when they (the patients) have reached this state of complete surrender that they can be cured by such transference."

But however thorough the transference, however complete the surrender, transference—this mental and emotional shifting—can't build cells or join nerves and arteries in the twinkling of an eye. This, as

---

* In this chapter again I am much indebted to Dr. Vallet and his publishers Flammarion & Co. for material drawn from his valuable book, *La Vérité Sur Lourdes.*

doctors remind us over and again, is a *slow* and *progressive* process. No mere swift emotional change could accomplish it.

One of the favorite explanations of Lourdes cures by rationalist doctors is that they are produced by "unknown natural forces"—unknown today, but whose laws science may uncover tomorrow. I have heard interesting discussions on this by groups of doctors at the Medical Bureau.

Most of them appeared to discount this theory—because of the *irregularity of method* which, as we have seen, is one of the outstanding characteristics of Lourdes cures. They would point out that the action of the forces of nature is always general, universal, permanent and unchanging. The law of gravity, for example, works just the same for the learned scientist who falls from the seven-story window of his Paris apartment as for the savage in Africa who falls from the top of his coconut tree; for the Eskimo in Iceland, the tea-planter in Ceylon, or for any man any time, anywhere in the world.

So would it have to be with the "unknown natural forces" alleged to be responsible for Lourdes cures. They would have to act the same for all persons under similar conditions. Though their formulas are still unknown, their operation would have to show the characteristics of *generality, universality, permanence* and *changelessness:* the undeviating marks of the forces of nature.

But with Lourdes cures we see the exact opposite. Here, these "unknown forces" act neither constantly nor uniformly. They act today, but not tomorrow; for some people, but not for others. They have their privileged persons. They show a special fondness for the pilgrimage season. They appear less active during the winter.

Can we reasonably say, the AMIL doctors ask, that these are characteristics giving evidence of the action of natural forces?

Here, then are various theories and hypotheses—probably none of them acceptable to both the religious and the scientific-minded, certainly none of them satisfactory to all. The reader must decide for himself, or delay decision if he thinks that further evidence is necessary. But before leaving this question of causes, there is a point worth noting—a point that we arrive at through the facts of our experience.

Our physicists, in their accounts of the recent discoveries of physical science speak of forms of energy so fine that they can be known and described only through their effects. A Lourdes cure, as we have repeatedly seen, involves a profound spiritual as well as physical experience, and a profound and permanent spiritual transformation. These being the effects, we logically infer that the producing cause behind them must partake of the same qualities—in even larger measure: that the force which produces such profound spiritual transformation must be a force of tremendous spiritual power.

To bring about both physical and spiritual transformation, revolutionizing the whole being in an instant, it must be a magnificent force indeed.

25

First-hand Statements by the "Cures"

No scientific hypothesis up to the present accounts for the phenomena," says Dr. Carrel.

For myself, I have been interested in putting together first-hand statements by the Cures—comments made to me and to others about their sensations and subjective experiences at the moment of the cure and after. Similarities and repetitions among these, reports of the same sort of feelings among people of widely different types and ages, backgrounds and regions, may stimulate the reader's conjecture and further inquiry, as they have mine.

The two principal spots where cures occur are the baths and the Procession. At the baths, especially, many Cures speak of temporary but agonizing pain.

Elizabeth Delot (cancer of the stomach), cured at her first bath, felt "intolerable pain—a terrible burning and stabbing in the stomach and abdomen—as though they were holding her under the blows of a fiendish hammer." On coming out of the water, all this gave place to "a remarkable sense of well-being—a sense of vigor and appetite." She is cured!

Madame Gestas, cured at her second bath, of adhesive peritonitis—felt "diabolical pain, as though my whole insides were being torn out." Back at the Asile she felt better—began to eat. The cure made itself evident from that time on.

Fernand Legrand "felt as though his arms and legs were being broken to pieces"—a moment of utter agony. Only a moment, though —then he sat up and began to help the brancardiers to dress him.

Joachime Dehant, whole ulcered leg was cured at the second bath, felt "terrible pain, followed by a feeling of ease and disappearance of pain." She went home wearing boots she had brought as an act of faith.

Francis Pascal uttered loud cries. His mother thought he had a convulsion.

John Traynor: At his ninth and last bath his legs became violently agitated—almost emptied the whole bath of its water. On his way to the baths, earlier during his visit, he "felt something burst in my chest, and blood flowed freely from my mouth." After that, "some change had taken place in me which marked the end of my epileptic fits. I never had another."

Madame Augault, partially cured at first bath, felt excruciating pain for the brief instant of her immersion in the water. "Sensation of being put in boiling oil." But the compression in her abdomen seemed to disappear. Calmed down on her return to the hospital. In the afternoon Procession, again great pain—"as though my insides were being torn out" (like Gestas). Everything quieted down at the passing of the Blessed Sacrament. From that precise moment as the Host was raised above her, "as though by enchantment," her sufferings vanished. Her energies had a rebirth—she could get up and walk!

Achille Billet, cured at the baths of a suppurating wound in the foot, of four years—felt "agonizing pain in affected foot and leg" at the moment of his cure. "Fine," afterwards.

Abbé Fiamma, cured at first bath of varicose veins with ulcerations —felt intense pain, "like the insertion of a red-hot iron under the skin." Francois Macary, cured of the same disease, felt no pain at all but woke up in the middle of the night cured, having simply put Lourdes water on his legs.

Patients do not always feel pain but it seems that in a great many cases they do. Constance Piquet, cured at the third bath of cancer of the breast, felt no attendant pain or disturbance. Swelling disappeared, everything normal.

Rose Martin (cancer of the uterus) "felt something moving inside —through my whole being. Not painful, not tearing—but moving." "It was your cure, madame!" said the Sister.

Madame Pouxvieille (stomach ulcer) at the second bath felt something extraordinary taking place within her, and then felt considerably better. From that time on, she was cured; felt "as though a current were running through her body."

Many accounts of spiritual healing speak of an "electric current" running through the body. Charles McDonald called it "a glow." The first bath had no effect as regards his illness. But at the second bath he "felt the first glow of health." "When leaving the bath I felt more fit than I had ever felt in my life."

Both McDonald and Joachime Dehant brought clothes with them to wear home for the return trip—as normal persons. In these cases, a psychiatrist might say that a powerful suggestion was conveyed to the subconscious, impressing it with the complete acceptance of a perfect cure; no complexes, no inhibitions. And the cure was accomplished.

Another striking case was that of Monsieur Vion-Dury, totally blind for seven years, afflicted with two detached retinas. Dipping a finger in Lourdes water, he passed it over his eyes; then felt violent pain "as though someone had thrust a knife into his eyes." He thought the Sister had made a mistake and given him the ammonia bottle. But on that instant his sight was completely recovered. The case was the subject of a paper by Dr. Dor of Lyon, who had treated him, at the Congress of Ophthalmology in Paris.

Madame Pierson, suffering from contraction of the arms and legs with palsy, following encephalitis, took a partial bath in the piscine. Violent pain—"as though her right arm were being torn off." Immediately afterward the arm and hand could move with ease. Next day recuperation was complete.

Mademoiselle Maria Raedt, afflicted for several years with pyelonephritis and cystitis, the day before her departure from Lourdes felt a sensation of "tearing" in the lower abdomen, and of intolerable pain. Her illness was finished.

I have not heard any similar reports on this pain question from healing centers other than Lourdes, though they may of course exist. At Lourdes, especially at the baths, intense pain seems to be a very common characteristic.

While many cures occur at the baths, many others—and some of the most notable—have occurred at the Procession of the Blessed Sacrament. Sometimes peacefully, sometimes, at the baths, accompanied by intense and painful sensations. "With the cures that take place at the passing of the Blessed Sacrament," says Dr. Vallet, "we observe similar phenomena which seem to indicate the intervention of some superior force."

Nina Kin, a girl who had been horribly burned by the upsetting of a demijohn of sulfuric acid—nerves of the leg involved—had been unable to move for six months. She felt herself "lifted up by a violent impulse" and started to walk after the Procession.

Marguerite Savoye, twenty years old, a living corpse weighing forty pounds, had not left her bed or taken any solid nourishment for six years. As the Blessed Sacrament passed, "a violent and irresistible impulse" raised her on her bed and threw her abruptly to earth. She found herself at the foot of her litter on her knees. "I am cured!" she cried. "I am cured!"

Mademoiselle Guimard of the Bordeaux, paralyzed seventeen years, at the moment when the Blessed Sacrament came near her, experienced an indefinable feeling and motion "like the sweep of waves" which raised her from her litter. "This sensation," she says, "I can neither forget nor explain—but it certainly proceeded from a force outside of and superior to my own nature." She said she "became conscious of a violent movement of the knee—a violent force which suddenly took possession of her and *flung* her from her litter."

Gargam, the atheist—"in pieces" after his terrible railway accident —also declared that he had the sensation of "being thrown from his litter to the ground." "Hurled" was the word he used.

John Traynor records that "his arm began to agitate violently" at the Procession, as his legs had at the baths. He burst his bandage and freed the arm—now active again after being paralyzed for eight years.

Here are other interesting comments:

Jeanne Fretel, cured at Communion and at the Grotto, said: "I had the sensation that someone took me under the arms to help me sit down. I found myself in a sitting position. Looking round, I could see no one. As soon as I was seated I had the feeling that the same hands that helped me to sit down took my hands to put them on my abdomen"—which she discovered, had suddenly become flat and normal. She thought she was dreaming, but came back to full consciousness, cured.

Sister Marie-Marguerite, also cured at Communion and "moved to go there by what seemed a superhuman force," records that "it seemed to me that a hand, both gentle and powerful, passed over my legs, which suddenly became deflated. New life flowed through them. The bandages fell to the floor."

The reader will have noticed how many cures occur at, or just after, the moment of Communion—at the Grotto, at the Altar of Bernadette, or when the Host is raised over the sick at the passing of the Sacrament at the Procession. That is, at the moment when emotional intensity and spiritual fervor (their own and others') is at its height: when the intense emotional force of the crowd, and the spiritual exaltation of the priests and bishops, of their own families and attendants, reaches its climax.

Marie-Louise Arnaud was cured at the moments when she was praying for her dead brother, at the Grotto. She had just taken Communion. She did so, "completely absorbed in the thought of my brother and oblivious of myself and my illness." Turning her face on the pillow to hide her tears, she suddenly discovered that her limbs and sight were normal. She was cured!

Madame Charette (tumor of the liver) was cured while lying in front of the Grotto after a particularly painful "crisis." Cured just after Communion—she has been in flourishing health ever since.

Ernestine Guilloteau, a skeleton weighing forty-six pounds, dying of tuberculous peritonitis and supposedly on the very verge of death, got up and followed the Blessed Sacrament up the steps to the Rosary Church. She did this in a state of semi-consciousness, at the moment when, believing herself dying, she was thanking the Blessed Virgin for the great happiness of dying there before Her wonderful Grotto. Suddenly she found herself walking and following the Sacrament into the Church.

Many *miraculés* speak of this state of "unawareness" of what was going on in the physical world, of being transported, in spite of and "beyond" themselves and their normal consciousness.

Mademoiselle Clauzel was cured at Mass, between the Elevation and the Communion. At this moment her family noticed "signs of agitation" in the invalid which they took to be the result of the very long ritual. In reality it was her cure, which at first she did not dare believe. She records "a sense of profound well-being"—not of agitation but of "a wonderful force acting within her, renewing her entire being." She knew beyond the shadow of a doubt that she was cured. She went to the altar and offered her thanksgiving. "It seemed to me," she said, "that I was no longer touching the ground."

Jeanne Fretel said she never knew how she got to the Grotto from the Altar of Bernadette where she was cured. She felt as though she "must have flown there."

Mrs. Feely, cured at the baths of a diseased lung, knew "a supreme joy and peace—breath-taking! The next thing I knew I was at the

Grotto. Never knew how I got there. I felt as though I were floating—flying." She looked around to see if people were noticing her—afraid they would think her "queer." She knelt down and gave thanks; afterwards she ran all the way up the steep steps to the top of the Basilica. Her pilgrimage doctor, meeting her, gazed at her astounded.

John Traynor appears to have been in a detached subjective state for some twenty-four hours after his cure. He ran to the Grotto and prayed, came back to the Asile and dressed himself, went into chapel, and served Mass for the officiating priest. Then he had breakfast, went through a long series of interviews and events during a crowded day, still not fully conscious of what had happened to him. "Although I knew I had received a great favor from Our Lady, I had no recollection of all the illness that had gone before."

In the train on the way home, he was "still in a sort of daze"—until one of the bishops came in and talked to him. "John, do you realize how ill you were, and that you have been miraculously cured?"

"Then," said Traynor, "everything came back to me, the memory of my years of illness, the sufferings of the journey, and how ill I had been in Lourdes too . . . Suddenly I realized fully what had happened."

The repeated references by the Cures to "hands" helping them, "a violent force" hurling them to the ground and so on, will interest those who believe in the influence upon human beings of beings in another world. Early man—and men of modern times also—have believed that spirits "gone before" could help mortals in their physical as well as moral need. According to Catholic doctrine, God may sometimes use the saints, angels, and other beings to assist in work of spiritual or physical transformation. Prayer, ritual, the lifting of the heart in meditation—all are regarded as aids. But these are all considered preparatory disciplines, essential to a cure but not to be confused with the final Cause and Creator.

Our American Indians have some interesting beliefs, in the matter of preparatory prayers and rituals. Mary Austin, who spent much of her life among them, quotes the words of an old Indian chief who offered prayers for the cure of her servant:

"He said you couldn't get help from the Friend simply by asking. You had first to get to Him. You had to make a veritable motion of your own soul—*here*. (He moved his hand over his solar plexus.) When you had climbed up to the Friend by rhythmic motions and sounds, then you came close to Him, and the thing you wanted happened."

Mrs. Austin added: "I discovered that the value of sustained rhythmic movements and sounds, so much used by the Indians, lay in their power to break the tension of immediate circumstances and their hold upon the attention . . . a completely integrated movement, persisted in until all the rhythms of the physical body are gathered together in it to the exclusion of all bodily sensations."*

A completely integrated movement: the prayer and faith at Lourdes perpetually going up as with one voice, certainly produces such a movement and constitutes a tremendous living force of which even the most callous and indifferent must be aware.

Apropos of relaxing tension and "letting go," we note that patients of Lourdes are often cured (1) when they are not thinking about themselves and their cure; (2) when they are praying for someone else; (3) when they have stopped hoping and have given up altogether—as with Ernestine Guilloteau and her mother.

Lydia Brosse was completely unconscious of her cure when it came. Nothing (apparently) had happened, at the baths or during her stay at Lourdes. Greatly depressed, she was on her way home. When she had stopped hoping, given up, *let go,* the cure came. Lydia unaware of it, had to be told by another patient of her change in looks.

Cures often occur when the recipient is absorbed in the thought of God or of some absent loved one. In such cases the person praying forgets all about himself—his personal problems, tensions, fears and anxieties—and becomes single-pointed, overwhelmed by a great, impersonal, selfless feeling for his neighbor, and by faith and reliance on a Higher Being or God. His own being is permeated with the consciousness of this Higher Being. Then the "miracle" of transformed physical structure takes place.

We have reviewed a series of facts—and some speculations—with regard to Lourdes cures. My own deepest impression has to do with the atmosphere of the place. *Prayer* is the essence and heart of that atmosphere. Constant prayer, constant repetition of certain liturgies, hymns, responses—the Rosary, the Station, the Hail Marys—over and over, thousands of times, creates a spiritual and mental atmosphere surround-

* From Mrs. Austin's *Can Prayer Be Answered?* with kind permissions of Rinehart & Company, Inc.

ing the patient; opening his whole being to spiritual forces of renewal and transformation. The very air he breathes conveys this to him.

Faith too plays a major part. "I had tremendous faith," said Madame Pellegrin. "Well, madame, I had great faith!" declared the mother of little Francis Pascal. "How much the faith of those Sisters meant to me!" said Rose Martin, and Jeanne Gestas, and half a dozen others. "It did something to me, madame—it seemed to roll a stone away!" (Probably unlocked certain inner resistances and long-standing psychological blocks and disbeliefs.) The nurses, the brancardiers, the priests and everybody around them, are sending out this strong faith all day and every minute.

Last but by no means least, that ever-present spirit of *devotion:* the great wave of love and compassion pouring out over those rows upon rows of sick, every hour and every second throughout the Domaine. Thousands of people moving together as one being, acting in unison in faith and prayer and overflowing love and service; thousands of lives moving in concentrated purpose in one direction—a single motion, a single intent. What a rhythm *this* must produce! What an effect it must have on those receptive eager souls.

It may be that the wavelength brought about by constant prayer, constant spiritual "recollection" by people at the highest level of thinking and giving, produces a psychological condition that has a definite effect upon the patient. His own psychic and spiritual state, and that of his relatives, nurses, and others around him, may play an important part too in opening the way for a cure. The presence or absence of moral or psychological blocks must also have something to do with it.

All these are contributing *conditions*—but none of them can be a *cause.* No one of them can create new bone or tissue instantaneously. That, Catholics say, can be done only by a Divine Creator—God.

26

The End of the Road

Now, what does it all add up to? What stays with you? What is most important? And why is it important to *me*—asks the everyday normal person leading a healthy normal existence here at home. What significance has all this in relation to *my* everyday life and affairs?

Each of us must make his own appraisal. But for me personally, this is the core of it and the summing up:

Lourdes is important because it offers the thing most needed by every human being: spiritual assurance, solid ground to stand on. In a recent Town Hall poll, the major anxiety of modern men and women was found to be not money, or health, or even war. More than twenty thousand men and women gave as their major worry, *spiritual insecurity:* "The need for some solid spiritual and moral basis of life," "Something to believe in, to hang on to," "Something I can really be sure of, something I *know* is there."

Swept away from the old moorings, buffeted about between science and psychiatry, Kinsey and Comte, the menace of the guided missile and the super-bomb, now in the panic science has laid upon them, they desperately search for something to hold on to, some inner haven, since no physical refuge can be relied on.

For me, Lourdes gives that solid rock, that inner fortress; takes us back to the lost spiritual foundations so many thousands and millions are longing to find again.

Lourdes is one of the wonders of the world today, yes; from a scientific point of view, from a psychological point of view, from a human-interest point of view. But more than this—far more—Lourdes holds the answer to the problems of a sick humanity. Here is healing not only for a few thousand suffering individuals: here is the answer, the key, to the healing of a sick world.

Time and again a *miraculé* will say: "Well, we had tried everything else—doctors, medicines, hot springs, therapies. They all failed. There was nothing left. So we had to go to Lourdes. We *had* to try God!"

I heard the same thing at one of the big international conferences in Geneva. Going in to see the Chief of one of the top Commissions, I found him reading the Bible. In the midst of all the hubbub and confusion—telegrams, visitors, special messengers, transatlantic telephone calls—there he sat, with the Book in his hand, quietly reading.

"Well! Isn't this rather unusual?" (He was anything but a religious man.)

"Well," he said, with a tired smile across his littered table, "we've tried everything else. I guess you have to come back to it, don't you? You have to come to it sooner or later."

A sick person—or a sick world. Sooner or later.

Today we are told, not only by Communists but by many supposedly intelligent people in our own communities, that God and the Scriptures are myth and foolishness; that the idea of a superhuman power is "mediaeval superstition"—old wives' tales. The "rational intelligent" modern man is "old-fashioned" and "behind the times" if he believes in such things.

He is behind the times if he doesn't. The position of the nonbeliever, a Nobel-prize-winning physician has assured us, can no longer be sustained. Facts prove that there *is* a superhuman power. For at Lourdes—and at other healing centers—we see a superhuman power in action, doing what human power has repeatedly proved unable to do.

"That is actual which acts," says Dr. Carl Jung.

"It Acts—therefore It Exists," is the quiet assertion that rules this Domaine.

So Lourdes offers first this great message: *The fact of a higher-than-human Power* which we see here, undeniable and in actual operation. "If miracles occur, then God exists," as more than one skeptic has admitted. The fact of the existence of that Power, that man may have access to it, receive help from it, be healed of his ills and woes through it—this fact has been proved at Lourdes not once but hundreds and thousands of times. Sometimes physically, sometimes spiritually, or both.

The cures at Lourdes come about (as Dr. Blanton says) through surrender to a Higher Power—through complete dependence and reliance upon that Power. This is the process with Lourdes cures and the cures at other healing centers. It is the same with the cures that occur at Alcoholics Anonymous—where "surrender to a power greater than ourselves" is the keystone of the entire program;* with the "conversions" of the orthodox churches, and with practically every form of spiritual healing and transformation.

This Power exists (all teach). It can do what I cannot do. If I turn to it in faith and trust, it will help me. It will deliver me from my ills and problems, heal my iniquities, cure my diseases.

"Is there really such a Higher Power?" people ask doubtfully.

If there isn't, what cause is producing all these effects? Certainly no man or group of men is producing them. That is actual which acts. Here is a Power which we see in daily operation before our eyes, in concrete physical conditions.

Of the nature of the Power we are as yet woefully ignorant. We shall learn more about it when we seek further, try hard enough to find out more; when we try as hard to discover the secrets of Life as men have tried to discover those of death and destruction.

But we do know this much: It Acts; therefore It Exists. There is a higher-than-human Power. Man is in contact with it—blurred, only partial thus far, perhaps—*but contact.* He can approach the Power by asking humbly, sincerely—and it responds to him.

This we know from actual facts of human experience, from tens of thousands of cases, not only at Lourdes but in many other places. And it is the most important knowledge in the world for every living being in it. God—not the hydrogen bomb—is the greatest Fact of present-day existence. This is the Fact of Lourdes.

So, the first great Lourdes declaration: *God is true.* And the second: *The Miracles are true.* The man with the palsy, the boy with the deaf and dumb spirit, the woman with the infirmity of twelve years, the soldier's son, the man with the withered arm, and many with much worse, are there before our very eyes.

These are no longer "quaint stories" of olden time, to be glossed over, "interpreted," glibly explained away in the light of the "higher

* Dr. Harry Tiebout says the root disease of the alcoholic is his idea of his own omnipotence. If you can get him to give *that* up, he has a chance for a cure. It is true of every disease—and of the world's illness also.

criticism." They are facts of present-day experience: facts to be honestly acknowledged and respected.

Robert Hugh Benson, son of an Archbishop of Canterbury, puts it like this after his own visit to Lourdes:

> For over thirty years I had been accustomed to repeat the accepted formula—that "the age of miracles is past," that "they were necessary for the establishment of Christianity but that they are no longer necessary now, on rare occasions perhaps"—and in my heart I knew my foolishness . . . As for Lourdes, I spoke of hysteria and autosuggestion and French imaginativeness and the rest of it.
>
> As a child on Sunday afternoons I used to walk with my father and listen to his discourse. As an Anglican clergyman I used to teach in Sunday schools or preach to children. As a Catholic priest I used occasionally to attend a catechism. At all these times the miraculous seemed singularly far away. We looked at it across twenty centuries. It was something from which a lesson might be drawn, upon which the imagination might feed, but it was a state of affairs as remote as the life of prehistoric man; one assented to it, and that was all.
>
> Here at Lourdes it was a present vivid event. I sat at an ordinary glass window, in a cassock made by an English tailor, with an Englishman beside me, and saw the miraculous happen. (Five times in one afternoon, he said, "the finger of God flashed down" and one of those dying figures rose and walked victoriously up the steps into the Church.) Time and space disappeared, the centuries shrank and vanished, and behold we saw that which prophets and kings have desired to see, and have not seen.*

The Miracles are true. The Scriptures are true.

The longer one stays at Lourdes, the more one is impressed with

---

* From "Lourdes" by Robert Hugh Benson. By kind permissions of the literary Executors of the late Mgr. Benson and of the Manresa Press.

the literal truth of many passages in the Bible that, of late years, learned critics have insisted we should consider purely allegorical.

And this has a direct bearing on the spiritual insecurity of the present generation. One of the chief causes of moral breakdown during the past half century has been increasing disbelief in the Scriptures and in a Supreme Being whose moral law is the blueprint for sane human behavior. Without such belief we have no moral yardstick, no universal gauge of reference.

Our forefathers went through their terrific problems, wars, privations, sacrifices, because they had an unshakable faith in God and His divinely inspired Revelation, giving the laws of life by which they were meant to live.

How do we know that these laws given in the Bible truly are the basic moral law for us? Again, for the pragmatist, by effects. Because when we break them, we and our world know chaos. When we break the laws laid down for a moral human nature, we rapidly revert (as in recent years) to the state of the jungle.

There are some things in the Scriptures, no doubt, that directly apply to the times in which they were written; some that do not apply today. But—and here is the never-to-be-forgotten point: there is much in them that is everlasting and eternal. Scientific theory changes every twenty-four hours. The great spiritual principles taught us by Christ and the Prophets and seers have stood unchanged for centuries. No modern psychiatrist has invented any substitute for them. On the contrary, the psychiatrists are going back to them, and preaching these principles themselves now, more and more emphatically.

The Fact of God—the Miracles—the truth of the Scriptures: these are great lessons, great gifts of Lourdes. But these are not all. There is still the innermost core of it, the thing that makes Lourdes take hold of you, never to let you go.

When I have these discussions with myself, trying to push through to the innermost secret—seeing those restless throngs, those eager, seeking faces—a certain text in the Bible comes back to me again and again:

"They looked for a city . . . a city which hath foundations"—foundations of love and devotion and unselfishness, just genuine friendship, *caring people*—"whose builder and maker is God."

To my mind, that is the secret of Lourdes.

Here the homesick millions find what they are looking for, what they have been searching for, hungering after, ever since they were born.

The greatest thing at Lourdes is not the cures. It is not the rediscovery of the Scriptures. It is not the rediscovery of God, vital as that is. That is only half of it. The other half is putting God into actual everyday living.

The greatest thing about Lourdes is the spirit in which life is lived there: the Brotherhood of Man in actual performance, the Beloved Community, *the human dream come true*.

"You can't run any community today on the principles laid down by Christ," we are told. "It isn't practical. It isn't normal. It won't work. It just can't be done!"

At Lourdes you see it *being* done—joyfully, successfully—every minute of the day. You yourself are part of its being done. That's why it seems "home" to the homesick hearts of men and women from all over creation. The way we were meant to live. A life based on Love instead of Power—of helping one another, serving the weak, sharing among the strong. No wonder thousands of practical people yearn for the few precious days or weeks each year when they can return to it—the most normal of all atmospheres.

Lourdes says the way to happiness is to give, not grab. It is every man's nature to give. Economic systems, exploitations, and tyrannies have forced him into the false position of fighting his brother, fighting to *get*. The modern human being is a mass of frustrations, conflicts, and diseases, in consequence.

Lourdes releases him—to be himself: furnishes him an outlet for self-giving. So it seems like heaven. The one way to peace and bliss, every great prophet has told us, is to give yourself away. From the human standpoint, to give yourself to your fellow men; from the superhuman, to give yourself to God: to the Highest. We are all trying to find our way back—into that one normal and natural condition.

We set out on Pilgrimage the minute we are born: out into the glittering world of our own omnipotence, our arrogant self-sufficiency; and some of us wander into a very far country indeed before finally we "come to ourselves" and make the swing-around, back to the place whence we came forth.

Every race, every religion, tells of this eternal quest, this perennial journey. The Chinese call it "the Old Road"; the Hindus "the Path of Return"; in Christianity we read of it in the story of the Prodigal Son.

Everybody knows it is there—that Road of Return. Everybody

knows that sooner or later he has to take it. Even the people who are yelling loudest about "sentimental eyewash" and "mediaeval superstition": even they, the self-styled atheists and agnostics know it, deep down in their hearts. The more loudly they howl, the less sure they are of themselves.

Every man is born with that picture—the image of the Goal—deep within him; and never loses it, no matter how low he may fall. The folklore of every people sings of it.

The road to Lourdes is the Road Back Home. Every man must take it, for in the end (as all us sick find out) there is nowhere else to go. In the end, everyone must "come to Lourdes"—the shining city, the beloved community, the city of brothers—the Father's House: the end of the long road where we pilgrims of all faiths and races come Home.

THE MIRACLE OF LOURDES

≈ *PART FOUR* ≈

Cures Since 1955

Recounted in this chapter, among others, are some of the details of two of the last three cures of tuberculosis recorded in Lourdes (the third appears in Chapter 28). Almost half of the miraculous cures up to 1948 were cures of tuberculosis. The only "treatment" until then was the fresh air, good food, and rest at the numerous sanatoriums in Europe, and/or to collapse a part of a lung by mechanical or surgical means. As there was no effective drug therapy, when cases of tuberculosis were suddenly cured at Lourdes there was little doubt that these would be considered miraculous cures. In fact, many rather skeptical physicians have remarked that with tuberculosis now a curable disease, there is not much need for Lourdes today!

Since tuberculosis was so prevalent, thousands of cases came to Lourdes on pilgrimage, but with not much hope of a cure. Lydia Brosse and Maddalena Carini were happy exceptions.

Included here too are the only three miraculous cures of multiple sclerosis recorded and recognized up to now in Lourdes. These three cures (Thea Angele, Alice Couteault and Brother Leo Schwager) illustrate the difference between miraculous cures and natural remissions. The normal course of this disease is one of alternating remissions and relapses before the final stage of permanent disability progressively worsens until death occurs. When there is a natural remission, it is a gradual process requiring a period of convalescence, during which the muscles slowly regain their power to make full movement possible.

This is in marked contrast to the speedy recovery of these three *miraculés.* Each of the three patients was in a state of grave illness and disability, and was suddenly cured at Lourdes. All their symptoms disappeared, and no long convalescence was needed. Within hours, they each regained full vigor and mobility, sufficient for them to return immediately to their former occupations. Alice Couteault rode a bicycle the day after she returned home from Lourdes. Moreover, their cures were permanent. No sign of a recurrence ever appeared, and all of them remained well for over twenty years afterward.

27

Miraculous Cures from 1955 to 1963

Miss Lydia Brosse's cure of multiple tuberculous abscesses in 1930 was described by Ruth Cranston (Ch. 18, p. 180ff.) as one of those who were cured on the train going home. In good health afterward, she often returned to Lourdes in the ensuing years, and made a special pilgrimage there in 1955, the twenty-fifth anniversary of her cure. On that occasion, she called at the Medical Bureau, where her case was examined by the thirteen doctors present. They confirmed both the permanence of her cure and the decision made by their former colleagues at the B.C.M. in 1931 that the cure was extraordinary. They also decided that the dossier should be presented to the International Medical Committee of Lourdes for further assessment.

One of the committee members, Prof. Oberlin, was delegated to produce a full report. The main problem, which led to some discussion, was the absence of bacteriological information giving the precise cause of Miss Brosse's numerous abscesses. However, the whole history of her illness was consistent with a chronic tuberculous infection. Moreover, the sudden and permanent restoration to health, after the local application of Lourdes water to her wounds and two baths daily in the Piscines, was dramatic. Although she left Lourdes in a corpse-like condition, only four hours later, on the train going home, she suddenly felt better, hungry, free from pain, and her abscesses were healing. She could sit up unaided. When the train arrived at the St.-Raphaël station,

Miss Brosse walked from it with remarkable ease. The ambulance and stretcher awaiting her arrival were not needed.

All this information enabled the committee to accept her cure unanimously as medically inexplicable. The next stage in the procedure was to present her dossier to the bishops of her present and former dioceses. In 1930, Miss Brosse lived in the Diocese of Toulon-Fréjus, but by 1956 she had moved into the Diocese of Coutances. After due inquiries, on August 5, 1958, the Bishop of Coutances declared her cure miraculous, saying, "We judge and declare that the cure of Miss L. Brosse, which occurred on October 11, 1930, in the pilgrimage train returning from Lourdes, was miraculous, and must be attributed to a special intervention of the Blessed Virgin, Immaculate Mother of God."

It had been a long wait—twenty-eight years since her cure. She continued to visit Lourdes regularly to give thanks for her years of freedom from tuberculosis. Miss Brosse died in September 1984, at the age of ninety-five.

Miss Maddalena Carini was cured of tuberculosis in 1948. The delay before declaring her cure miraculous was due to the twelve years taken for investigations.

Miss Carini, born at Bereguardo, Pavia, Italy, in 1917, lost her father and two aunts to tuberculosis. She, too, contracted the infection. Beginning in 1935, she displayed signs of tuberculosis: pleurisy at age ten; Pott's Disease of the spine at age thirteen, requiring sanatorium treatment; tuberculosis peritonitis at age seventeen; tuberculous pericarditis and abscesses of the upper femur by 1947.

During this long, eighteen-year history of chronic infection, her general condition steadily deteriorated. She became anemic, was often feverish, and lost weight. Her abdomen became distended. She had difficulty walking, due to the bone and cardiac complications. Her family nursed her at home in the early years, but later she spent much of her time in the hospital.

The hospital doctors were not very happy about letting Miss Carini travel anywhere, but she did get permission to go to Lourdes in 1947. On returning to the sanatorium as ill as ever, she was mocked for her faith. . . . Undaunted, she went to Lourdes again the next year with the UNITALSI Pilgrimage. While reciting the Rosary at the Grotto on August 15, 1948, she suddenly felt a sensation of warmth and "creepiness" in the chest, and had palpitations. This was followed immediately by a feeling of well-being. The next day, during the Blessing of the Sick, she experienced similar sensations. At this stage, she realized she was cured. Her distended abdomen, bone pains, and angina had all vanished.

Miss Carini decided to keep the secret of her cure to herself, so she did not inform the doctors until the next day, August 16, on the return journey to Milan. They found a remarkable improvement in her, and this was confirmed at the hospital in Milan. A year later, her doctor, Dr. Bonizzi, stated, "We are in the presence of a *restitutio ad integrum,* complete and absolute, of all the symptoms which had affected the lungs, circulation, viscera, ovaries and bones." Another senior physician, Dr. Villa, declared that her "cure was contrary to all logical expectation, considering her past medical history."

A year later, Miss Carini returned to Lourdes and was examined at the Medical Bureau, where the doctors wanted to see her medical reports and X-rays. When these proved satisfactory, the Medical Bureau, in 1950, concluded that her cure was "medically inexplicable" and referred the case to the International Committee of Lourdes. The Committee concurred with the findings of the Medical Bureau. The Canonical Diocesan Committee in Milan also accepted their decision, enabling Cardinal Montini, Archbishop of Milan, to declare, in 1960, that her cure was a "miraculous fact."

Miss Carini has remained well since. In thanksgiving, she founded a religious order, "La Famille de l'Ave Maria," with its mother house at San Remo. In their work for the sick and the poor, this order tries to extend to them the same loving care as the Blessed Virgin showed to its foundress.

Mrs. Alice Couteault came from Bouillé-Loretz, in France, where she was born in 1917. She was married, and had a child in 1938. Apart from phlebitis, her health was good. Her illness (multiple sclerosis) began in July 1949 with early symptoms causing spasticity of the legs together with loss of balance, which made walking increasingly difficult. Deterioration progressed, with disturbances of vision and loss of speech and of sphincter control. She developed a tremor of the hands which made eating, sewing, and writing awkward. Her loss of weight gave her a gaunt, emaciated appearance.

Mrs. Couteault felt her only hope lay in joining the Anjou Pilgrimage to Lourdes. Her husband, a nonpracticing Catholic, was against her undertaking the journey, but he did accompany her to the station, wheeling her along the platform to the ambulance coach. She arrived in Lourdes on May 12, 1952, in a very poor state after the arduous journey by train.

From the moment of her arrival in Lourdes, Mrs. Couteault began to feel some improvement and regain her appetite. After being taken to the Baths on May 15, she experienced a strange sensation of faintness, palpitations, and tinnitus (ringing in the ears). In the afternoon she managed to walk a few steps in the ward at the Accueil Notre Dame. During the Procession of the Blessed Sacrament she recovered her speech and was surprised to hear herself making the responses to the invocations along with the crowd, who, if they can, all take part. But she realized she was getting the words mixed up, so she said little out loud, fearing she would be embarrassed. After being wheeled back to the Accueil Notre Dame, she jumped down from her stretcher and walked perfectly without any help.

Mrs. Couteault was examined at the Medical Bureau on May 16. It was determined that all neurological signs of her illness had disappeared, apart from a minimal tendency of the eyeballs to oscillate, and absent corneal reflexes.

Being a reserved person and not wanting to advertise her cure, Mrs. Couteault remained in a wheelchair in Lourdes, and on the homeward-bound train she traveled with the other sick pilgrims. Her husband had engaged an ambulance and was waiting at the station among all the other relatives and friends who had come to greet the returning pilgrims. On the train, word had gone around that no one was to alight from the train until Mrs. Couteault had stepped onto the platform and walked on her own to greet her husband. But Mr. Couteault was looking for his invalid wife in a wheelchair, and at first he neither noticed nor recognized her. When they eventually came face to face and he realized it was his wife standing before him, he fainted. He was taken home in the ambulance he had engaged for his wife, and remained in bed, speechless, for three days. His first words on recovery were to ask his wife to send for the priest to thank God for this cure.

Mrs. Couteault returned to Lourdes regularly following her cure. She was checked at the Medical Bureau in 1953 and 1954, and by the International Medical Committee of Lourdes in Paris in 1955. There was no doubt—she had been completely cured of multiple sclerosis. Msgr. Henri Vion, the Bishop-Coadjutor of Poitiers pronounced the cure miraculous in 1956.

Brother Leo Schwager, a lay brother in the Benedictine Congregation of Ste. Odile, in Switzerland, was one of the only three persons to be miraculously cured of multiple sclerosis in Lourdes. He was born in 1924, and his early years were marked by accidents: a tumble from his bicycle left him unconscious; a kick from a horse during his military service also rendered him unconscious; and after a steep dive, he needed resuscitation on being rescued from the water. He survived all these traumas, but fell victim to multiple sclerosis in 1947. During the next five years, he showed the common features of this disease, aggravated in 1951 by a transient paralysis. By then, he could stand up for no more than ten minutes at a time. In 1952, Brother Leo left for Lourdes, full of confidence in God and the Blessed Mother. After receiving holy communion on April 30, he prayed for a cure with even greater fervor. After mass he went into the Piscines, and emerged with a feeling in his legs as though he might be able to walk again. But he could not. He prayed in his wheelchair at the Grotto, surrounded by many sick people. He found time before the afternoon Procession to go into the Baths again. After that his legs no longer felt numb and heavy.

Brother Leo's own description of his faith and cure is recorded. While waiting for the Blessing of the Sick, he recalls, "I prayed with all my heart. As the Blessed Sacrament came near to me, my confidence increased yet more. I hoped and said this prayer: 'Lord, if Thou wilt, Thou canst cure me. Holy Mother, pray for me!' All at once I felt something like an electric shock and immediately got out of my wheelchair without knowing what had happened to me. I fell on my knees; my eyes were fixed on the Blessed Sacrament right to the end of the ceremony . . . and I was lost in prayer." Only then did he realize that he had been cured. Overcome with joy, he felt at peace. Professor Barbin, Consultant Surgeon of the Medical Faculty in Nantes, was walking in the Procession that day and observed this spectacular cure. He actually heard the thud when Brother Leo fell onto his knees, and was most struck by his facial expression. He wrote later: "He had an air of blissful ecstasy, with eyes fixed on the Blessed Sacrament as it was carried away from him. I noticed that at the same time he seemed breathless, as if affected by great emotion, hardly able to take a deep breath." Professor Barbin was present at the Medical Bureau when Brother Leo was examined the following day.

By May 3, when his appetite had returned, Brother Leo realized fully that on April 30 his paralysis, numbness of the limbs, intense headaches, and backache had gone for good, after five years of dreadful disability.

Dr. Jeger, the doctor in charge of Brother Leo's pilgrimage, also examined the monk at the end of his pilgrimage. In his report he described in detail the absence of all previous symptoms, and how he walked normally and was psychologically sound, adding, ". . . he does not give the impression of being nervy, anxious or a man disturbed."

Brother Leo returned to Lourdes in 1956, 1957, and 1958, working as a brancardier. He was declared healthy at the Medical Bureau, but did not bring his medical records right away. In 1958, Dr. Pelissier, President of the Medical Bureau, announced that this instant and extraordinary cure had been maintained for six years without a relapse. Professor Thiebaut, Consultant Neurologist and member of the International Medical Committee of Lourdes, agreed that the cure was medically inexplicable. He asked the Bishop of Tarbes and Lourdes to present the case to the Archbishop of Lausanne, Geneva, and Fribourg for further confirmation. This came in 1960, when the cure was proclaimed miraculous. Brother Leo is now the bursar of his Congregation, goes on pilgrimage to Lourdes annually, and remains well.

Miss Thea Angele was also one of the three miraculous cures of multiple sclerosis at Lourdes. She is German, born September 24, 1921, at Oberlangensee, Neukirch (Württemberg) and was a shorthand typist before this illness. She was not unaccustomed to sickness, having already undergone three operations, as well as fracturing her wrist twice. Her multiple sclerosis began in 1944 and progressed until 1946, by which time she was bedridden. Dr. Kohler confirmed the diagnosis. She was admitted to the Neurology Clinic at Tübingen, where the prognosis was anything but favorable. Alcohol injections into nerves to relieve the pain were ineffective. She became extremely emaciated and declined into a stupor.

Fortunately, she had earlier expressed a wish to be taken to Lourdes. She was put on the Pax Christi Pilgrimage train at Ulm station on May 15, 1950. She was apparently dying—one of the doctors commented, "How could one send a dying person on a thirty-hour journey to a foreign country?" On arrival in Lourdes, two days later, she was taken directly to the Accueil Notre Dame and given the Last Rites. Next morning, after her first immersion in the Baths, her medical officer noticed a slight change: a smile on her face. The following day, Miss Angele went into the Baths twice. After the morning immersion, she could drink and swallow; after the one in the afternoon, her pain vanished. On May 20 she was taken for yet another immersion. When she came out, Dr. Wimmer, in charge of the Pax Christi Pilgrimage, said, "What happened made a great impression on me. Smiling, Thea turned her head towards me, opened her mouth, and spoke to me for the first time, saying, 'Doctor, I am terribly hungry.'" After a hearty meal, she joined in the Procession of the Blessed Sacrament. Immediately afterward, first she could lift her left arm, then flex and extend her legs. She visited the Medical Bureau, where, Dr. Wimmer said, "The paralysis disappeared under the very eyes of the doctors." Her muscle power was returning. The next day, after another immersion at the Baths and a check at the Medical Bureau, Miss Angele got up for the first time and walked to the Accueil Notre Dame chapel.

The return journey by train was comfortable and without incident. On arrival at her own home, she was able to get out of the car unaided. The transformation from a dying woman to one in good health was truly incredible. When she was examined in July by her doctor, she had regained her normal weight and was free of all symptoms of multiple sclerosis. She visited the Medical Bureau in 1952 and in 1955; she was still well, and had gone back to work.

Ten years after the cure of her illness, Miss Angele had become a nun, taken the name of Sister Maria Mercedes, and was living at the Convent of the Immaculate Conception in Lourdes. At that time, Professor Thiebaut studied her dossier on behalf of the International Medical Committee of Lourdes and presented a favorable report. The following year, Msgr. Théas, Bishop of Tarbes and Lourdes, declared her cure miraculous. Sister Maria Mercedes is still alive.

Mr. Evasio Ganora was born in Italy in 1913. He became the father of five children and was a farmer at Casale Monferrato. After enjoying excellent health for thirty-six years, the onset of his illness, with anorexia, loss of weight, fever, and sweats, caused consternation. When his liver and spleen became enlarged, and swollen lymph nodes appeared in his neck and armpits, blood tests and a gland biopsy revealed the cause to be Hodgkin's Disease. There followed a steady deterioration, despite radiation treatment, twenty blood transfusions, and a whole range of such cytotoxic (toxic to cells) drugs as were available at that time. In 1949–50 it was well known that this disease usually proved fatal, and Mr. Ganora was in what seemed a hopeless state.

He demanded to be taken to Lourdes. At the end of May 1950, he joined the OFTAL Pilgrimage, but required constant supervision en route because of his extremely grave condition.

On his first day in Lourdes (June 1, 1950), he was carried to the Baths. After the immersion he immediately felt a great warmth throughout his body, and, to everyone's surprise, was able to walk back to the Accueil Notre Dame. The next day, his health seemed perfectly normal, and he was strong enough to walk up the Calvary Hill. Two days later, he helped as a brancardier. When he was examined at the Medical Bureau, all signs of his disease had gone. His case was assessed again in 1953 and 1954 at the Medical Bureau in Lourdes. In 1955, the International Medical Committee of Lourdes asked two famous specialists in pathology for detailed studies of this case, and for their opinions. They concurred with the diagnosis of Hodgkin's Disease; the slides from their studies are at the Medical Bureau for all to see. The Medical Bureau and the International Medical Committee of Lourdes agreed that Mr. Ganora had been cured instantly and completely in Lourdes on June 2, 1950.

An examination in 1955 by the Diocesan Medical Committee of Casale Monferrato revealed a lymph node in Mr. Ganora's left armpit, but his blood count revealed no abnormality at all, and the lymph node disappeared spontaneously. In the next few months of 1955, he was reexamined by the Medical Bureau, the International Committee of Lourdes, and then by the Canonical Committee again. Their favorable reports enabled the bishop to declare this cure miraculous.

Although his health remained excellent, Mr. Ganora did not live for very long following his cure. In 1957 he fell under his tractor and was crushed, while working on his estate. His premature death (even though accidental) only seven years after his cure from Hodgkin's Disease could raise doubts as to the miraculous nature of the cure—this disease can relapse, even after seven years, and even with modern therapeutic measures. But in Mr. Ganora's case, where the diagnosis was proved with certainty by blood tests and a gland biopsy, the suddenness of the cure, without convalescence or relapse, marks it as extraordinary and medically inexplicable.

Miss Edeltraut Fulda was born in Vienna in 1916, and inherited from that great city a love of music and dance. Even at school, her thoughts and energy were expended far more on dancing than on academics. Though she could not afford dancing lessons, she practiced hour after hour at home for school performances. When she left school, she went on the stage with her sister, appearing either in the chorus or in a twin act. Before long, they were invited to dance in Austria, Italy, Switzerland, and Hungary.

Her career was often interrupted by illness. Attacks of abdominal pain eventually necessitated an operation for a perforated ulcer in 1937. In 1938, her right kidney was removed (due to an accumulation of mineral salts and inflammatory disease). Shortly afterward, signs of Addison's Disease appeared. This is a condition in which there is a hormonal imbalance due to adrenal-gland insufficiency. Miss Fulda lost weight, could eat very little, and developed a bronze pigmentation of the skin—all symptoms typical of Addison's Disease. At that time, the only way to control this disease was the use of corticosterone, which she received in one form or another between 1938 and 1950. Her life quite literally depended on this very expensive drug. Her parents sold their home to meet the cost.

Miss Fulda was taken to Lourdes, in August 1950, by her mother. They traveled together, but not as part of a pilgrimage. A Dutch hospitaller took an interest in them when she noticed that they were by themselves. She accompanied them to the Medical Bureau, where Dr. Leuret and Dr. Pelissier met them, gained Miss Fulda's confidence, and encouraged her to go into the Baths. After the first immersion, on August 11, she began to feel better, could sit up, and could eat all that was put before her. She went into the Baths again on August 13, 14, and 15. On August 14, on her own initiative, she authorized the cessation of her corticosterone treatment. She has remained well ever since. She lives an energetic normal life, and has married.

Miss Fulda was examined in Lourdes on August 16, 1950, by Dr. Leuret, and again in 1952 and 1954. On the last check, twenty-five doctors at the Medical Bureau agreed that there had been a definitive cure, "no medical explanation could be given to account for it," and that "it was beyond the laws of Nature." In 1955 the International Committee passed the cure, stating that "for more than ten years this suprarenal [adrenal] insufficiency was treated with the appropriate hormones, which had been essential for her survival. Suddenly this indispensable medication could be stopped at a stroke and indefinitely, without a relapse. The cure has lasted for four years, which is truly remarkable and extremely rare. It merits to be upheld by us." Then, on May 15, 1955, having taken into consideration the medical findings and the criteria laid down by Pope Benedict XIV, Cardinal Innitzer, Archbishop of Vienna, declared the cure miraculous.

Not many people have described and published a full account of their cures. Miss Fulda did just that. Her autobiography, *I Shall Be Healed,* was published in German in 1959 and later translated into French and English. In it, her passionate love of dancing, her frightful experiences going from hospital to hospital for thirteen years, having one operation after another, being often near to death, and her marvelous pilgrimage to Lourdes are all vividly described. She is a person of forceful character and unswerving faith, and was never deeply resentful of her illness or of high-handed treatment. Rather, she used these experiences to develop even further her unshakable trust in God.

As one critic of her book commented: "Often we don't hear God speaking because of the noise of the world, because we fear the silence in which His voice can be heard. Then it happens that God must speak out loud. He shouts to us in a miracle like Edeltraut's."

Miss Henriette Bressolles was cured in 1924, but it was not until thirty-three years later (1957) that her cure was recognized as miraculous by the Church.

Miss Bressolles was born in Nice and later lived in Lyons. She was the daughter of an army officer and was attracted to life in the Army, so she worked as a military nurse in the French Field Ambulance Service during the First World War. She won many medals and citations, and was proposed for the Légion d'Honneur.

On July 6, 1918, Miss Bressoles was on the battlefield in the region of Dormans when she was called to the aid of a soldier with shrapnel injuries. Struggling to lift him, she felt a "crack" and a sharp pain in her spine. Despite difficulty straightening her back, she refused to be evacuated. That evening, a burst of gunfire knocked her to the ground; an hour later she was found unconscious, with a leg wound caused by shrapnel. She recovered, but it was only a few months before signs of paralysis of the right leg appeared (in April 1919). The paralysis was due to Pott's Disease (tuberculosis) in her dorso-lumbar vertebrae, associated with her active service. In the hospital, where a plaster cast immobilized her spine and leg, the paralysis became complete after she developed meningitis. Thereafter she was incontinent and had no sensation in her legs. The meningitis was treated with anti-meningococcal serum, without great success. In March 1920, she went home from the hospital and was given a 100 percent service pension, which was later increased to 125 percent because of the gravity of her illness. During the next few years, she suffered more attacks of meningitis, developed uremia, and by 1924 was gravely ill. In February of that year, her mother promised to take her to Lourdes as a last resort.

They arrived in Lourdes on July 3, 1924, in time for the afternoon Eucharistic Procession. As the Blessed Sacrament was carried in front of her, Miss Bressolles sensed a feeling of lassitude and was covered in perspiration. She was taken to the Grotto afterward, where she prayed intensely. After experiencing another strange and painful "crack" of short duration, she indicated to her mother that she was cured. Already she could straighten her right foot, move the right leg, and raise herself up on her stretcher. All pain had gone. Next day, her spinal support was removed. All sensation had returned, but her joints remained rather stiff, hindering walking. Twenty-four hours later her cure was confirmed. It took a few weeks before her full strength was restored; she still needed a stick for support in September.

Dr. Fighiera and Dr. Lavezzari, in Nice, both reported that all signs of her disease, present when she set out for Lourdes, had disappeared completely. On October 5, 1924, after the B.C.M. had investigated the case, its President, Dr. H. Marchand, declared that Miss Bressolle's incurable illness was cured in Lourdes without any effective treatment being administered. The circumstances of the cure's occurrence were beyond the realm of medicine, and it was impossible to explain it by the current knowledge of human science.

Twenty-five years later, in 1950, Dr. Leuret, then President of the Medical Bureau, sent the dossier to Msgr. Rémond, Bishop of Nice, whose Canonical Commission was instructed to make a double inquiry —at Lyons, where Miss Bressolles lived after 1941, and at Nice, where she lived at the time of the cure. The report of this Canonical Commission stated: "We acknowledge that the cure of Miss Bressolles can be considered as presenting all the guarantees required by the official criteria and by theology, and classed as miraculous." The Bishop of Nice officially declared in 1957 that the cure of Miss Henriette Bressolles at Lourdes in 1924 should be recognized as miraculous.

Miss Bressolles died from a heart attack in 1961 at the age of sixty-five, never having had any recurrence of her former illness.

Miss Marie Bigot was born in 1922 at La Boussie, in the Diocese of Rennes, France. She was cured of three disabilities, resulting from an infection of the brain system and surrounding tissues, on three separate visits to Lourdes.

In her early years, she often had quite severe skin infections, such as impetigo and infected dermatitis, requiring treatment in a hospital, since this was at a time when antibiotics were nonexistent. The only operation she had was an appendectomy.

Miss Bigot's really serious illness began in 1951, when her already poor eyesight deteriorated until her visual acuity was only 3/10. Glasses did not improve it. Doctors could find nothing abnormal in her eyes, except for pallor of the retina. By April 1951, she was very ill, with frontal headaches and fever. Despite treatment, she became semi-comatose. Increased cranial pressure made an operation necessary that same month. Four cranial nerves were found to be embedded in adhesions. They were dissected free by the neurosurgeon. He made the diagnosis of posterior fossa arachnoiditis and encephalomyelitis.

No real improvement followed the operation. By September of that year, she developed a paralysis of the right side of the body, deafness in the right ear, and very poor vision in both eyes. By 1952, her right eye was completely blind and the left one nearly so. Her deafness, by then, was total, and she could walk only with help.

In this desperate state, for which such treatment as she had had proved useless, Miss Bigot decided to go to Lourdes. When she returned from her first pilgrimage, in 1952, her condition remained unchanged. At this point she began to learn Braille.

A year later, she made her next pilgrimage to Lourdes. This time, during the Blessing of the Sick, her paralysis disappeared, but she remained blind and deaf.

On her third pilgrimage in October 1954, at the close of the Blessing of the Sick, she described vividly what happened to her: "Suddenly I heard what seemed to me to be a loud noise—I was afraid. I did not know what had happened to me. I had clearly heard the crowd singing 'Queen of the Rosary'—Then, I heard the sick person next to me say, 'Marie, you can hear!' I replied, 'Hush.' " That same afternoon, Miss Bigot lost all the pain and stiffness in her neck which had caused her much trouble on the train coming to Lourdes. Next morning, she was examined at the Medical Bureau and her hearing was found to be normal.

Before leaving Lourdes, Miss Bigot took a last bath at the Piscines. She emerged with a terrible headache and pain in her eyes. The pain was so intense that she commented to her nurse, "I will certainly not arrive back at St.-Malo alive!" During the return journey she slept badly on an upper bunk in the ambulance coach. At about 2 A.M., she "saw," as one does with the eyes closed. What she saw was something resembling streaks of lightning. When she asked someone if there was a storm, No, came the answer, there had not been a storm that night. What Miss Bigot saw was the series of platform lights as the train sped through a station. Her vision had returned. This was confirmed by Dr. Debroise on the train.

Before this cure was proclaimed miraculous on August 15, 1956, by Cardinal Roques, Archbishop of Rennes, the dossier was thoroughly studied by the Medical Bureau of Lourdes in 1955 and the International Medical Committee of Lourdes in 1956. Professor Thiebaut reported on the full sequence of events, explaining how the disabilities were linked to the infected spinal membrane, affecting the adjacent parts of the brain stem. He also described how there had been three separate but complete cures: those of her paralysis, her deafness, and her blindness. Miss Bigot never again displayed any neurological symptoms, and has remained well.

Providentially, Mr. G. Rouquier was taking photographs of the sick in Lourdes in 1954 for his film *Lourdes et ses Miracles,* and among those on the film was Marie Bigot. After her sudden cure, he took another photograph of her. She is the only miraculously cured person who was photographed just before, and just after, her cure.

Miss Yvonne Fournier was born in Paris in 1923. When she was only seventeen years old, she caught her left arm in the moving belt of a machine, which dragged on it so violently that the arm became quite useless. It hung lifeless, her hand was cold, and the forearm was swollen due to static edema.

The severe pain in her swollen and paralyzed arm was so unbearable that Miss Fournier asked for it to be amputated. This request was refused. Instead, between 1940 and 1945 several neurosurgeons operated on her cervical sympathetic nervous system, hoping to ease the pain. Among these specialists was Professor Leriche, who was renowned for his knowledge of the sympathetic nervous system. These operations gave only transitory relief. She also had twenty-two sessions of physiotherapy and radiation therapy, but these proved to be of no help. Her persistent pain and disability were recorded fully by Professor de Léobardy of the School of Medicine in Limoges. On his evidence she was awarded a 70 percent disability pension.

In this serious state, Miss Fournier went on pilgrimage to Lourdes in 1945. On August 18, intense pain in her shoulder disturbed her sleep. The next day, at 8:45 A.M., she was carried to the Piscines and took her first bath. As she came out of the water, she immediately felt strength returning in her arm and could move her fingers. The numbness had gone, as had the pain. She was examined twice at the B.C.M. while still in Lourdes. The dramatic improvement was clearly present on the first visit, but it took a little time for the reabsorption of all the edema and for restoration of full muscular power.

In 1946, Professor Thiebaut reported on the case to the B.C.M., stating that the traumatic injury had produced complete paralysis of the left arm, which had been unresponsive to surgery and physiotherapy for five years; and that her sudden cure in Lourdes in 1945 was medically inexplicable. He explained to the International Medical Committee in 1959 how the extremely violent traction in 1940 had overstretched the brachial plexus (a complex of nerves lying in the armpit and supplying shoulder, chest, and arm), causing all the trouble. There was no evidence at all of any neurotic factor. Members of the Committee agreed with the inexplicable nature of this sudden and complete cure. In December 1959, her bishop, Cardinal Feltin of Paris, declared the cure to be miraculous.

This case so captured the public imagination that the cure was described on French television programs in 1954 and 1960. Miss Fournier herself appeared on television and told her own story. Since then, she has returned to Lourdes many times, usually with the French National Pilgrimage, and has remained in good health. Professor Salmon, Consultant Orthopedic Surgeon of Marseilles and a member of the International Medical Committee of Lourdes, was so impressed with her case that he wrote a pamphlet telling the whole story of her cure.

Mrs. Ginette Nouvel was cured in 1954 of Budd-Chiari Disease, in which there is venous obstruction in the liver. Her cure is the only one of its kind in the official list of cures.

Mrs. Nouvel was born in 1928 at Carmaux (Tarn). Her illness began suddenly, in November 1953, with epigastric pain and vomiting of bile-stained fluid. Next morning, in a state of collapse, she was taken to a hospital in Carmaux in need of emergency surgery. The suspected pancreatitis was not found; instead, the surgeon discovered an enlarged, purplish liver. Her distended abdomen contained 500 cubic centimeters of ascitic (serous) fluid. The surgeon had no option but to close the abdomen, as there was nothing he could do to alleviate the situation. She recovered from the operation, but more fluid accumulated and her condition remained grave. The fluid required tapping (up to two liters) every five days. In 1954, another exploratory operation was done with the idea of taking a liver biopsy and constructing a porto-caval anastomosis. This proved impossible, and instead, the hepatic artery was ligatured. Despite all the help and advice of eminent surgeons and physicians, Mrs. Nouvel's condition continued to deteriorate. Her blood became abnormal, and tapping her fluid now yielded up to eight liters at a time. She became emaciated, had a distended abdomen, and suffered from indigestion and diarrhea. Dr. Marchal of Carmaux wrote on August 28, 1954: "She must travel lying down. Prognosis is very grave: incurable disease; the outcome will be death. . . ." With this report, she left for Lourdes on September 20.

Mrs. Nouvel described her cure quite simply: "In Lourdes I was plunged into the Baths on the twenty-first, twenty-second and twenty-third of September. I was lowered into the bath on a rubber mattress on the first day, and had the sensation that my abdomen had suddenly gone down, before I could get my breath back (the water was icy cold) and even before I was lifted out. I said to myself: 'It's only an impression because you thought you were going to be cured, but that is all.' . . . So I said nothing to anyone. On the twenty-second and twenty-third I felt nothing amiss whatsoever . . . and went home." The journey home was comfortable. At home she felt well, her diarrhea and nausea had ceased, her kidneys and ovaries worked normally again. She required no further draining of ascitic fluid, though this took three months to disappear completely. Her blood returned to normal and she gained weight, which this time was not due to excess fluid. Having regained her former vigor and sense of well-being, she resumed her usual occupations.

Mrs. Nouvel was examined at the Medical Bureau in 1955, 1956, and 1957, where the collective decision was that she had been completely cured in an extraordinary way. In 1960 her case was submitted to the International Medical Committee of Lourdes and was investigated by Professor Mauriac, of Bordeaux. His report to the committee stated that Mrs. Nouvel had been cured of a very grave illness, Budd-Chiari Disease, at the Piscines in Lourdes. There had been a quite sudden change for the better at the Baths, and the improvement was eventually complete. In April 1961, the committee accepted these findings and concluded that the cure was extraordinary. After examination of the dossier by the Canonical Commission, Msgr. Dupuy, Archbishop of Albi, declared on May 31, 1963, that the cure of Mrs. G. Nouvel was "miraculous and must be attributed to the special intervention of the Blessed Virgin, the Immaculate Mother of God."

Mrs. Nouvel frequently returned to Lourdes through 1969. At the beginning of 1970 she became ill again, and seemed to present symptoms similar to those of her original illness, sixteen years before. After weeks of unsuccessful treatment, a variety of medical investigations were undertaken to establish if there had been a recurrence of Budd-Chiari Disease. These led to her death from an intestinal perforation, caused by an instrumental error during a laparoscopy.

It was so rare for a *miraculé* to have a recurrence of the original disease that serious thought was given to this case some years later. As an independent witness, Dr. Claudine Thozet recorded her assessment in her M.D. thesis on "The Stability of Cures of Lourdes." She discussed two aspects of the Nouvel cure: Was the cure proved? Was the cure inexplicable?

Regarding the first point, it seems that all the records supported the existence of Budd-Chiari Disease; the fact that Mrs. Nouvel's cure followed her visit to the Baths in Lourdes in 1954; the fact that it lasted until 1961. Although it took three months for the last trace of edema to disappear, her health had completely returned to normal without any effective treatment. Six years afterward, the Medical Bureau confirmed the definitive, total, and lasting cure of a disease which is usually fatal within six months.

Concerning the second point, Dr. Thozet wrote in 1975, fourteen years after the report of the International Medical Committee: "The survival for sixteen years is now not considered unique . . . but is utterly exceptional after such an illness, where, whatever the treatment, death supervenes as a rule. Therefore the conclusion reached by the medical control at Lourdes regarding the inexplicable nature of this cure seems to me to be consistent."

In the light of more recent research, the International Medical Committee in 1977 insisted on a review of this case, bearing in mind the peculiar circumstances of her death. This new inquiry, led by Professor Barbin, arrived at the following decisions:

—This case remains quite exceptional, and medically inexplicable in the original phase. The manner of her death does not really affect the first decision.
—A recurrence of the previous illness had probably

occurred in this case, but only after a long period (sixteen years) of complete remission. Although her death may not be looked upon as directly linked to this recurrence, one must admit it was an indirect consequence.

≈ **28** ≈

The Last Five Cures, 1965–78[*]

Since the first publication of this book, thirty years ago, only four cures have been declared extraordinary and later proclaimed miraculous. Two were declared miracles in 1965, one in 1976, and the last in 1978. The most recent extraordinary cure (Delizia Cirolli) occurred in 1976 and now awaits the decision of her bishop.

The four people who were miraculously cured, two French and two Italian, were all born within eleven years of one another (1929–40), and their respective cures spanned twelve years (1958–70). Their names are well known today; each has a photograph and a citation on display at the Medical Bureau.

Elisa Aloi. This young lady's cure will always be imprinted on my mind, because I was fortunate enough to be in the Procession of the Blessed Sacrament on June 3, 1959, when the President invited all doctors there to attend the review of Miss Aloi's case the next day at the Medical Bureau. With no hesitation, I joined the other doctors on this momentous occasion.

Tuberculosis was still the prevalent disease in those days. Elisa's parents died from it, and Elisa, who had been born at Patti, in Sicily, in 1931, developed it too. When she was seventeen years old, a chronic tuberculous infection appeared first in her right knee and then spread during the next ten years to most of her large joints and also to her

[*] This section is by Dr. Vivienne d'Andria.

spine. The disease led to one abscess after another, often complicated by secondary infection. During this decade, she was in the hospital more than she was at home. Treatment included fifty operations to drain the abscesses, use of the only available antibiotics (penicillin and streptomycin), and a plaster-of-paris cast from pelvis to feet. It was all very frustrating for both Elisa and her doctors. In 1957, weak, wasted, and immobilized, she went on pilgrimage to Lourdes.

No change for the better took place during or after this pilgrimage to Lourdes. In fact, after it she developed a septic arthritis of the left knee which required her admission to Messina Hospital in 1958. Professor di Cesare, of that hospital, later stated: "The patient had never obtained any benefit from either the medication or the surgical operations carried out at the various hospitals where she had been admitted." That same year, Elisa went on pilgrimage to Lourdes again, in her plaster cast, and with four fistulas (abnormal passages leading from an abscess to the body surface) draining pus from the underlying abscesses. There she asked for the direct application of Lourdes water to the fistulas. By the third day in Lourdes, all of them had ceased to discharge. She wanted the plaster cast removed, but this was refused until her return to the hospital of San Angelo, in Messina, Sicily. By then, all the fistulas had remained dry and were healing.

Professor di Cesare certified, on June 11, just seven days after she left Lourdes, that "she was completely cured and so well that one could hardly believe it was the same person who had left for Lourdes in such a desperate state." This was in 1958, ten years after the onset of her illness. She was twenty-seven years old.

Elisa returned to Lourdes in 1959 and 1960, and was examined thoroughly at the Medical Bureau. After this, the doctors had no uncertainty in declaring unanimously that the cure of Elisa Aloi was extraordinary. At the examinations she was clearly in robust health, and was remarkably athletic, considering her earlier tuberculous infection of so many bones and joints. Moreover, the scarred skin over her knee, for example, had not adhered to underlying tissues, as would have been expected in a natural cure, but glided over it like silk.

In 1961, Professor M. M. Salmon presented a favorable report of her case to the International Medical Committee of Lourdes, which accepted it. In 1965, Msgr. Fasola, Archbishop and Archimandrite of Messina, declared Elisa Aloi's cure of multiple tuberculous bone and joint infections to be miraculous.

Elisa Aloi has revisited Lourdes several times since. She has remained in perfect health, needing only an appendectomy. She was married in 1965 and is now Signora Varacalli. Her husband commented in 1971, "I think the birth of our four children is the best evidence of my wife's cure."

Miss Juliette Tamburini was born in Marseilles in 1930. Her disease began when she was twelve years old, but did not reveal itself until six years later, when a fistula opened on her left thigh. The fistula was secondary to the underlying bone infection—a chronic staphylococcal osteitis. This was confirmed by bacteriological examination of the pus from the fistula, and by X-rays, which showed a cavity in the bone. Between 1948 and 1959, Miss Tamburini spent many months in the hospital undergoing local antibiotic treatment and repeated curettage and drainage operations, all of which proved to be ineffective. The long history of opening and closing of the fistula was characteristic of this sort of chronic bone infection.

In addition, Miss Tamburini was prone to nosebleeds during her long illness. Cauterization used in their treatment led to a perforation of her nasal septum. Despite skin grafting and blood transfusions, etc., the frequent and heavy nosebleeds persisted for eight years.

When Miss Tamburini set off by train for Lourdes on her Diocesan Pilgrimage in the care of Dr. Bouyala, in July 1959, she was in a weak state and quite dejected. Her fistula was open and draining profusely and normally required frequent change of dressings. Due to the offensive odor, this could not be done en route in the ambulance coach. In Lourdes, she attended the Blessing of the Sick on her first three days, but was far too afraid to venture into the icy water of the Baths. Instead, on July 15, her fistula was irrigated with 10 cubic centimeters of Lourdes water from the taps near the Grotto. The discharge from the fistula dried up almost immediately, and the fistula itself disappeared almost as quickly, with a sudden ejection of the gauze plug as it closed. Both Dr. Bouyala and the Pilgrimage nurse witnessed the change in the fistula, having seen it both before and after the irrigation with Lourdes water.

During that night, although weak from several nosebleeds, Miss Tamburini found new strength of mind. She decided to go into the Piscines the next day. She was taken there on a stretcher and bathed on the sixteenth and again on the seventeenth of July.

From that date, the fistula remained dry and sealed and she had only one further nosebleed—on the way home. Her general health improved rapidly. Her wasted leg muscles regained their strength, enabling her not just to lead a normal life, but to walk miles as the leader of the Cubs in her locality. The only vestige of her illness is a five-by-one-inch scar on her lower thigh.

The next year, Miss Tamburini returned to Lourdes to give thanks for her cure. On this visit, in 1960, she was examined at the Medical Bureau, where it was confirmed that her weight had gone up by almost nine pounds and there was no sign of a relapse. She was checked again in 1961 and 1963. In 1961, X-rays showed the bone returning to normal, and by 1963 it was completely normal. The Medical Bureau then passed the cure as extraordinary and inexplicable.

The International Medical Committee of Lourdes appointed Professor M. M. Salmon to report on this cure in 1964. He had followed Miss Tamburini's illness for many years, having been the first surgeon to operate on her. The Committee, having heard his report and discussed the case, declared that:

> On her arrival in Lourdes in July 1959, Juliette Tamburini suffered from a fistula in the left thigh; the fistula was due to chronic osteitis of femur, a disease spanning eleven years and resistant to all therapy.
>
> The disease, up to then without any real and lasting tendency to amelioration, was suddenly modified on 17.5.59.
>
> This cure, instantaneous, without convalescence, must be placed amongst the medically inexplicable, extraordinary cures.

On May 11, 1965, after the Canonical Committee had studied her dossier, the Bishop of Marseilles declared her cure miraculous.

Since that time, Miss Tamburini has been a faithful pilgrim to Lourdes, returning in 1966, 1967, 1970, and 1971, giving her services as a handmaid. In Marseilles she works as a night attendant at the Hôpital Sainte Marguerite.

This cure attracted so much public attention that Miss Tamburini was invited to appear on television. In the course of the interview, she recalled, in her straightforward, unassuming way, the events leading up to her cure. "I was too weak to give an account of it. My mother did not believe it! Only when I arrived back in Marseilles was I told, 'You are cured!' I never asked for a cure; I only went to Lourdes to obtain enough faith to sustain me in my illness."

Vittorio Micheli enlisted in the Army, like most fit young men in Italy, choosing to join the Alpine Corps close to his home, in Trento, in the north of the country. He was about twenty-two years old.

He had not been in military service long before severe sciatic pain and a swelling in his left buttock limited hip movement. He was admitted to the Verona Military Hospital in 1962, and X-rays and a biopsy revealed a pelvic sarcoma. This malignant growth had invaded much of the left half of his pelvic bones, destroying the acetabular cup, into which the head of the femur (thighbone) fits and in which it rotates. In fact, the rounded head of the femur had moved 4 centimeters (about 1 1/2 inches) upward and was embedded in the mass of malignant tumor, leaving his left leg hanging limp and virtually useless. The leg looked, but actually was not, 4 centimeters short. At this time, barely four months after the first symptoms appeared, the only treatment was to encase the pelvis and leg in a plaster cast. Amputation and radiation therapy, which in any event would have been only palliative, were not available at any of the military hospitals in which he had been a patient.

Weakened, without appetite and unable to walk, Mr. Micheli set off on a pilgrimage to Lourdes on May 24, 1963. There he took several baths in the Piscines. By June 1, he suddenly felt much better and was free from all bone pain. None of the doctors in Lourdes or in Italy believed a cure was possible. Yet he was able to walk again, still wearing the plaster cast, one month after his return from Lourdes. By February 1964, his X-rays revealed that normal bone structure and configuration of his hip were present and complete. The only abnormality was the position of the acetabulum, which had re-formed 4 centimeters higher than its original position. This meant that his shoe had to be built up. When the plaster cast was removed, Mr. Micheli was discharged from the hospital, in April 1964. The army authorities declared him physically unfit for further military service, which was a disappointment to him, but not a surprise, since even at that stage the Italian doctors still did not believe the cure would be permanent. But it was. Soon after that, he resumed work in Trento, took long walks in the Alps, and was married.

In 1967, the Medical Bureau, after full examination, accepted the cure of Vittorio Micheli as extraordinary. Professor M. M. Salmon, a consultant orthopedic surgeon, was asked to present the report on this case to the International Medical Committee of Lourdes. After two years of deliberation, the committee officially agreed with the Medical Bureau. In 1976, this cure, now obviously permanent, was declared miraculous by Archbishop Gottardi of the Diocese of Trento, who said: ". . . this cure is an intervention of the power of God, the Creator and Father, through the intercession of the Immaculate Virgin."

Each instance of a Lourdes cure is unique and requires several years for a full and meticulous assessment. Vittorio Micheli's case was no exception. He himself was quite certain of his cure while still in Lourdes, but his Italian doctors were so skeptical that it was not until August, two months later, that they took X-rays of his hip to see if there had been any alteration. These revealed a marked reduction of the tumor mass. Although they were amazed, they were not really convinced of the cure until the following February. By then, the X-rays showed a normal hip joint. With such an extensive part of the pelvic bones affected, complete recalcification took time.

The time lag between Mr. Micheli's cure and his doctors' official recognition of that cure is easily explained. Mr. Micheli was serving in the Army and was treated in military hospitals, where he was subject to military procedures in a medical setting. Also, it was difficult to be aware of a cure, because his plaster cast had not been disturbed for months. Once all the facts were known, it became obvious that Vittorio Micheli's cure had been a "sudden" one, because at a particular moment the tumor had ceased to grow, then had begun to shrink, and finally had vanished. This is the crucial criterion of a miraculous cure, but it is not essential to observe literally all the changes at each given moment. The hidden details come to light as time passes.

One might ask why, in this case, the bones did not return immediately to their normal form and composition. The answer is that the cancer had destroyed the normal structure of the bones. Once the body was freed from the cancerous process, the bones could start to regain their normal features by the slow process of recalcification. In Vittorio Micheli's case, the evolution of these changes can be seen in the sequence of his X-ray films following his pilgrimage to Lourdes.

Professor M. M. Salmon ends his full report on this cure by describing the work of doctors: "In Medicine, we are trained to assess facts. First we 'observe' facts, then, try to 'explain' them." He continued, "We must judge the facts with moderation, consideration, good sense, sympathy and medical humility—the humility of a Carrel, a Pasteur. We must guard against the sin of the spirit which always *attempts* through arrogance to seek an explanation. When a doctor does not find a valid explanation, he must assume a spiritually human attitude and accept in all good faith, with loyalty and impartiality, the case as 'inexplicable.' Believers and unbelievers must let the facts speak for themselves—so that the believer does not see extraordinary cures everywhere . . . and the unbeliever does not take refuge in useless denial or skepticism."

The facts in Mr. Micheli's case are indisputable:

—He had a sarcoma of the pelvis and did not undergo any specific treatment.

—At Lourdes, he suddenly felt better and sensed he was cured.

—A completely destroyed hip articulation was spontaneously reconstructed, enabling his once useless limb to become sound and his walking to become normal after one month.

—The cure was lasting; eight years later he was still fit.

—No medical explanation could be given.

There was a unique sequel to this cure. Professor Salmon presented Vittorio Micheli's case at a clinical meeting in Marseilles in 1971. The theme of the meeting was "Bone Sarcomata," which had attracted both French and foreign doctors, consultants in general and orthopedic surgery, cancer and pathology, all with a particular interest in bone sarcomata. The dossier was introduced as "a cure of a sarcoma of pelvis said to be spontaneous." Full clinical details were described, but no reference was made to Lourdes. The diagnosis was confirmed at the meeting by Professor Nezelof, Professor of Pathology at the Faculty of Paris. None of the consultants could suggest a valid explanation of the cure, the general improvement of the patient, or the reconstruction of the acetabulum. Only afterward did Catholics, Protestants, Jews, et al., learn that the cure had taken place at Lourdes.

A résumé of this case in the *Orthopedic Surgical Review* (Vol. 57, No. 4, June 1971, p. 323) said:

> In this extraordinary observation, considerable destruction of the iliac bone was followed by a reconstruction without any therapeutic, medical or surgical intervention, other than a biopsy.
>
> The histological specimens examined, nevertheless, appeared to confirm the malignancy of this sarcoma of pelvis. The pilgrimage to Lourdes, in desperation, followed.

This publication in a review of national and international reputation was something quite new. Previously, it would have been unthinkable that Lourdes should be cited in a highly scientific journal. This in itself demonstrated the professional competence of the work being done by the Medical Bureau and the International Medical Committee of Lourdes. In addition, it illustrated the respect and good faith shown by their colleagues regarding the high standard of work the doctors produce in Lourdes.

Mr. Serge Perrin was born in 1929 in Angers, France. His cure was the last one in Lourdes to be declared miraculous, and he was the very first person to be cured during the ceremony of the Anointing of the Sick.

Mr. Perrin was an accountant, married, and had three children. Apart from partial deafness caused by otitis media (an inflammation of the middle ear), and severe sunstroke at the age of sixteen, he was a healthy young man. His family history, however, did include evidence of hypertension and cardio-vascular accidents.

One morning in February 1964, when he was thirty-five years old, he woke up with a severe headache, some speech impairment, and a partial right-side paralysis. After three months off from work, he recovered and remained well for almost five years. Then, in December 1968, there was a recurrence of the paralysis. This time it was progressive, caused by bilateral insufficiency of the carotid arteries in his neck. This left him with poor vision and so disabled that he was unable to attend to his personal needs. He was also afflicted with frequent "cerebral attacks." Such treatment as was tried proved useless. Professor Pecker, a neurosurgeon from Rennes, decided against operative intervention and gave a poor prognosis.

In May 1969, Mr. Perrin made his first pilgrimage to Lourdes. When he returned home, he was in the same physical state and feeling discouraged. It was clear that he was quite incapable of working again or, indeed, of looking after himself. His family was more optimistic, and persuaded him to return to Lourdes; on April 26, 1970, he accompanied his wife and daughter to the Shrine, really only to please them. He had himself lost all hope of a cure and only prayed for "greater faith to die well." However, he did have a longing to attend the Anointing of the Sick ceremony and insisted on being taken to it, even though he had just spent his worst night ever, when it was feared he might die.

On May 1, 1970, he was in his wheelchair in the St. Pius X Basilica. During the Anointing of the Sick ceremony, he suddenly sensed a feeling of warmth in his toes. The feeling spread to his legs, and a few hours later his vision returned and his paralysis vanished. As he was about to leave for home, he realized that he was perfectly well—cured. He was free from cerebral attacks, could walk unaided, and could see without spectacles.

These changes were witnessed in Lourdes by Dr. Sourice and seven other medical officers of the Angers Pilgrimage. At home, Mr. Perrin was examined by Professor Pecker, who had treated him for the illness. The professor was astonished to find his patient cured. The blockage seen earlier in the arteriograms was no longer present. Although the cause of the obstruction was in some doubt, it was considered that "this sudden cure is most unusual after an ischaemic cerebral lesion" (injury of brain tissue due to lack of blood flow).

Serge Perrin has remained well since, has shown no sign of relapse, and has resumed his occupation.

The medical and ecclesiastical assessment of this cure was to set a precedent in Lourdes, a new trend in the order and thoroughness with which a case is examined. The medical examination was a model piece of research, and the canonical investigation reached a new height in detailed deliberations. The considerations of the International Medical Committee of Lourdes were, for the first time, undertaken at a later stage in the full procedure. The ultimate aim of this scholarly assessment remained the same: to decide if the recognition of divine intervention in a human situation applied to this particular cure.

First the Medical Bureau examined Serge Perrin in Lourdes in May 1970, in October 1971, and in 1972. During these interviews, as many as 174 doctors were present. At the last meeting, the doctors agreed that the cure was extraordinary, certain, and lasting.

Next, in 1974 the Diocesan Medical Commission of four doctors appointed by Msgr. Mazerat, Bishop of Angers, examined the dossier from the Medical Bureau. The commission affirmed the "unusual and scientifically inexplicable character of the cure." Then members of the International Medical Committee of Lourdes were given the case to examine. The committee also appointed two consultants (Dr. Mouren, Professor of the Faculty of Medicine, Chief Physician in nervous diseases at the Hospitals of Marseilles; and Dr. Bartoli, Chief Ophthalmic Surgeon at the Centre Hospitalier at Troyes) to give expert opinions. The consultants agreed on the organic nature of the disease and its virtual *restitutio ad integrum*. On October 17, 1976, the fifteen doctors present at the meeting unanimously declared:

> Serge Perrin presented a case of recurring organic hemiplegia, with ocular lesions, due to cerebral circulatory defects, without it being possible to define accurately the nature and the site of the vascular lesions. The cure of this condition, without any effective treatment, by its instantaneous character, absence of convalescence, definitely proved and stable for six years, may be considered as acquired in a completely unusual way, from a medical point of view.

The next step was the Canonical Commission. In 1977, this commission proceeded with its lengthy but fascinating assessment of the miraculous character of the Perrin cure and its value as a sign.

The members first took note of the detailed medical reports, which they did not presume to judge, not being medically qualified. They accepted all the aspects noted in the International Medical Committee's report. Still, a medically inexplicable cure is not *per se* a miracle attributable to God. The commission had to establish that the cure could not be due to any psychological factor or to a preternatural cause which did not come from God. Their task was to seek for positive signs that would substantiate the recognition of the cure as attributable to God alone, displaying the direct and particular extraordinary action of His power and goodness.

Psychic causes were easy to eliminate. There was no evidence of neurosis, autosuggestion, emotional shock, etc. In any case, psychic factors could not possibly have influenced the organic changes involved in the cure. Moreover, Serge Perrin was not expecting to be cured and had not asked for it. In fact, he had given up all hope of a cure and was taken by surprise when it happened.

As for preternatural satanic powers, these were excluded by the whole style of his life and personality. The cure had taken place in a highly religious context, in a place of prayer, and during the administration of a sacrament. Lourdes is not a center for medical treatment, but a world center for prayerful pilgrimages. Here, crowds of pilgrims pray unceasingly to God, in response to the requests made in 1858 by The Lady. In Lourdes, Serge Perrin prayed as intensely as he could. He was surrounded by his relatives and friends, who also prayed with him and for him, and it was immediately after he had been anointed that he felt cured. The Sacrament of the Anointing of the Sick has been known to cure physical ills, and it was the particular intervention by God, through this sacrament, that cured him instantly. The inexplicable medical cure which was so closely linked to prayer and anointing prompted the Canonical Commission to declare that "God has given us a sign which leads us to believe that this cure is certainly the result of a direct and extraordinary intervention, which ipso facto merits to be declared 'miraculous.'"

After the members of the Canonical Commission had pondered all these aspects of a miraculous cure, they asked the Bishop of Angers, in May 1978, to consider that in the cure of Serge Perrin, which had been established as instantaneous, without convalescence, lasting, extraordinary, and medically inexplicable, God had given a sign; that this sign was worthy of being declared miraculous; and that through this cure Christians should be exhorted to recognize and welcome the appeal that God was making to their faith.

The final step in the procedure of assessing this cure was taken on June 17, 1978, when Msgr. Orchampt, Bishop of Angers, proclaimed this cure as miraculous and invited Christians to see in this sign the work of the merciful love of God.

The last Lourdes cure to be classed as extraordinary was that of a young girl from Sicily. *Delizia Cirolli* was born on November 17, 1964, at Paternò. She was the eldest of four children. In May 1976, when she was eleven and a half years old, Delizia was diagnosed as having a malignant tumor of the right knee. The diagnosis was confirmed by X-rays and a bone biopsy. Her parents refused permission for an amputation or radiation therapy. The prognosis was virtually hopeless with or without these measures, and they realized how upset, frightened, and homesick Delizia had been in the hospital. And she had never been really at ease with the medical staff, so they decided to take her home.

Delizia was popular in her class, although she was frequently absent because of her illness. Her popularity made it easy for her teacher to collect enough money to send Delizia and her mother to Lourdes. They set off in August 1976 and stayed in a hotel so as to be as far away as possible from hospitals, wards, doctors, and nurses. At the Shrine, Delizia attended the ceremonies, went into the Baths, and was frequently at the Grotto. At the end of her pilgrimage there was no apparent change in her condition.

Between August and December, her condition became steadily worse, and she was confined to bed. Her mother prepared her burial robes, according to the local custom. But Delizia belonged to a praying family and a praying local community, and her mother in particular had great faith in Lourdes and never failed to give Lourdes water to Delizia every day.

One morning in December, when she was clearly close to death, Delizia asked her mother to bring her clothes, saying that she felt a great urge to get up and go out into the street. Though she was astonished by such a request, her mother not only brought the clothes, she helped Delizia to dress. The little girl immediately got out of bed, went outside and ran about fifty yards down the street. A few minutes later she returned, exhausted but tremendously happy. Naturally, she was weak after her long illness and immobility, but her knee bore her weight easily and never gave her any further trouble. After this event she quickly regained her strength and energy.

Delizia returned to Lourdes annually for many years with the UNITALSI Pilgrimage, from eastern Sicily. She was first examined at the Medical Bureau in 1977, and in 1980 the Medical Bureau accepted her case as an extraordinary cure of Ewing's Sarcoma of the knee.

When the International Medical Committee of Lourdes was asked in 1980 to assess Miss Cirolli's case, the committee agreed in principle with the extraordinary nature of the cure as certified by the Medical Bureau. But it postponed its endorsement until the actual nature of the original disease had been further discussed. The problem was due to the similarity in appearance between a Ewing's Sarcoma and a solitary bone metastasis of a neuroblastoma (a malignant tumor of nerve tissue), and in the unusual tissue structure of both these diseases. There are, however, marked clinical differences between these two diseases: the number and locations of the bone lesions, the presence or absence of a primary tumor elsewhere, and the age at onset.

The prognoses for these two kinds of tumor were quite different, too. A Ewing's Sarcoma had never been found to regress spontaneously. Even with ultramodern treatment, only 50 percent of children with this sarcoma are alive after five years. As for the second kind (sympathoblastoma), in children under two years old—but never in children twelve years old—these tumors have been known on very rare occasions to disappear spontaneously. Published cases are available for study or reference.

Whatever the classification may be, Delizia's cure is still extraordinary or exceptional because:

> –it happened either in a potentially fatal disease—Ewing's Sarcoma—for which no specific treatment was given (95 percent likelihood of failure); or
> –it is the first known and published case of a metastatic neuroblastoma in a child of this age (5 percent likelihood of cure).

In Delizia's case the tumor began and disappeared in 1976. Early X-rays clearly revealed a malignant growth at the upper end of the right tibia (the bone just below the knee); later ones showed the bone structure and configuration gradually returning to normal. The only remaining abnormality was a slight deformity at the site of the lesion. The cure dated from the sudden change in December, when the tumor ceased to grow and started to regress. It took some time after that for the recalcification of the bone to be completed. Since that December, Delizia has enjoyed good health, has qualified as a nurse, and has recently married.

In 1982, after sifting all this information, the International Medical Committee of Lourdes declared that this cure was "a completely exceptional event in the strictest sense of the term, contrary to all known information and expectation in medical experience, and hence inexplicable."

Delizia's bishop has not yet made public his decision. This is by no means the first time a bishop has taken some years before announcing his verdict.

The fourteen miraculous cures described in this and the preceding chapter have many features in common. They were all directly connected with a pilgrimage to Lourdes, where health was regained in a variety of events and places. They were the first cures to be thoroughly assessed and medically authenticated by the recently formed International Medical Committee of Lourdes, after the Medical Bureau had classed them as extraordinary (with the single exception of Miss Bressolles, who was cured in 1924 and seen only by the Bureau Constatations Médicales). After this exacting assessment, these cures were all declared sudden, complete, and lasting, as well as unexpected and astounding. No medical or scientific explanation was ever put forward to account for any of them.

The diseases involved were grave and incurable, with a hopeless prognosis. Each presented a unique history and mode of cure. None of them had any aftereffects, apart from minimal vestiges showing that there had been an earlier disease, e.g. scars.

All these people remained free from their former diseases, without relapse or recurrence, with the one exception of Mrs. Nouvel. Even so, she lived free of disease for sixteen years following her cure from an illness which normally is rapidly fatal.

A miraculous cure, of course, does not confer life-long immunity from other illnesses. Barring accidents, sooner or later everyone succumbs to a fatal disease. Mr. Ganora, Miss Bressolles, and Mrs. Nouvel have died.

They have all returned to Lourdes time and again after being cured, where they render thanks, help other sick people, and visit the Medical Bureau.

All this has been brought to the world's notice through the vital role of the Medical Bureau, along with the other medical and canonical commissions. The Medical Bureau's long and very creditable history reveals how the doctors have found a way to help the sick and handicapped, to sift out the extraordinary cures from all the others, and to help establish Lourdes as a world center for pilgrimages.

Having been proclaimed miraculous by the Church, these cures are now an official witness to the Lord at work in the world today, still relieving suffering and healing the sick. Through these miracles, the love of God for mankind is clearly displayed.

Changes in Staff and Facilities Since 1955

Ruth Cranston could have foreseen only some of the changes that were to come about in the next decades. One place holds all the information about these changes: the Medical Bureau. Practically everything of importance connected with its members, their patients, and cures sooner or later has some association with this institution. It is a hive of activity, the focal point of the International Medical Association of Lourdes, and is run by the one and only resident doctor.

There the President of the Medical Bureau works in apparent isolation but can and does call upon the wisdom and experience of any of its fifteen thousand members. As most of them are in Lourdes for only a few days each year, the real burden of the work falls upon him. He is the person who must use his initiative to think out and implement desirable improvements—in conjunction, of course, with the Lourdes authorities.

The role of the President of the Medical Bureau is most important in any review of the changes in Lourdes since 1955. Three doctors have had that honor in the past thirty years: Dr. Joseph Pelissier, Dr. Alphonse Olivieri, and Dr. Theodore Mangiapan. Each had a secretary, but the only person who acted as a liaison between the public and the Medical Bureau throughout those thirty years was Mrs. Winifred Feely. The valuable contribution of each of these four people can be gleaned from a brief chronological survey of their main achievements.

Dr. Pelissier assumed office on the death of his renowned predecessor, Dr. François Leuret (President, 1947–54). Dr. Leuret's death marked the end of the immediate post-war era, when the pilgrimages were back in full swing and the moment was ripe for radical changes appropriate to modern times.

Dr. Leuret had paved the way for the smooth transition of the Bureau des Constatations Médicales into the Medical Bureau, and the appointment of some of its senior members to the newly constituted National Medical Committee. By 1954, this had expanded into the International Medical Committee of Lourdes, whose members included doctors and specialists from other nations as well as from France. This new arrangement not only forged a closer link with the Bishop of Tarbes and Lourdes (who automatically became its Chairman), but also provided other bishops, where applicable, with a more highly professional commentary on extraordinary cures.

During Dr. Leuret's presidency, eight cures were declared miraculous and the dossiers of cures outstanding from 1920 to 1940 were brought to the attention of bishops, but without much success.

One of Dr. Leuret's wishes was to ensure that the Centenary Year, 1958, would be marked with as much solemnity as his predecessor had managed for the Fiftieth Anniversary, in 1908. For this, he laid much of the groundwork on which Dr. Pelissier could build.

Dr. Joseph Pelissier (President, 1954–59)

Dr. Pelissier was born July 7, 1876. His connections with Lourdes dated back to 1905, when he began to go to Lourdes regularly, spending most of his time there as a brancardier in the Hospitalité de Lourdes. He specialized in neuropsychiatry.

Dr. Pelissier was by nature rather taciturn and aloof, and he was already close to eighty upon assuming office. His few years as President centered around the work initiated by Dr. Leuret. This included the final declaration of six extraordinary cures as miraculous—those of E. Fulda, E. Ganora, A. Couteault, M. Bigot, H. Bressolles, and L. Brosse —and the completion of two new building projects that were to bring real benefit to the sick pilgrims.

One of these projects was designed to provide an adequate supply of Lourdes water and to modernize the baths and taps. The new Piscines were officially opened in 1955. They contained fourteen baths with spacious dressing rooms and waiting areas, replacing the outdated nine baths in the old Pavilions. When these latter were demolished, a convenient length of wall was freed for the new brass push-button taps at a suitable height in place of the old *robinets*. Unseen, but of vital importance, was the completion of a complex circulation system for the water from the Spring to the baths and taps. This guaranteed a constant supply through an extensive system of pipes, huge reservoirs, electric pumps, and decanting and pressure chambers throughout the pilgrimage season.

Exploratory work had been undertaken at that time to determine exactly how water arrived at the Spring. Until then, no one knew just which Pyrenean streams discharged their water there. It was the Abbé Georges Michelin who carefully monitored (using dyes) the underground streams traversing the limestone rock behind the Grotto. He discovered that one central stream, arising at the Col du Portalet, thirty-one miles, as the crow flies, to the south of Lourdes, collecting water en route from twenty-six collateral streams, finally surfaces at the Grotto. This confirmed yet again the purely natural formation of the Spring.

The other major project was the enormous underground Basilica, dedicated to Pope Pius X and opened on March 25, 1958, by Cardinal Roncalli, Patriarch of Venice, the future Pope John XXIII. In those days the Pope did not travel abroad. Instead, Pope Pius delegated the Cardinal as his Papal Legate. This legate certainly did not travel in style —he blessed this large Basilica from a Jeep!

Constructed in concrete, the Basilica was custom-built to the design of Pierre Vago, a French architect. Devoid of steps, apart from those surrounding the raised central altar, and with four huge doorways, it is perfectly suited to the smooth entrance and exit of twenty thousand people, many of whom are lame or in wheelchairs. The Basilica is unadorned except for the ornate Blessed Sacrament Chapel and the mighty organ with its sound of trumpets. By all standards, this building with its skeletal fish-bone shape is a brilliant piece of architecture that gracefully lends itself to a lively community spirit. It has made possible the gathering together of all pilgrims and invalids under one roof for the International Mass every Sunday and Wednesday, and has provided a venue for the Blessing of the Sick and the Procession of the Blessed Sacrament when the weather is inclement—all too often in the Pyrenees. Fortunately, this Basilica (the largest in the world after St. Peter's Basilica, in Rome) was ready for the influx of nearly five million pilgrims in the Centenary Year, the highest number ever.

Also during Dr. Pelissier's years at the Medical Bureau, three special types of pilgrimage came to Lourdes for the first time. One was the Gypsy Pilgrimage, bringing over three thousand Gypsies in more than three hundred caravans; no accommodation problem for them! Their flamboyant dress and painted caravans, not to mention their monkeys, made an attractive and colorful sight.

Another type of pilgrimage was the first Handicapped Children Pilgrimage Trust, in 1957. Two years earlier, Dr. Michael Strode, the doctor in charge of Chailey Heritage, a resident school for handicapped children in Sussex, England, had ventured to Lourdes with four of his pupils, unsure of how they would behave and of how they would be received. He had no need to be anxious.

The outing was so successful that he brought forty-three girls and boys in 1957. This past Easter, the Thirtieth Annual HCPT Pilgrimage was five thousand strong: twenty-five hundred children without their parents were accompanied by twenty-five hundred helpers, along with nearly fifty doctors and the same number of priests, all from the United Kingdom and the Republic of Eire. This number of children may seem far too large, but Dr. Strode makes sure that no child is lost in the crowd. The children are in groups of ten, to create a family atmosphere. They stay in hotels and usually meet in groups, except for the full Pilgrimage Mass in the Pius X Basilica, when all five thousand "raise the roof" in prayer and song. To finance this great enterprise, green shield stamps are collected all through the year, and then exchanged for cash.

The third special type of pilgrimage was the first organized American pilgrimage, bringing sick pilgrims, following publication of *The Miracle of Lourdes,* in 1956. On the staff of this pilgrimage were Dr. Marcus Schaaf, Nurse Margaret Barrett, and Mr. John Hodgson. This pilgrimage became an annual event; it is called the National Rosary Pilgrimage of the U.S.A.

Dr. Joseph Pelissier died in November 1959, at the age of eighty-three.

Dr. Alphonse Olivieri (President, 1959–72)

Like all his predecessors, Dr. Olivieri was born in the nineteenth century, on August 26, 1890. He, too, had retired from active practice when appointed President of the Medical Bureau, but his connection with Lourdes dated back to 1935. Married, with eight children, he became both a classical scholar and a surgeon. He was a native of Corsica, and his closest colleagues, apart from his French associates in

Lourdes, were those from Italy. His relationships with English-speaking doctors were of necessity limited by the language barrier.

Dr. Olivieri wrote a book entitled *Are There Still Miracles in Lourdes?* Before it was published in July 1969, the rough draft he had prepared in 1960 was extensively revised by Dom B. Billet. The book was written in French, and it was never possible to publish it in English. It proved to be a highly popular volume, and Dr. Olivieri lived to see its third edition brought out.

There was a real need for an authentic book for the layman describing the investigation of cures as well as giving factual accounts of recent cures, including those declared miraculous during Dr. Olivieri's presidency. These were the cures of Y. Fournier, M. Carini, T. Angele, G. Nouvel, J. Tamburini and E. Aloi. All these cases had already been researched and accepted by the Medical Bureau and the International Medical Committee of Lourdes under Dr. Pelissier. Although Dr. Olivieri had supervised the early assessment of two more miraculous cures (V. Micheli and S. Perrin), the full accounts of these were not published until the fourth edition of his book was issued.

Dr. Olivieri was instrumental in requesting an up-to-date analysis of Lourdes water taken from the taps. This was done by chemists from the Institute of Hydrological Research in Nantes in 1964, and it confirmed the earlier reports. Since it was the first analysis to be done following the installation of the new circulatory system, it was satisfying to know that the materials used in its construction had not affected the chemical composition of the water at all.

In 1971, the first Mentally Handicapped Pilgrimage came to Lourdes. Some of these pilgrims had met in groups in Canada, where Professor John Vannier, of Toronto, formed them into the Faith and Light Movement, whose pilgrimage is now an international event, held once every ten years. Children and parents accompany the handicapped.

Another special type of pilgrimage began in 1968, when facilities were made available for those paralyzed with poliomyelitis. Setting up all the cables for respirators in the Domaine is such a huge task that this pilgrimage is held only for five days every five years. In 1978, these pilgrims had to make a hasty departure after only four days, because of the imminent National French Railway strike. During that week-long strike, only those pilgrims traveling by air or auto, and those already there, kept the ceremonies going on a very reduced scale. It made for an unusually quiet atmosphere. For instance, there were only two doctors following the Procession of the Blessed Sacrament each afternoon.

In Dr. Olivieri's time, the Anointing of the Sick was restored to its original status. It is a ceremony of great joy and spiritual grace to the sick. For centuries, this sacrament had been confined solely to those in danger of death; hence its name—Extreme Unction. It was administered to one individual at a time, usually in a hospital or at home. In this new community ceremony, hundreds of sick people receive a special blessing and anointing in the Domaine. These people are by no means all gravely ill, so they can more easily appreciate the value of this sacrament. Though it began as a Lourdes specialty, it has become an annual event in many parishes elsewhere, and is commonly celebrated on February 11, the Feast Day of the Apparitions.

Posterity will remember Dr. Olivieri most for his book. However, those who knew him personally in Lourdes will remember him as of outstanding character. He was a retiring, dignified person with a deep faith, whose professional competence and integrity were universally recognized. Wholeheartedly committed to his work at the Bureau, he was always gracious in dealing with people. He was devoted to the Church; his return to the Medical Bureau after early mass at the Grotto each morning, and his figure behind all the other doctors following the Blessed Sacrament in the afternoon procession were familiar sights in Lourdes. Upon handing over the presidency to his successor, he remarked that, of his long professional career, "my time at the Medical Bureau in Lourdes has been the most delightful period of my life."

Dr. Theodore Mangiapan (President, 1972–   )

The appointment of Dr. Mangiapan as President of the Medical Bureau heralded the start of a new era in the medical history of Lourdes. After his elderly predecessors who took office in their retirement, it was quite a change to have a relatively young, energetic doctor at the helm. In fact, he was the first President of the Medical Bureau to have been born in the twentieth century. The times were changing, as well. Medicine was becoming more and more sophisticated. The ideals of Vatican II were being put into practice. Pilgrims and invalids were arriving in Lourdes in ever greater numbers, and from more distant lands. There was a need to inform Catholics and non-Catholics alike of the deeper meaning of Lourdes.

Dr. Mangiapan studied medicine at the Medical Faculty of Marseilles, and graduated with distinction in 1952. After war service, he was appointed as a teaching assistant to the two Chairs of Medical and Surgical Pediatrics in Marseilles, and took a special interest in hematology. He is married, with three children, now grown. Although, in his early years, he devoted much of his time to charitable work, in 1963 he had an urge to do something more. He began going to Lourdes, working as a doctor on the pilgrimage from his own diocese. This had become an annual event when Msgr. Donze, then the Bishop of Tarbes and Lourdes, invited him to take up the full-time occupation of President of the Medical Bureau. His steadfast faith earned him the name of "militant Christian." He is utterly dedicated to Lourdes, an indefatigable worker, and quite accustomed to burning the midnight oil. He spends more than half the year at the Medical Bureau, and in winter attends to its affairs from his home in the South of France.

Dr. Mangiapan is a tall, bespectacled Frenchman who is very easy to find in a crowd. With unfailing regularity he is at the Medical Bureau during business hours, ready to meet with doctors and pilgrims and try to solve their problems. This task alone demands endless patience and forbearance, and is time-consuming. At 4:30 P.M. he can be found at the Grotto, quietly murmuring his Rosary, fingering the beads in hands joined behind his back, ready for the Procession of the Blessed Sacrament to begin. As it moves slowly away from the Grotto, he is easily seen with other members of the International Medical Association of Lourdes, head and shoulders above them all, and always in the last row. Those who have not yet observed his presence can hear his powerful voice speaking or singing the responses in all the common languages. During the Procession he is always alert to the needs of pilgrims along the promenade to the Rosary Square. Afterward, at the foot of the Basilica steps, he uses to the full his only opportunity of finding all the doctors assembled together.

A variety of building projects have received practical ideas in their planning stages from Dr. Mangiapan, who always strives to ensure that the sick pilgrims have suitable accommodation, whether in hostel or hospital.

On the far side of the River Gave de Pau stands the new Reception Center, the Accueil Ste. Bernadette, with 360–80 beds, opened in 1977. Then followed a scheme to modernize the two old centers: the Sept Douleurs Hospital, built in 1874 and now called the Accueil St. Frai, and the Asile, built in 1908–10 and recently renamed the Accueil

Notre Dame. This year [1987], the Renal Dialysis Center Unit should be completed and in use, after ten years of negotiation.

Suitable accommodations and transport were essential for the disabled, both old and young. Mr. Richard Glithero, from Surrey, England, spearheaded the foundation and development of the Across Trust in 1972. The trust sent its first jumbulance from London to Lourdes the next year. Now a fleet of ten jumbulances carry three thousand extremely ill or seriously handicapped pilgrims to Lourdes every year. These people cannot travel to Lourdes by any other means. They stay at specially designed hostels like Hosanna House (1975), the Chalet Across (1976) and Chalet l'Astazou (1982), where there is greater freedom and privacy at minimal cost.

The Italians organized something similar, though on a much greater scale, in 1972, when UNITALSI purchased the Hotel Bethanie and transformed it into the Salus Infirmorum, which can accommodate 250 pilgrims. This enables eleven to twelve thousand "walking sick" to come annually from Italy.

In the Domaine, extra facilities were needed for the disabled, such as ramps for wheelchairs, lifts, and the loop system for the deaf. Another small improvement in 1974 was the exposure of the Spring for all to see. Under an illuminated plate-glass cover, the crystal-clear water can be seen literally emerging from the rock of Massabielle.

A movement that has attracted thousands of pilgrims to Lourdes in recent years is the Charismatic Renewal. These throngs of young people really need much of the Domaine to themselves. Their vociferous ceremonies contrast with their silent prayer and contemplation when at the Grotto. The big problem for Dr. Mangiapan was to assess the physical cures these people claimed—made all the more difficult because they brought no medical records, were not medically examined after a cure, and never visited the Medical Bureau.

Since it is so distinct from miraculous cures, "Charismatic Healing" was selected as the main subject at the 1984 meeting of the International Medical Committee of Lourdes, in Paris.

Dr. Martine Laffitte-Catta spoke about charismatic healings, explaining that they are not classed as miracles, as defined by canonical rules. Nor are they usually extraordinary events; but are considered normal ones in which the goodness and compassion of God are evident. These healings are gradual and occur in less serious disorders often with a strong psychological component. Generally they happen where there is intense faith and prayer, especially during group prayer meetings, where the faith, hope, and love of those close to the sick persons contribute to the healing process. In such circumstances, the sick can more readily abandon themselves to the Lord and forget their spiritual shortcomings. Dr. Laffitte-Catta emphasized that, in charismatic healing, the healing power of God and the healing power of man are not set apart, but work together. In each, the love of God in healing mankind is shared.

Bishop Donze pointed out that healings in a religious context were attributed long ago to the faith of the sick people and their companions. Now they are seen as signs of the merciful love of God. He stressed that the allegations or witnesses of healing are personal and that it would be desirable to have the Medical Bureau give more attention to them.

Fr. Monléon, O.P., spoke on the theological and pastoral implications of unusual healing, which extends far beyond the limited scope of miraculous cures, is defined simply as being inexplicable, and is recognized by the Church. Charisms, on the other hand, are manifestations of the Holy Spirit, bestowed on the Church for the good of all. Their many and varied nature is not just preternatural or due to human talents. A charism refers more to the actual healing of the sick person and its effects than to the person with the power of healing. After mentioning healings in the Bible and in Church history, Fr. Monléon showed that healings were far from limited to the Charismatic Renewal, but throughout history had commonly occurred at religious gatherings, especially among the poor. They were never isolated bodily affairs, were unexpected and often dramatic, always being closely associated with psychological and spiritual factors. The subsequent conversion and thanksgiving of the cured person and his companions clearly showed the grace of God working through these healings.

Two memorable events in the recent history of Lourdes were the International Eucharistic Congress in 1981 and the visit of Pope John Paul II in 1983. The medical requirements for both these events were planned for and shepherded throughout by Dr. Mangiapan—no small achievement, considering that up to 250,000 pilgrims were expected at each.

The attempted assassination of the Pope ten weeks earlier prevented His Holiness from presiding at the Eucharistic Congress. As his legate, he sent Cardinal Gantin of Dahomey (Benin), West Africa, who was the Prefect of the Commission for Justice and Peace in Rome. Fortunately, the Pope had recovered sufficiently from his injuries to deliver a televised broadcast from his hospital ward in Rome to the pilgrims in Lourdes. His words were probably the most moving of the whole Congress; the crowd was obviously closely united spiritually and emotionally with their Pontiff. He held his vast audience spellbound, though he was still pale and drawn and his voice was much weaker than usual.

With people attending the Congress from 102 nations (the most impressive of whom were the Africans, resplendent in their national costumes and bubbling over with an innate and joyous faith and simplicity), there was inevitably a language problem at the first-aid stations. This was solved by inviting one hundred multilingual doctors; among them were contingents from Great Britain and Ireland. In their gum boots and sou'westers they weathered the numerous thunderstorms, drying out on the blisteringly hot Sunday at the International Mass, when the main casualties suffered from fits, faints, falls, feet, and forgotten pills.

Pope John Paul II did not make his longed-for pilgrimage to Lourdes until two years later. This was the first time a reigning Pope had trod in the footsteps of Bernadette. And he could have chosen no better day for his visit than the day he came: August 15, 1983, the Feast of the Assumption of Our Lady into Heaven.

Improving the quality of medical care has always been one of Dr. Mangiapan's priorities. To that end, he established the *Bulletin;* in it, he has published many articles on topics related to the role of doctors at Lourdes. In 1973, he invited Fr. John Godefroid, O.P., Head Chaplain of the National Rosary Pilgrimage, to contribute articles for the *Bulletin* on religious topics relevant to medicine. Fr. Michel de Roton, a former Rector of the Sanctuaries, has also contributed several articles. As well as these, the *Bulletin* now brings news of the International Medical Association of Lourdes, book reviews, often a prayer, and articles by other distinguished doctors. Recently published was an account of the latest cure (Delizia Cirolli), for which all the investigations had been supervised by Dr. Mangiapan.

One of Dr. Mangiapan's ambitions was to encourage doctors with an interest in Lourdes to meet together in their own countries (already the custom in Italy and France) for mutual cooperation and discussion of pilgrimage matters. At least one country set up a Lourdes Medical Association, thanks to the foresight and enterprise of Dr. Bernard Smits, who gathered a dozen doctors together in 1974 to discuss the project. The next year, the Lourdes Medical Association in Great Britain was established and is still flourishing. This organization holds an annual weekend conference; on the agenda are the Annual General Meeting, mass celebrated by one of the bishops, lectures on topics related to pilgrimage problems, and a day's-end banquet. This association has brought about a great *esprit de corps* among its members, and indirectly has raised the medical standards of British pilgrimages.

Dr. Mangiapan will be especially remembered for his painstaking research into the Archives of the Medical Bureau. In 1983, the Bureau (formerly the Bureau des Constatations Médicales—B.C.M.) celebrated its Centenary Year. Time has shown how this important institution has put its mark on the history of Lourdes: by fulfilling its exacting duties of verifying alleged cures in a competent manner. Since its inception, membership has steadily increased, with new young doctors registering every year, ensuring continuity. Dr. Mangiapan arranged the records in the Archives in orderly fashion and has used this vast store of information in many publications. He helped to revise the fourth edition of Dr. Olivieri's book, adding new statistics and more personal details of sick pilgrims and their cures. He is in demand on television in Western Europe, since he brings with him such a great store of detailed knowledge of past and present Lourdes. He represents the Medical Bureau at great festivities associated with the sick in Rome, Fatima, and elsewhere, and is often asked for advice on modern apparitions such as those at Medjugorje.

In fourteen years as President of the Medical Bureau, Dr. Mangiapan has used his administrative, innovative, and literary skills in the many and varied developments of the medical side of Lourdes. There is virtually no one associated with Lourdes who has not benefited from his presidency.

Mrs. Winifred Feely (Lourdes Hospitality, Lecturer, 1950–85)

No account of the changes in the Medical Bureau would be complete without reference to Mrs. Winifred Feely, particularly since she was already firmly established there when Ruth Cranston was writing her book. Mrs. Feely provided a very real continuity as Dr. Leuret left, Drs. Pelissier and Olivieri came and went, and Dr. Mangiapan came into the presidency. It is no wonder that she is known as the "living memory" of Lourdes, for she alone at the Bureau has met and remembers well so many people connected with it, having lived through the changes there for thirty-five years.

Mrs. Feely was a convert and was herself cured of a serious illness at the Baths in Lourdes in 1950. Given a new lease on life, she wanted to show her appreciation by offering her services, and had already been accepted to work at the Baths when Dr. Leuret suggested something else. He needed help at the Medical Bureau, and realized that Mrs. Feely's native English and fluency in French, along with her other qualities, would be a great asset there. She accepted his invitation and started at the Bureau in 1950. But she did not stay very long in the little office under the Rampe of the Esplanade. On her own initiative, with the blessing of the Bishop of Tarbes and Lourdes and the good will of Dr. Leuret, she set up her own office on the ground floor at the rear of the Pavillon des Salles de Conférences. In addition, she looked after the suite of new rooms there, including the Library. The whole floor became known as the "other half" of the Medical Bureau. Here Mrs. Feely worked and dwelt during the greater part of each pilgrimage season, hospitably greeting and helping any and every person who crossed the threshold. She always found time to chat with pilgrims, and she gave lectures on Lourdes at the Bureau. Her love of Lourdes, her great sincerity, her personal memories, and her sense of humor never failed to impress her audience. She also built an enormous correspondence with devotees of Lourdes. If all her letters, which were beautifully written and contained fascinating histories and observations, could be gathered into one volume, it would reach encyclopedic proportions and be a veritable modern history of Lourdes.

Mrs. Feely never stayed very long in her own home, in Somerset, England. She spent the winter months traveling in the United States, lecturing to vast audiences, who were spellbound by her portrayals of life in Lourdes. As a fortuitous result of this work, she raised large sums of money that contributed handsomely to the equipping and maintenance of the Medical Bureau, the building of the new Baths, and the renovation of the two old Centres d'Accueil.

In August 1985, Mrs. Feely retired, at the age of eighty-eight, and returned to Somerset. Naturally her interest in Lourdes remains, and she still keeps abreast of her huge correspondence with her friends of Lourdes. Her pen—and her voice on the telephone—are far from idle. She will be greatly missed by English-speaking pilgrims, by Dr. Mangiapan, with whom she worked closely, and by the authorities in Lourdes, who treated her as a confidante.

Ever deeply committed to Lourdes, she epitomized the "grace of

Lourdes," always available with her kindness, generosity, and big-heartedness. May she enjoy a long and happy retirement!

Mrs. Feely's successor has been appointed. Although she has learned a little about the job from her predecessor, a hard task lies ahead. Pilgrims and Dr. Mangiapan will give her every help and encouragement to rise to the demands she will encounter.

APPENDIX B

Lourdes, Then and Now

Dr. Barbara Coventry first came to Lourdes in 1960. She is a general medical practitioner—a family doctor—a member of I.M.A.L. and of the Hospitalité Notre Dame de Lourdes. Since 1979, she has been a Councillor to the Hospitalité for the English-speaking countries.

If Ruth Cranston revisited Lourdes today, what would she see? What has changed in thirty years? The same polyglot crowds stream toward the Grotto, the same suffering faces turn pleadingly upward. "That dark rent in the mountain," the Grotto of Massabielle, looks wider, more open. The Gave de Pau seems to have retreated eastward. The stone below the same statue in the same niche above our heads is worn smoother by the passage of a million hands. At the back of the Grotto, the Spring of Bernadette, source of healing and renewal, now trickles and dances at our feet beneath a panel of glass.

Many of the impedimenta have gone, though the blackened crutches left here by early pilgrims still hang above our heads. There is space now for sick pilgrims on stretchers and in wheelchairs to pass through below the statue, to touch the rock, to see the Spring.

The same little black-clad peasants of Southern Europe still murmur their rosaries. But air travel and paid holidays for all have brought new colorful figures—Japanese, Chinese from Malaya and Hong Kong, Koreans in exquisite kimonos and obis, Indians in saris, Danes, Yugoslavs, and Poles in national dress, the tall graceful men and women of

Africa. There are Vietnamese, the sad women of Lebanon, a group from Israel, and the sick groups from Australia.

Pope John Paul II came here in 1983—a new departure for a Pope and for Lourdes. In the late 1950s, for the first time, the total number of non-French exceeded the number of French pilgrims. An average year now brings fifty-five thousand registered sick in the Domaine Hospitals, fifteen thousand known sick in hotels, more than eight hundred thousand walking pilgrims, and an unknown number of visitors of no recorded grouping. In 1983 America brought her first pilgrimage with sick people requiring hospital facilities. An English society now specializes in the gravely ill, the dying, and the seriously disabled. Pilgrims and pilgrimages come in winter, too; they cannot wait for the next season to start.

Beyond the Grotto now stand racks to burn the myriad candles lit in petition. The Baths have been rebuilt, then reordered again. Mothers and children have a separate compartment, with large and small baths and their own entrance. The waiting area is covered, and rows of benches are provided. Organized prayers at the Baths are said in many languages, each pilgrimage taking a turn. The voice of America mingles with the "public school" accent of Ampleforth and the hoarse cries of Catalonia. Inside, the pilgrim has available simple directions and prayers in seven languages. The bath is a little slower, the prayers simpler than in Ruth Cranston's time. There are no partial baths now. The emphasis is on silence and prayer. The *hospitaliers* and *hospitalières* of the Piscines are trained to be quiet, smiling, devout and strictly adherent to a carefully worked-out drill for safety's sake. They are well aware that they are privileged to assist in this highly prized act of prayer, to share in this devotion peculiar to Lourdes.

Across the Gave (River), now spanned by one covered and two open bridges, the Prairie is seamed with paved roads. A permanent altar faces the Grotto. Here large and small groups can hold their ceremonies out of earshot of pilgrims at prayer. A new hospital of 360 beds was opened there in 1977—light, airy, and equipped with modern wards, a chapel, and dining, rest, and transit halls. The older hospitals have been brought up to date—750 beds in the Accueil Notre Dame, 540 at Notre Dame des Douleurs. A transit system allows entrance of pilgrimages directly from the highway, with departure from a separate exit. Another building, the Hospitalet, lodges pilgrimage helpers. Downstream are marquees (large tents or shelters) for conference and a slide show. The largest may soon be replaced by a permanent chapel, perhaps ecumenical.

Back across the Esplanade lies the new Medical Bureau, with conference facilities. Outside, ramps lead down to the Underground Basilica, opened in the Centenary Year, 1958, and capable of holding twenty-five to thirty thousand pilgrims. That same year saw the completion of the Cité St. Pierre, the City of the Poor, on the mountain. Ten years later came its neighbor, the Campsite, for young people.

Bartres Hosanna House, English-funded, French-staffed, lodges one handicapped pilgrim and one helper in each room. In 1958, the foundation stone was laid at Bartres for a dialysis unit, equipped to strict standards, with each section totally separate and self-contained to prevent cross-infection.

Vatican II brought the Catholic Church closer to the laity and closer to its separated brethren. It brought modification and expansion of the ceremonies of Lourdes. No longer are the side altars occupied by a succession of individual masses. Rather, concelebrations by a cardinal, some bishops, and as many priests as can fit around the altar appear regularly. Mass is said in the vernacular, with Latin only reemerging when a universal language would be helpful. Religious programs are more varied. Daily mass and Blessing of the Sick, of course; on other days, Stations of the Cross by sick and well together, Blessing of the Hands of Helpers, preparation for and celebration of the Sacrament of the Sick, and participation in turns by the sick from various hospitals in the Torchlight Procession.

In 1967 the first Protestant group came to pray. In 1982, ecumenism leapt forward with the first Anglican pilgrimage, led by three bishops and given facilities to use St. Joseph's Chapel, within the Domaine, and to have their place in the Processions.

In addition to the original diocesan pilgrimages, there are now many smaller groups, always including some sick pilgrims, organized by tourist agencies whose vocation to bring pilgrims to Lourdes is as profound as that of any professional hospitaller. The casual visitor is provided for. "One-Day Pilgrims" of all European languages have their own quasi-permanent chaplains, their own programs—mass, prayer, baths, tour of historic sites—their own banners and places in the processions. Linked to this is the "Service des Touristes et Isolés." This provides for anyone, sick or well, belonging to no fixed group. It is maintained under a *permanent* of the Sanctuaries, aided by a number of hostesses speaking a variety of languages. The "Service des Malades et

Handicapés Isolés" began through the devotion of a retired police officer from Normandy. Each year, he lodged in cheap hotels for as long as he could afford and made daily rounds of the hotels seeking out sick visitors in need of transport around the Domaine. I met him at the bedside of a dying youngster from Polynesia who was lodging in a hilltop hotel, within sight of, but unable to reach, the Sanctuaries. One man's loving care answered this youngster's prayer and inspired this service. Provision has also been made for pilgrims with personal problems. The *Porte Ouverte* ("Open Door") is under the Rampe, and there anyone can walk in and talk to a sympathetic listener.

The Hospitalité Notre Dame de Lourdes (Ruth Cranston's "Hospitallers") includes men and women of many nationalities. Their membership list reads like a gazette of the world. In 1975, the Branche Masculine, until then wholly French, took in its first foreign Councillors; the Branche Féminine followed in 1979—American, Belgian, English, Irish, Italian, Spanish, Swiss. The Lourdais themselves take part and assure winter service. Every hotel, every souvenir shop of the "commercial side" of Lourdes either numbers among its staff one or more members of the Hospitalité or contributes in some way to the work of the Domaine. Père Joseph Bordes, the Rector of the Chaplaincy, formerly a parish priest of Lourdes town, said, "Until I came to work in the Sanctuaries, I had no idea how many of my parishioners were involved in the Domaine. I was dumfounded." Trainees must be soundly recommended as to ability and character. They serve a six-year apprenticeship before making their Consecration into the Hospitalité— a life commitment to service in Lourdes and in their lives at home.

Les Permanents have changed too. A new bishop, discreet and wise, has brought Lourdes into the twentieth century. The old Hospitalité chaplain, pastoral friend to all his *hospitaliers,* made way for a man with a taste for organization, founder of the school for Trainee Hospitaliers. In 1972, a younger Medical Bureau President of restless, searching intelligence followed Dr. Olivieri to carry on the tradition of his noble predecessors.

And what of the pilgrims? It is said that fewer stretcher sick are seen in Lourdes now. Is this true? If so, why? There may in fact be fewer stretchers. The welfare state now extends throughout Europe and beyond. The expectation is one of state responsibility for caring for illness—welfare care and welfare cure. It is harder for today's patient to accept an unfavorable outcome to his affliction.

Certainly the sick in wretched condition, primitively clothed and cared for, with deep bedsores, ill-constructed colostomies, and old-fashioned apparatus have disappeared. The trend of modern medicine is to keep the seriously ill ambulant as long as possible. Yet there are groups and pilgrimages devoted precisely to the most gravely ill. It is a fact that many pilgrimages from overseas come by air, and each stretcher costs the price of two seats. It is also true that many pilgrimages include men and women whose only disability is old age. Yet, each year, some desperately ill pilgrims are brought, with attendant doctor and nurse, to bathe in the Spring. Often, in fact, such people, having attained their heart's desire—this final journey of prayer and reaffirmation—die in Lourdes, as the local graveyards attest.

The pattern of illness has changed with advancing medicine. Tuberculosis, paralytic poliomyelitis, and rheumatic heart disease are now rarities. Other diseases now predominate: multiple sclerosis, neuromuscular disease, the disastrous results of traffic accidents, kidney disease, and cancerous conditions. The last polio pilgrimage, in 1983, numbered thirty-six pilgrims in respirators, all born before the advent of poliomyelitis vaccine in 1963. This group now makes up its numbers with pilgrims gravely handicapped by chronic sickness or traffic accidents. Blood dyscrasias (abnormalities) and leukemias are said to be more common in this age of radiation. Heart and arterial pathologies, the stress diseases of modern life, seem to be the price of today's industrial society. And always with us is the sad group of congenitally and incurably sick children. Psychiatric illness is not yet susceptible of objective proof and, therefore, is not the subject of investigation by the Medical Bureau. However, the Faith and Light Pilgrimage, first held in 1971 and repeated twice, brought mentally handicapped pilgrims of many nations together to pray and process in scenes of spontaneous enjoyment and gaiety.

In the early days, people brought their hopelessly sick and dying to Lourdes. Some were dramatically cured. The Lourdes described by Ruth Cranston still had something of that same expectation. Does that hope still exist? Few fully documented cases have been declared medically inexplicable by the doctors. Even fewer have been accepted as miraculous by the Catholic Church. Sixty-four cures in 126 years, among so many millions. What, then, do all these pilgrims, sick and well, come so far for?

I suppose that, among the acutely sick, the rapidly advancing disease of younger people, there must be a strand of hope. "Might I be the one among so many?" Also, clearly there are now a sizable proportion of chronically sick and elderly people who expect not medical relief but something different: companionship, a change of scene, equality with the healthy, participation in their Church, comfort of spirit. And perhaps some of the pilgrims of today come to Lourdes as others seek out Indian gurus, Buddhist monasteries, way-out religions—as a means of escape from the welfare state into the world of the spirit. Perhaps they are no longer asking "Can I be cured?" but "How can my spirit live in my crippled body?" "How can my crippled spirit live in the world in which I find myself?" Perhaps they come to Lourdes to plunge themselves into prayer as they plunge themselves into the Source.

"Lourdes is one of the few places left where people are loved because they exist, not for what they do," said a psychiatrist in Lourdes in 1983. Is it only in Lourdes that "every man can be a first-born son" (Heb. 12:23)? Here we dare to love and be loved, to give and to receive, we dare to be good, to set sail again for perfection. Here, in the shadow of Mary, the humblest of the saints, suffering man dares to reach out to God, who is Love; who, through her, in the Incarnation, became one with us.

Dr. Barbara Coventry

Members of the International Medical Committee of Lourdes (June 1986)

Msgr. Henri Donze	Bishop of Tarbes and Lourdes	
Prof. Th. Kammerer	France	Psychiatry
Dr. J. L. Armand-Laroche	France	Psychiatry
Prof. J. Y. Barbin	France	General Surgery
Prof. H. Barrière	France	Dermatology
Prof. A. Beretta-Anguissola	Italy	Medicine
Prof. Ch. Boudet	France	Ophthalmology
Prof. U. Carcassi	Italy	Medicine
Dr. Ch. Chassagnon	France	Medicine
Dr. B. Colvin	Scotland	Orthopedic Surgery
Dr. B. J. Deasy	Ireland	Medicine
Dr. S. J. Dowling	England	Medicine
Dr. D. Pérez	Spain	Medicine
Prof. J. Gibert-Queralto	Spain	Medicine
Dr. S. J. Heffernan	Ireland	Medicine
Dr. P. Lance	France	Orthopedic Surgery
Prof. P. Mouren	France	Neurology
Prof. C. Puijlaert	The Netherlands	Radiology
Dr. L. Revol	France	Hematology
Dr. J. Rodier	France	Cardiology
Dr. J. Rousseau	France	Cancer
Dr. B. Smits	England	Gastroenterology
Dr. E. Theiss	Germany	Surgery
Dr. C. Trabucchi	Italy	Psychiatry
Dr. A. Trifaud	France	Orthopedic Surgery
Dr. C. Wijffels	The Netherlands	Thoracic Surgery
Dr. T. Mangiapan	France	Pediatrics

Questionnaire

After a full discussion, a new list of questions was agreed upon, as follows:

1. What is the diagnosis?_____
   _____
   _____

2. Has the diagnosis been established by adequate objective examination?   YES   NO

3. Are the subjective symptoms in accordance with the objective findings?   YES   NO

4. Does the comprehensive clinical picture rule out psychogenic overlay?   YES   NO

5. Was the disease serious   YES   NO
       –because of the degree of disability   YES   NO
       –because of its threat to life?   YES   NO

6. Does the prognosis rule out the possibility of spontaneous remission, natural cure, significant improvement or, long-term remission?   YES   NO

7. Can one rule out any treatment received as having played a part in the cure   –totally   YES   NO
                    or
       –partially   YES   NO

8. Can the cure be confirmed by irrefutable facts?
                             YES   NO

9. Has the sick person noticed the disappearance of subjective symptoms?   YES   NO

10. Did the cure appear completely contrary to the prognosis?   YES   NO

11. Was the cure sudden and consistent with the disappearance of objective pathological signs?   YES   NO

12. In the absence of signs of immediate regression of a cure, has there been a modification of the symptomatology that one could consider as the beginning of the process of cure?   YES   NO

13. Was the cure complete?   YES   NO

14. Were there any sequelae?   YES   NO

15. Were there any pathological repercussions?   YES   NO

16. Was the duration of the surveillance of the cure adequate enough to give the appearance that it is quite contrary to the prognosis?   YES   NO

Conclusion: Taking into consideration the way it was produced and sustained, does the established cure of M. _____ constitute a phenomenon which is

    —contrary to the observations and expectations of medical knowledge,   YES   NO

                       and

    —scientifically inexplicable?   YES   NO

Miraculous Cures (Listed in Order of Year of Cure)*

Name:	Mrs. Catherine Latapie-Chouat
Residence:	Loubajac
Disease:	Traumatic Brachial Palsy
Year of Cure:	1858
Age at Cure:	39 years
Cure recognized by:	Church (1862)

Name:	Mr. Louis Bouriette
Residence:	Lourdes
Disease:	Post-traumatic Blindness
Year of Cure:	1858
Age at Cure:	54 years
Cure recognized by:	Church (1862)

Name:	Mrs. Blaisette Cazenave (née Soupène)
Residence:	Lourdes
Disease:	Chronic Ophthalmitis
Year of Cure:	1858
Age at Cure:	50 years
Cure recognized by:	Church (1862)

* Names that appear in capital letters indicate people whose cases are mentioned or reported in this book.

Name: Mr. Henri Busquet
Residence: Nay
Disease: Tuberculous Cervical Lymphadenitis
Year of Cure: 1858
Age at Cure: 15 years
Cure recognized by: Church (1862)

Name: MR. JUSTIN BOUHOHORTS
Residence: Lourdes
Disease: Hypothrepsia with Retarded Motor Devel-
                               opment, or "Consumption"
Year of Cure: 1858
Age at Cure: 2 years
Cure recognized by: Church (1862)
Mention in this book: Chapter 3, p. 37–39

Name: Mrs. Madeleine Rizan
Residence: Nay
Disease: Cerebral Thrombosis
Year of Cure: 1858
Age at Cure: 58 years
Cure recognized by: Church (1862)

Name: Miss Marie Moreau
Residence: Tartas
Disease: Panophthalmitis of Right Eye
Year of Cure: 1858
Age at Cure: 17 years
Cure recognized by: Church (1862)

Name: MR. PIERRE DE RUDDER
Residence: Jabbeke, Belgium
Disease: Ununited Fracture of Left Leg
Year of Cure: 1875
Age at Cure: 52 years
Cure recognized by: Church (1908)
Mention in this book: Chapter 16, p. 161–64

Name: MISS JOACHIME DEHANT
Residence: Gesves, Belgium
Disease: Chronic Gangrenous Leg Ulcer

Year of Cure:	1878
Age at Cure:	29 years
Cure recognized by:	Church (1908)
Mention in this book:	Chapter 3, p. 39–40

Name:	Miss Elisa Seisson
Residence:	Rognonas
Disease:	Hypertrophy of the Heart
Year of Cure:	1882
Age at Cure:	27 years
Cure recognized by:	Church (1912)

Name:	Sr. Eugenia (Marie Mabille)
Residence:	Bernay
Disease:	Chronic Pelvic Inflammatory Disease with Multiple Fistulae
Year of Cure:	1883
Age at Cure:	28 years
Cure recognized by:	B.C.M., Church (1908)

Name:	Sr. Julienne (Aline Bruyère)
Residence:	La Roque
Disease:	Cavitating Pulmonary Tuberculosis
Year of Cure:	1889
Age at Cure:	25 years
Cure recognized by:	B.C.M., Church (1912)

Name:	Sr. Josephine-Marie (Anne Jourdain)
Residence:	Goincourt
Disease:	Pulmonary Tuberculosis
Year of Cure:	1890
Age at Cure:	36 years
Cure recognized by:	B.C.M., Church (1908)

Name:	Miss Amélie Chagnon
Residence:	Poitiers
Disease:	Tuberculous Arthritis of Knee and Dactylitis
Year of Cure:	1891
Age at Cure:	17 years
Cure recognized by:	Church (1910)

Name: Miss Clémentine Trouvé (Sr. Agnès-Marie)
Residence: Rouille
Disease: Osteomyelitis of Right Foot with Fistulae
Year of Cure: 1891
Age at Cure: 14 years
Cure recognized by: B.C.M., Church (1908)

Name: Miss Marie Lebranchu (Mrs. Wuiplier)
Residence: Paris
Disease: Pulmonary Tuberculosis
Year of Cure: 1892
Age at Cure: 35 years
Cure recognized by: Church (1908)

Name: Miss Marie Lemarchand (Mrs. Authier)
Residence: Caen
Disease: Pulmonary Tuberculosis with Leg Ulcer-
                         ation and Lupus
Year of Cure: 1892
Age at Cure: 18 years
Cure recognized by: B.C.M., Church (1908)

Name: Miss Elise Lesage
Residence: Bucquoy
Disease: Tuberculous Arthritis of Knee
Year of Cure: 1892
Age at Cure: 18 years
Cure recognized by: B.C.M., Church (1908)

Name: Sr. Marie de la Présentation
Residence: Lille
Disease: Chronic Abdominal Tuberculosis
Year of Cure: 1892
Age at Cure: 44 years
Cure recognized by: Church (1908)

Name: Fr. Cirette
Residence: Beaumontel
Disease: Spinal Sclerosis
Year of Cure: 1893

Age at Cure: 46 years
Cure recognized by: Church (1907)

Name: Miss Aurélie Huprelle
Residence: St. Martin-le-Noeud
Disease: Pulmonary Tuberculosis
Year of Cure: 1895
Age at Cure: 26 years
Cure recognized by: B.C.M., Church (1908)

Name: Miss Esther Brachmann
Residence: Paris
Disease: Tuberculous Peritonitis
Year of Cure: 1896
Age at Cure: 15 years
Cure recognized by: B.C.M., Church (1908)

Name: Miss Jeanne Tulasne
Residence: Tours
Disease: Pott's Disease of the Spine, Clubfoot
Year of Cure: 1897
Age at Cure: 20 years
Cure recognized by: B.C.M., Church (1907)

Name: Miss Clémentine Malot
Residence: Gaudechart
Disease: Pulmonary Tuberculosis
Year of Cure: 1898
Age at Cure: 25 years
Cure recognized by: B.C.M., Church (1908)

Name: Mrs. Rose François (née Labreuvoies)
Residence: Paris
Disease: Lymphangitis of Right Arm with Fistulae
Year of Cure: 1899
Age at Cure: 36 years
Cure recognized by: Church (1908)

Name: Rev. Fr. Salvator
Residence: Dinard
Disease: Tuberculous Peritonitis
Year of Cure: 1900

| Age at Cure: | 38 years |
| Cure recognized by: | B.C.M., Church (1908) |

Name:	Sr. Maximilien
Residence:	Marseilles
Disease:	Hydatid Cyst of Liver, Phlebitis of Left Lower Leg
Year of Cure:	1901
Age at Cure:	43 years
Cure recognized by:	B.C.M., Church (1908)

Name:	Miss Marie Savoye
Residence:	Le Cateau-Cambrésis
Disease:	Rheumatic Mitral Valvular Heart Disease
Year of Cure:	1901
Age at Cure:	24 years
Cure recognized by:	B.C.M., Church (1908)

Name:	Mrs. Johanna Bezenac (née Dubos)
Residence:	St. Laurent-des-Batons
Disease:	Cachexia (unknown origin), Impetigo of Face
Year of Cure:	1904
Age at Cure:	28 years
Cure recognized by:	Church (1908)

Name:	Sr. Saint-Hilaire
Residence:	Peyreleau
Disease:	Intestinal Tumor
Year of Cure:	1904
Age at Cure:	39 years
Cure recognized by:	B.C.M., Church (1908)

Name:	Sr. Sainte-Beatrix (Rosalie Vildier)
Residence:	Évreux
Disease:	Laryngo-bronchitis, probably tuberculous
Year of Cure:	1904
Age at Cure:	42 years
Cure recognized by:	B.C.M., Church (1908)

| Name: | Miss Marie-Thérèse Noblet |
| Residence: | Avenay |

Disease:	Dorso-lumbar Spondylitis
Year of Cure:	1905
Age at Cure:	15 years
Cure recognized by:	B.C.M., Church (1908)

Name:	Miss Cécile Douville de Franssu
Residence:	Tournai, Belgium
Disease:	Tuberculous Peritonitis
Year of Cure:	1905
Age at Cure:	19 years
Cure recognized by:	B.C.M., Church (1909)

Name:	Miss Antonia Moulin
Residence:	Vienne
Disease:	Chronic Osteomyelitis of Right Femur with Fistulae, Arthritis of Knee
Year of Cure:	1907
Age at Cure:	30 years
Cure recognized by:	B.C.M., Church (1910)

Name:	Miss Marie Borel
Residence:	Mende
Disease:	Pyelo-nephritis with Colonic Fistulae
Year of Cure:	1907
Age at Cure:	27 years
Cure recognized by:	B.C.M., Church (1911)

Name:	Miss Virginie Haudebourg
Residence:	Lons-le-Saunier
Disease:	Tuberculous Nephritis and Cystitis
Year of Cure:	1908
Age at Cure:	22 years
Cure recognized by:	B.C.M., Church (1912)

Name:	MRS. MARIE BIRE (née Lucas)
Residence:	Ste. Gemme-la-Plaine
Disease:	Blindness of Cerebral Origin, Bilateral Optic Atrophy
Year of Cure:	1908
Age at Cure:	41 years

Cure recognized by:	B.C.M., Church (1910)
Mention in this book:	Chapter 3, p. 42–44

Name:	Miss Aimée Allope
Residence:	Vern
Disease:	Chronic Abdominal Fistulous Tuberculosis
Year of Cure:	1909
Age at Cure:	37 years
Cure recognized by:	B.C.M., Church (1910)

Name:	Miss Juliette Orion
Residence:	St. Hilaire-de-Voust
Disease:	Pulmonary and Laryngeal Tuberculosis, Mastoiditis
Year of Cure:	1910
Age at Cure:	24 years
Cure recognized by:	B.C.M., Church (1913)

Name:	Mrs. Marie Fabre
Residence:	Montredon
Disease:	Chronic Inflammatory Bowel Disease, Uterine Prolapse
Year of Cure:	1911
Age at Cure:	32 years
Cure recognized by:	Church (1912)

Name:	MISS HENRIETTE BRESSOLLES
Residence:	Nice
Disease:	Pott's Disease with Paraplegia
Year of Cure:	1924
Age at Cure:	c. 30 years
Cure recognized by:	B.C.M., Church (1957)
Mention in this book:	Chapter 27, p. 292–93

Name:	MISS LYDIA BROSSE
Residence:	St.-Raphaël
Disease:	Chronic Abdominal Fistulous Tuberculosis
Year of Cure:	1930
Age at Cure:	41 years
Cure recognized by:	B.C.M., M.B., I.M.C., Church (1958)
Mention in this book:	Chapters 18, 27, pp. 181, 283

Name: SR. MARIE-MARGUERITE (Françoise
                    Capitaine)
Residence: Rennes
Disease: Chronic Left Renal Abscess, Cardiac Crises
Year of Cure: 1937
Age at Cure: 64 years
Cure recognized by: Church (1946)
Mention in this book: Chapter 23, p. 247–49

Name: Miss Louise Jamain (Mrs. Maître)
Residence: Paris
Disease: Pulmonary, Intestinal, and Peritoneal Tu-
                    berculosis
Year of Cure: 1937
Age at Cure: 22 years
Cure recognized by: B.C.M., Church (1951)

Name: [Boy] FRANCIS PASCAL
Residence: Beaucaire
Disease: Blindness and Paralysis of Lower Limbs
Year of Cure: 1938
Age at Cure: 3 years, 10 months
Cure recognized by: B.C.M., Church (1949)
Mention in this book: Chapter 22, p. 233–39

Name: MISS GABRIELLE CLAUZEL
Residence: Oran
Disease: Rheumatic Spondylosis
Year of Cure: 1943
Age at Cure: 49 years
Cure recognized by: B.C.M., Church (1948)
Mention in this book: Chapter 21, p. 216–23

Name: MISS YVONNE FOURNIER
Residence: Limoges
Disease: Leriche's Syndrome (traumatic)
Year of Cure: 1945
Age at Cure: 22 years
Cure recognized by: B.C.M., M.B., I.M.C., Church (1959)
Mention in this book: Chapter 27, p. 295–96

Name:	MRS. ROSE MARTIN (née Perona)
Residence:	Nice
Disease:	Carcinoma of the Cervix
Year of Cure:	1947
Age at Cure:	45 years
Cure recognized by:	M.B., N.M.C., Church (1949)
Mention in this book:	Chapter 23, p. 253–56

Name:	MRS. JEANNE GESTAS (née Pelin)
Residence:	Bègles
Disease:	Adhesive Peritonitis
Year of Cure:	1947
Age at Cure:	50 years
Cure recognized by:	M.B., N.M.C., Church (1952)
Mention in this book:	Chapter 23, p. 250–53

Name:	Miss Marie-Thérèse Canin
Residence:	Marseilles
Disease:	Pott's Disease of the Spine with Tuberculous Peritonitis with Fistulae
Year of Cure:	1947
Age at Cure:	37 years
Cure recognized by:	M.B., N.M.C., Church (1952)

Name:	MISS MADDALENA CARINI
Residence:	San Remo, Italy
Disease:	Peritoneal, Pleuro-pulmonary, and Bone Tuberculosis with Coronary Disease
Year of Cure:	1948
Age at Cure:	31 years
Cure recognized by:	M.B., N.M.C., Church (1960)
Mention in this book:	Chapter 27, p. 284–85

Name:	MISS JEANNE FRETEL
Residence:	Rennes
Disease:	Tuberculous Peritonitis
Year of Cure:	1948
Age at Cure:	34 years
Cure recognized by:	M.B., N.M.C., Church (1950)
Mention in this book:	Chapter 21, p. 209–16

Name: MISS THEA ANGELE (Sr. Marie-Merce-
                        des)
Residence: Tettnang, Germany
Disease: Multiple Sclerosis
Year of Cure: 1950
Age at Cure: 29 years
Cure recognized by: M.B., I.M.C., Church (1961)
Mention in this book: Chapter 27, p. 288–89

Name: MR. EVASIO GANORA
Residence: Casale, Italy
Disease: Hodgkin's Disease
Year of Cure: 1950
Age at Cure: 37 years
Cure recognized by: M.B., I.M.C., Church (1955)
Mention in this book: Chapter 27, p. 289–90

Name: MISS EDELTRAUT FULDA (Mrs. Haid-
                        inger)
Residence: Vienna, Austria
Disease: Addison's Disease
Year of Cure: 1950
Age at Cure: 34 years
Cure recognized by: M.B., I.M.C., Church (1955)
Mention in this book: Chapter 27, p. 290–92

Name: MR. PAUL PELLEGRIN
Residence: Toulon
Disease: Post-operative Fistula following a Liver
                        Abscess
Year of Cure: 1950
Age at Cure: 52 years
Cure recognized by: M.B., N.M.C., Church (1953)
Mention in this book: Chapter 21, p. 223–26

Name: BRO. LEO SCHWAGER
Residence: Fribourg, Switzerland
Disease: Multiple Sclerosis
Year of Cure: 1952
Age at Cure: 28 years

Cure recognized by:	M.B., I.M.C., Church (1960)
Mention in this book:	Chapter 27, p. 287–88

Name:	MRS. ALICE COUTEAULT (née Gourdon)
Residence:	Bouillé-Loretz
Disease:	Multiple Sclerosis
Year of Cure:	1952
Age at Cure:	34 years
Cure recognized by:	M.B., I.M.C., Church (1956)
Mention in this book:	Chapter 27, p. 285–86

Name:	MISS MARIE BIGOT
Residence:	La Richardais
Disease:	Arachnoiditis of Posterior Fossa (blind, deaf, hemiplegic)
Year of Cure:	1953, 1954
Age at Cure:	31 years (1953)
Cure recognized by:	M.B., I.M.C., Church (1956)
Mention in this book:	Chapter 27, p. 293–95

Name:	MRS. GINETTE NOUVEL (née Fabre)
Residence:	Carmaux
Disease:	Budd-Chiari Disease (hepatic vein thrombosis)
Year of Cure:	1954
Age at Cure:	26 years
Cure recognized by:	M.B., I.M.C., Church (1963)
Mention in this book:	Chapter 27, p. 296–99

Name:	MISS ELISA ALOI (Mrs. Varacalli)
Residence:	Patti, Italy
Disease:	Tuberculous Arthritis with Multiple Fistulae of Right Leg
Year of Cure:	1958
Age at Cure:	27 years
Cure recognized by:	M.B., I.M.C., Church (1965)
Mention in this book:	Chapter 28, p. 300–2

Name:	MISS JULIETTE TAMBURINI
Residence:	Marseilles

Disease:	Femoral Osteomyelitis with Fistulae, Epistaxes (Nosebleeds)
Year of Cure:	1959
Age at Cure:	22 years
Cure recognized by:	M.B., I.M.C., Church (1965)
Mention in this book:	Chapter 28, p. 302–4

Name:	MR. VITTORIO MICHELI
Residence:	Scurelle, Italy
Disease:	Sarcoma of Pelvis
Year of Cure:	1963
Age at Cure:	23 years
Cure recognized by:	M.B., I.M.C., Church (1976)
Mention in this book:	Chapter 28, p. 304–7

Name:	MR. SERGE PERRIN
Residence:	Lion d'Angers
Disease:	Multiple Stroke Syndrome
Year of Cure:	1970
Age at Cure:	41 years
Cure recognized by:	M.B., D.M.C. (Diocesan Medical Commission), I.M.C., Church (1978)
Mention in this book:	Chapter 28, p. 307–10

Cures Mentioned in Text (Not Officially Recognized by the Church)

Name:	CATHERINE LAPEYRE
Residence:	Toulouse
Disease:	Cancer of the Tongue
Year of Cure:	1889
Age at Cure:	—
Cure recognized by:	— (cured away from Lourdes)
Mention in this book:	Chapter 16, p. 167

Name:	MR. GABRIEL GARGAM
Residence:	—
Disease	Spinal Cord Injury-Paralysis, Gangrene of Feet
Year of Cure:	1901
Age at Cure:	32 years
Cure recognized by:	B.C.M.
Mention in this book:	Chapter 3, p. 40–42

Name:	MISS MARIE BAILLY
Residence:	Lyon
Disease:	Tuberculous Peritonitis
Year of Cure:	1902

Age at Cure:	22 years
Cure recognized by:	B.C.M.
Mention in this book:	Chapter 17, p. 173–75

Name:	MISS ERNESTINE GUILLOTEAU
Residence:	Thouars
Disease:	Tuberculous Peritonitis
Year of Cure:	1908
Age at Cure:	24 years
Cure recognized by:	B.C.M.
Mention in this book:	Chapter 12, p. 134–35

Name:	FR. FIAMMA
Residence:	Paris
Disease:	Ulcerated Varicose Veins of Both Legs
Year of Cure:	1908
Age at Cure:	—
Cure recognized by:	B.C.M.
Mention in this book:	Chapter 13, p. 143–44

Name:	MR. JOSEPH DUNCAN-BOTHMAN
Residence:	Dover, England
Disease:	Chronic Suppurating Infection of Middle Ear, Total Deafness
Year of Cure:	1910
Age at Cure:	16 years
Cure recognized by:	— (cured away from Lourdes; use of Lourdes water)
Mention in this book:	Chapter 16, p. 167–68

Name:	MR. LUCIEN BELHACHE
Residence:	Toulouse
Disease:	Spinal Injury followed by Pott's Disease
Year of Cure:	1922
Age at Cure:	22 years

Cure recognized by: B.C.M.
Mention in this book: Chapter 13, p. 142–43

Name: MR. JOHN TRAYNOR
Residence: Liverpool, England
Disease: Gunshot Wounds, Paralysis, Epilepsy
Year of Cure: 1923
Age at Cure: 40 years
Cure recognized by: B.C.M.
Mention in this book: Chapter 14, p. 145ff.

Name: MISS MARIE-LOUISE ARNAUD
Residence: Montpellier
Disease: Disseminated (Multiple) Sclerosis
Year of Cure: 1925
Age at Cure: 49 years
Cure recognized by: B.C.M.
Mention in this book: Chapter 12, p. 129–31

Name: MRS. CÉLESTINE GARDELLE
Residence: Crevant
Disease: Malignant Tumor of the Nasal Cavity
Year of Cure: 1925
Age at Cure: 54 years
Cure recognized by: B.C.M.
Mention in this book: Chapter 16, p. 168–70

Name: MISS ELIZABETH DELOT
Residence: Boulogne
Disease: Metastasized Cancer of the Stomach (to
                            Liver)
Year of Cure: 1926
Age at Cure: 46 years
Cure recognized by: B.C.M.
Mention in this book: Chapter 12, p. 127–28

Name:	MRS. AUGAULT
Residence:	Craon
Disease:	Fibroid Tumor of Uterus, Heart Condition
Year of Cure:	1926
Age at Cure:	49 years
Cure recognized by:	B.C.M.
Mention in this book:	Chapter 18, p. 177–80

Name:	[Boy] HENRI MIEUZET
Residence:	—
Disease:	Chronic Enteritis
Year of Cure:	1927
Age at Cure:	7 years
Cure recognized by:	B.C.M.
Mention in this book:	Chapter 12, p. 132–34

Name:	FR. ALBERT DESSAILLY
Residence:	Pau
Disease:	Tuberculous Laryngitis, Loss of Voice
Year of Cure:	1928
Age at Cure:	22 years
Cure recognized by:	B.C.M.
Mention in this book:	Chapter 13, p. 137

Name:	MRS. PILLOT
Residence:	Nancy
Disease:	Tumor of the Brain
Year of Cure:	1933
Age at Cure:	42 years
Cure recognized by:	B.C.M.
Mention in this book:	Chapter 16, p. 165–67

Name:	MR. FERNAND LEGRAND
Residence:	Gisors
Disease:	Polyneuritis of Spinal Nerves and Cord, Paralysis

Year of Cure:	1934
Age at Cure:	29 years
Cure recognized by:	B.C.M.
Mention in this book:	Chapter 13, p. 137–141

Name:	MR. ROBERT GUYOT
Residence:	Dourges
Disease:	Abscessed Left Kidney, spreading to Left Leg
Year of Cure:	1934
Age at Cure:	41 years
Cure recognized by:	B.C.M.
Mention in this book:	Chapter 13, p. 141–42

Name:	[Boy] YVES JOUCAU
Residence:	Paris
Disease:	Pott's Disease, cervical, abscessed
Year of Cure:	1934
Age at Cure:	7 years
Cure recognized by:	B.C.M.
Mention in this book:	Chapter 22, p. 239–41

Name:	MR. CHARLES McDONALD
Residence:	Dublin, Ireland
Disease:	Tuberculous Disease of the Vertebrae with Abscesses, Nephritis
Year of Cure:	1936
Age at Cure:	31 years
Cure recognized by:	B.C.M.
Mention in this book:	Chapter 8, p. 85–93

Name:	[Boy] GUY LEYDET
Residence:	St.-Étienne
Disease:	Infantile Encephalopathy with Idiocy, Quadriplegia
Year of Cure:	1946

Age at Cure: 7 years
Cure recognized by: B.C.M., B.M., N.M.C.
Mention in this book: Chapter 22, p. 242–46

Name: [Boy] GERARD BAILLIE
Residence: Dunkerque, Arras
Disease: Chorio-retinitis (bilateral) and Double Op-
                            tic Atrophy, Blindness
Year of Cure: 1947
Age at Cure: 8 years
Cure recognized by: M.B., N.M.C.
Mention in this book: Chapter 22, p. 227–33

Name: MISS DELIZIA CIROLLI
Residence: Paternò, Sicily
Disease: Malignant Tumor of the Right Knee
Year of Cure: 1976
Age at Cure: 12 years
Cure recognized by: M.B., D.M.C., I.M.C.
Mention in this book: Chapter 28, p. 310–12

Thanks are tendered to the following publishers through whose courtesy quotations and reprints appear in the volume: The Bruce Publishing Company for *After Bernadette* by Don Sharkey, 1945; Burns, Oates & Washburne, Ltd., for *The Crowds of Lourdes* by J. K. Huysmans, 1925; The Catholic Truth Society, for "I Met a Miracle" by Rev. Patrick O'Connor, 1951; Clonmore and Reynolds, Dublin, for *Miracle at Lourdes* by Charles Mc-Donald, 1953; *Commonweal Magazine;* Flammarion, for *La Vérité sur Lourdes* by Augustin Vallet, 1944; Harper & Brothers, for *Man, the Unknown,* 1939, and *Voyage to Lourdes* by Alexis Carrel, 1950; Manresa Press, for *Lourdes* by Mons. Robert Hugh Benson, 1921; Presses Universitaires, for *Guérisons Miraculeuses Modernes* by Drs. Leuret and Bon, 1950; Ratisbone Publishing Company, for *Heaven's Recent Wonders* by P. G. Boissarie, 1909; Rinehart & Company, Inc., for *Can Prayer be Answered* by Mary Austin, 1934; and *The Rosary Magazine,* for *The National Pilgrimage* by Contesse de Courson, 1921.

Readers wanting further information about Lourdes should address their local Catholic authorities. The author is not qualified, medically or ecclesiastically, to deal with personal problems regarding health, Pilgrimages, etc.

A reminder should be added, again stressing the very small percentage of physical cures *at this shrine. The journey to Lourdes is a deep spiritual experience and blessing, and should be so undertaken. Only one out of ten thousand of the sick is physically cured. True, you might be that one. The chances are 9,999 that you would not be. So if you go, go with the hope of getting the spiritual strength and inspiration—and leave the rest with God.*